diabetic LIVING®

Everyday COOKING

VOLUME 6

DIABETIC LIVING® EVERYDAY COOKING
IS PART OF A BOOK SERIES PUBLISHED BY
BETTER HOMES AND GARDENS SPECIAL
INTEREST MEDIA, DES MOINES, IOWA

QUICK TIPS

Helpful cooking or healthful eating tips appear on every page that has one of these color tabs. Look for them throughout the book.

Pork and Green Onion
Tortilla Pile-Ups
recipe on page 24

One of my biggest challenges is keeping my family healthy.

Juggling a full-time job and the schedules of my kids and husband can sometimes make mealtime tricky. That's why I'm glad to have *Everyday Cooking* to help me prepare wholesome and appealing meals.

I try to plan dinners ahead—knowing what I'm putting on the table when I wake up makes the 5 p.m. frenzy that much smoother. Although my family has favorites, I like introducing them to different dishes. A benefit for me is that the *Diabetic Living*® magazine professionals create and revise recipes each year to include in the newest volume of *Everyday Cooking*. With the calories counted, fats in check, and diabetic exchanges included, the lightened-up recipes are perfect for those with diabetes and just right for those who are interested in eating healthful, balanced meals.

Because each recipe is developed by registered dietitians, I know that the meals deliver health-smart amounts of calories, carbs, fats, and sodium. And the Better Homes and Gardens® Test Kitchen seal of approval assures me that each recipe is going to be easy to follow, taste great, and turn out well.

This volume will be my new go-to recipe collection when I'm looking for something nutritious and tasty to cook for breakfast, lunch, or dinner. And when I need a sweet indulgence, I know I can find a recipe for that, too. I hope you will enjoy dishing up these new recipes as much as I will.

Martha Miller Johnson
Editor, *Diabetic Living*® magazine

ON THE COVER:

Banana Split Cake Roll
recipe on page 139

Photographer: Kritsada Panichgul

3

Everyday COOKING

VOLUME 6

CONSUMER MARKETING

Vice President, Consumer Marketing	JANET DONNELLY
Consumer Product Marketing Director	HEATHER SORENSEN
Consumer Product Marketing Manager	WENDY MERICAL
Business Director	RON CLINGMAN
Production Manager	AL RODRUCK
Contributing Project Manager	SHELLI McCONNELL, PURPLE PEAR PUBLISHING, INC.
Contributing Photographers	JASON DONNELLY, JASON WALSMITH
Contributing Food Stylists	GREG LUNA, JENNIFER PETERSON, SUSAN STRALECKI
Test Kitchen Director	LYNN BLANCHARD
Test Kitchen Product Supervisors	JANE BURNETT, RD, LD; CARLA CHRISTIAN, RD,
Editorial Assistants	LORI EGGERS, MARLENE TODD

SPECIAL INTEREST MEDIA

Editorial Director	JIM BLUME
Art Director	GENE RAUCH
Managing Editor	DOUG KOUMA

DIABETIC LIVING® MAGAZINE

Editor	MARTHA MILLER JOHNSON
Art Director, Health	MICHELLE BILYEU
Assistant Art Director	ALEXIS WEST-HUNTOON
Senior Editor, Food & Nutrition	JESSIE SHAFER
Assistant Editor	LORI BROOKHART-SCHERVISH

MEREDITH NATIONAL MEDIA GROUP

President TOM HARTY

Chairman and Chief Executive Officer STEPHEN M. LACY

Vice Chairman MELL MEREDITH FRAZIER

In Memoriam — E.T. MEREDITH III (1933-2003)

Diabetic Living® Everyday Cooking is part of a series published by Meredith Corp., 1716 Locust St., Des Moines, IA 50309-3023.

If you have comments or questions about the editorial material in *Diabetic Living® Everyday Cooking*, write to the editor of *Diabetic Living* magazine, Meredith Corp., 1716 Locust St., Des Moines, IA 50309-3023. Send an e-mail to diabeticlivingmeredith.com or call 800/678-2651. *Diabetic Living* magazine is available by subscription or on the newsstand. To order a subscription to *Diabetic Living* magazine, go to *DiabeticLivingOnline.com*.

contents

Carrot Raisin Cookies
recipe on page 151

family-pleasing dinners

Coffee- and Smoked Paprika-Rubbed Steak with Buttermilk Dressing

Look no further than your own kitchen for healthful eats your entire family will enjoy. From favorite Asian and American fare to interesting Mexican and Mediterranean cuisine, these lightened-up dishes are sure to rival takeout. You'll find familiar favorites and new dishes, each loaded with good-for-you ingredients and featuring fabulous, fresh flavors.

Coffee- and Smoked Paprika-Rubbed Steak with Buttermilk Dressing

If smoked paprika is not available, use 1 teaspoon regular paprika and $1/2$ teaspoon ground cumin instead.

SERVINGS 4 (3 ounces cooked meat, 2 skewers, and about 1 tablespoon dressing each)
CARB. PER SERVING 11 g
PREP 25 minutes CHILL 2 hours BROIL 17 minutes
STAND 5 minutes

1	1-pound beef flank steak, trimmed of fat
1	tablespoon packed brown sugar*
$1^1/2$	teaspoons instant espresso coffee powder
$3/4$	teaspoon sweet smoked paprika
$1/2$	teaspoon garlic powder
$1/2$	teaspoon salt
$1/8$	teaspoon freshly ground black pepper
1	zucchini, cut into 1-inch pieces
16	cherry tomatoes
12	to 16 fresh whole mushrooms
1	recipe Buttermilk Dressing

1. Score both sides of steak in a diamond pattern by making shallow diagonal cuts at 1-inch intervals. In a small bowl combine brown sugar, espresso powder, paprika, garlic powder, salt, and pepper. Sprinkle evenly over both sides of steak; rub in with your fingers.

2. In a large saucepan bring a large amount of water to boiling. Add zucchini; cook for 2 minutes and drain. Thread tomatoes, mushrooms, and zucchini onto eight skewers.** Cover; chill steak and skewers for 2 to 24 hours.

3. Preheat broiler. Place steak on the unheated rack of a broiler pan. Broil 3 to 4 inches from heat for 17 to 21 minutes or until medium doneness (160°F), turning once. Add skewers to the broiler pan for the last 7 to 8 minutes of broiling or just until vegetables are tender, turning once. Transfer steak to a cutting board. Let stand for 5 minutes.

4. Thinly slice steak across the grain. Serve steak with vegetable skewers and Buttermilk Dressing.

BUTTERMILK DRESSING: In a small bowl whisk together 2 tablespoons low-fat buttermilk, 2 tablespoons light mayonnaise or salad dressing, 1 tablespoon snipped fresh chives, 1 teaspoon cider vinegar, 1 teaspoon Dijon-style mustard, $1/8$ teaspoon garlic powder, $1/8$ teaspoon salt, and $1/8$ teaspoon black pepper. Cover and chill for up to 2 days.

*SUGAR SUBSTITUTE: We do not recommend using a sugar substitute for this recipe.

**TEST KITCHEN TIP: If using wooden skewers, soak them in enough water to cover for at least 30 minutes before broiling.

PER SERVING: 240 cal., 9 g total fat (3 g sat. fat), 73 mg chol., 523 mg sodium, 11 g carb. (2 g fiber, 8 g sugars), 28 g pro.
Exchanges: 1 vegetable, 0.5 carb., 3.5 lean meat, 0.5 fat.

Beef and Vegetables in Peanut Sauce

To feed a family of four, simply double the ingredients for this quick-to-fix meal.

SERVINGS 2 (1 cup meat mixture and $^1/_2$ cup cooked rice each)

CARB. PER SERVING 36 g

START TO FINISH 20 minutes

- $^1/_2$ cup cold water
- 3 tablespoons powdered peanut butter, such as PB2 brand
- 1 tablespoon reduced-sodium teriyaki sauce
- 1 tablespoon cider vinegar
- 2 teaspoons honey
- $^1/_4$ teaspoon ground ginger
- $^1/_4$ teaspoon crushed red pepper
  Nonstick cooking spray
- 6 ounces boneless beef sirloin, cut into thin bite-size strips
- 1 clove garlic, minced
- 1 cup fresh snow pea pods, trimmed
- $^1/_2$ cup purchased shredded carrots
- $^1/_2$ of an 8.8-ounce pouch cooked brown rice (1 cup)

1. For peanut sauce, in a small saucepan stir together the cold water and peanut butter powder until powder dissolves. Stir in teriyaki sauce, vinegar, honey, ginger, and crushed red pepper. Bring to boiling, stirring occasionally. Boil gently, uncovered, for 1 to 2 minutes or until thickened; set aside.

2. Coat an unheated large nonstick skillet with cooking spray; heat over medium-high heat. Add beef and garlic to hot skillet. Cook and stir for 2 minutes. Add pea pods and carrots; cook and stir 2 minutes more or until vegetables are crisp-tender. Heat brown rice according to package directions.

3. Add the peanut sauce, stirring to coat; if necessary, heat through. Serve beef and vegetable mixture over the rice.

PER SERVING: 353 cal., 12 g total fat (4 g sat. fat), 34 mg chol., 345 mg sodium, 36 g carb. (3 g fiber, 10 g sugars), 26 g pro. Exchanges: 1 vegetable, 2 starch, 3 lean meat, 0.5 fat.

Texas Beef with Butternut Squash

Slow-cooked to fork-tender perfection, this saucy beef mixture is superb served over polenta or rice. A $^1/_3$-cup serving of either is enough to sop up the flavorful sauce.

SERVINGS 8 (2 ounces cooked meat and 1 cup vegetable mixture each)

CARB. PER SERVING 16 g

PREP 25 minutes **SLOW COOK** 8 hours (low) or 4 hours (high)

- $1^1/_2$ pounds beef chuck roast
- 4 cups $1^1/_2$-inch cubes peeled butternut squash
- 2 14.5-ounce cans fire-roasted diced tomatoes, undrained
- $1^1/_2$ cups no-salt-added beef broth or water
- $^3/_4$ cup chopped onion
- 1 4-ounce can diced green chiles
- 1 tablespoon ground ancho chile pepper
- 2 teaspoons unsweetened cocoa powder
- 1 teaspoon ground cumin
- 1 teaspoon dried oregano, crushed
- 3 cloves garlic, minced
  Hot cooked polenta or hot cooked rice (optional)
  Snipped fresh cilantro

1. Trim fat from beef roast and cut beef into 2-inch pieces. In a 5- to 6-quart slow cooker stir together beef, squash, tomatoes, beef broth, onion, chiles, chile pepper, cocoa powder, cumin, oregano, and garlic.

2. Cover and cook on low-heat setting for 8 to 10 hours or on high-heat setting for 4 to 5 hours. If desired, serve with polenta or hot cooked rice. Sprinkle each serving with cilantro.

PER SERVING: 258 cal., 13 g total fat (5 g sat. fat), 75 mg chol., 313 mg sodium, 16 g carb. (4 g fiber, 5 g sugars), 19 g pro. Exchanges: 1 vegetable, 0.5 starch, 2 medium-fat meat, 0.5 fat.

Beef and Vegetables
in Peanut Sauce

QUICK TIP
No peeking! Each time you lift the lid, you add 15 minutes of cooking time to your simmering slow cooker meal.

Texas Beef with Butternut Squash

Beef Medallions with Kasha Pilaf

Kasha, a nutty-flavor grain common in Eastern Europe, is buckwheat groats. Look for it in the international section of the supermarket or in health food stores.

SERVINGS 4 (3 slices meat and ³/₄ cup pilaf each)
CARB. PER SERVING 32 g
START TO FINISH 35 minutes

1½	cups water
²/₃	cup toasted buckwheat groats (kasha)
2	tablespoons olive oil
½	cup chopped red onion (1 medium)
2	large cloves garlic, minced
¼	cup dried cherries
¼	cup coarsely snipped fresh basil
1	tablespoon balsamic vinegar
½	teaspoon salt
1	pound beef shoulder petite tenders
¼	teaspoon Montreal steak seasoning
⅓	cup sliced almonds, toasted

1. In a medium saucepan bring the water to boiling. Stir in buckwheat groats; reduce heat. Simmer, covered, for 5 to 7 minutes or until the water is absorbed (you should have about 2 cups of cooked groats). Set aside.

2. In a large nonstick skillet heat 1 teaspoon of the oil over medium-high heat. Add onion and garlic; cook and stir for 2 to 3 minutes or just until onion begins to soften.

3. Drain cooked groats if necessary. Add onion mixture to the cooked groats. Stir in 4 teaspoons of the remaining oil, the cherries, basil, vinegar, and salt. Let stand at room temperature while preparing the beef.

4. Meanwhile, cut beef crosswise into 12 slices, each about 1 inch thick. Add the remaining 1 teaspoon oil to the same skillet; heat over medium heat. Evenly sprinkle beef pieces with Montreal seasoning. Cook beef pieces in hot oil about 6 minutes or until medium (145°F), turning once halfway through cooking time. Serve beef pieces over groats mixture. Sprinkle with almonds.

PER SERVING: 358 cal., 19 g total fat (4 g sat. fat), 65 mg chol., 407 mg sodium, 32 g carb. (5 g fiber, 8 g sugars), 29 g pro. Exchanges: 2 starch, 3 lean meat, 1.5 fat.

Beef Medallions
with Kasha Pilaf

Beefy Stuffed Shells

Double the goodness—a homemade vegetable mixture is both a binder for the meat filling and a sauce to spoon over the shells.

SERVINGS 6 (2 filled shells each)
CARB. PER SERVING 33 g
PREP 30 minutes **BAKE** 25 minutes

Nonstick cooking spray
12 dried jumbo shell macaroni
12 ounces extra-lean ground beef
1 tablespoon olive oil
1½ cups chopped fresh mushrooms (4 ounces)
1 cup chopped onion (1 large)
½ cup shredded carrot (1 medium)
¼ cup chopped celery
4 cloves garlic, minced
½ teaspoon dried Italian seasoning, crushed
1 14.5-ounce can no-salt-added diced tomatoes with basil, garlic, and oregano, undrained
¼ teaspoon salt
1 cup shredded reduced-fat Italian-style cheese blend (2 ounces)
1 medium tomato, chopped

1. Preheat oven to 350°F. Lightly coat a 2-quart square baking dish with cooking spray; set aside. Cook pasta according to package directions; drain. Rinse with cold water; drain again. Set aside.
2. Meanwhile, in a medium skillet cook ground beef until browned, using a wooden spoon to break up meat as it cooks. Drain off fat. Set meat aside.
3. In a large nonstick skillet heat oil over medium heat. Add mushrooms, onion, carrot, celery, garlic, and Italian seasoning; cook for 6 to 8 minutes or until vegetables are tender, stirring frequently. Add diced tomatoes and salt. Cook and stir for 2 minutes more. Remove from heat; cool slightly.
4. Spoon the tomato mixture into a blender or food processor; cover and blend or process until nearly smooth. Set aside ¾ cup of the pureed tomato mixture. Return the remaining pureed tomato mixture to the skillet. Stir cooked meat into tomato mixture in skillet. Spoon a rounded tablespoon of the meat mixture into each pasta shell.
5. Arrange filled pasta shells in the prepared baking dish. Spoon the reserved ¾ cup pureed tomato mixture over the shells.
6. Bake, covered, for 20 minutes. Sprinkle with cheese and fresh tomato. Bake about 5 minutes more or until heated through and cheese is melted.

PER SERVING: 310 cal., 9 g total fat (4 g sat. fat), 45 mg chol., 322 mg sodium, 33 g carb. (6 g fiber, 8 g sugars), 24 g pro. Exchanges: 0.5 vegetable, 2 starch, 2.5 lean meat, 1 fat.

Beefy Stuffed Shells

Meat on Call

Ground beef, turkey, or chicken is the go-to meat for making meals the whole family will love.

To brown the ground meat of choice ahead of time for casseroles, chilies, and soups, cook the meat fully. Drain off any fat by transferring the meat mixture to a colander and pressing with the back of a spoon. Place the meat in an airtight container and chill for up to 3 days. If you choose to freeze it, place the meat in a freezer bag, seal, label, press to an even thickness, and freeze for up to 3 months.

Spaghetti Squash with Chili

Spaghetti squash serves as a low-calorie option to pasta in this delicious chili dish.

SERVINGS 4 (1 cup chili and $\frac{1}{2}$ cup spaghetti squash each)
CARB. PER SERVING 32 g
PREP 20 minutes **BAKE** 45 minutes **COOK** 10 minutes

Nonstick cooking spray
1 2-pound spaghetti squash
1 pound extra-lean ground beef
$\frac{1}{2}$ cup chopped onion (1 medium)
1 clove garlic, minced
1 14.5-ounce can diced tomatoes and green chiles, undrained
1 15-ounce can no-salt-added corn, drained
1 8-ounce can no-salt-added tomato sauce
2 tablespoons no-salt-added tomato paste
2 teaspoons chili powder
$\frac{1}{2}$ teaspoon dried oregano, crushed
Fresh oregano leaves (optional)

1. Preheat oven to 350°F. Line a baking sheet with foil. Coat foil with cooking spray; set aside. Halve the spaghetti squash lengthwise and remove seeds and membranes. Place squash halves, cut sides down, on prepared baking sheet. Bake for 45 to 50 minutes or until tender.* Cool slightly. Using a fork, shred and separate the spaghetti squash into strands.

2. Meanwhile, for sauce, In a medium saucepan cook ground beef, onion, and garlic until meat is browned and onion is tender, stirring to break up meat as it cooks. Drain off fat.

3. Stir in tomatoes and green chiles, corn, tomato sauce, tomato paste, chili powder, and dried oregano. Bring to boiling; reduce heat. Simmer, uncovered, about 10 minutes or until desired consistency.

4. Serve meat sauce with spaghetti squash. If desired, sprinkle with fresh oregano.

*TEST KITCHEN TIP: To cook squash in the microwave, place, cut sides down, in a baking dish with $\frac{1}{4}$ cup water. Microwave, covered, on 100 percent power (high) for about 15 minutes or until tender. Continue as directed.

PER SERVING: 300 cal., 7 g total fat (3 g sat. fat), 70 mg chol., 566 mg sodium, 32 g carb. (8 g fiber, 17 g sugars), 29 g pro. Exchanges: 1 vegetable, 1.5 starch, 3.5 lean meat.

Chipotle Picante Meat Loaf

If you can't locate chipotle-style salsa, make your own by stirring 1½ teaspoons ground chipotle pepper into ⅔ cup medium salsa.

SERVINGS 4 (2 slices each)
CARB. PER SERVING 15 g
PREP 20 minutes **BAKE** 40 minutes **STAND** 10 minutes

Chipotle Picante Meat Loaf

Nonstick cooking spray
⅔ cup chipotle-style salsa
¼ cup refrigerated or frozen egg product, thawed
½ of a 10-ounce package frozen cooked brown rice, thawed (about 1½ cups)
¾ cup chopped fresh cilantro
2 tablespoons flaxseed meal
¼ teaspoon salt
1 pound extra-lean ground beef

1. Preheat oven to 350°F. Coat a foil-lined baking pan with cooking spray.
2. In a large bowl combine ⅓ cup of the salsa, the egg, rice, cilantro, flaxseed meal, and salt; add ground beef and mix well. Shape into an oval loaf about 8 inches long by 5 inches wide. Place in prepared pan. Bake, uncovered, for 40 to 45 minutes or until an instant read thermometer registers 160°F.
3. Spoon remaining ⅓ cup salsa over meat loaf or serve the salsa on the side. Let stand 10 minutes before slicing loaf. To serve, cut meat loaf into eight slices. If desired, serve with oven-roasted *Brussels sprouts* and *Yukon gold potatoes*.

PER SERVING: 256 cal., 8 g total fat (3 g sat. fat), 70 mg chol., 470 mg sodium, 15 g carb. (2 g fiber, 2 g sugars), 28 g pro. Exchanges: 1 starch, 3.5 lean meat, 0.5 fat.

Loaded Nachos

This slimmed-down version of the finger-lickin' snack favorite makes perfect during- or after-game fare.

SERVINGS 4 (16 chips, ¼ cup meat, ¼ cup cheese sauce, and ½ cup vegetables each)
CARB. PER SERVING 23 g
PREP 30 minutes **BAKE** 10 minutes

8 6-inch corn tortillas, cut into 8 wedges each
2 teaspoons unsalted butter
1 tablespoon flour
¾ cup fat-free milk
½ cup shredded part-skim mozzarella cheese (2 ounces)
½ cup shredded reduced-fat cheddar cheese (2 ounces)
1 ounce fat-free cream cheese, softened
¼ teaspoon paprika
¼ teaspoon ground turmeric
8 ounces extra-lean ground beef
¼ cup water

1 recipe Homemade Taco Seasoning
1 cup chopped tomato (1 large)
½ cup chopped green or red sweet pepper (1 small)
¼ cup sliced green onions (2)
1 fresh jalapeño chile pepper, stemmed, seeded, and thinly sliced (see tip, page 20) (optional)
½ cup chunky mild salsa

1. Preheat oven to 375°F. Place tortilla wedges in a single layer on a large baking sheet. Coat wedges with *nonstick cooking spray*. Bake for 10 to 13 minutes or until wedges are crisp and golden brown on edges. Set aside.
2. Meanwhile, for cheese sauce, in a small saucepan melt butter over medium heat. Stir in flour until combined. Whisk in milk until smooth. Cook and stir until thickened and bubbly. Cook and stir for 2 minutes more. Stir in mozzarella cheese, cheddar cheese, cream cheese, paprika, and turmeric. Cook and stir over medium heat until cheese is melted and mixture is smooth. Reduce heat to low. Hold cheese sauce over low heat until needed, stirring occasionally.
3. Meanwhile, coat an unheated large skillet with *cooking spray*. Heat skillet over medium heat. Cook beef in skillet until browned, using a wooden spoon to break up meat as it cooks. Drain off fat. Stir the water and Homemade Taco Seasoning into meat in skillet. Cook and stir for 3 to 5 minutes more or until most of the water has evaporated.
4. To serve, arrange tortilla wedges on four plates. Top with meat mixture, cheese sauce, tomato, sweet pepper, green onions, and, if desired, chile pepper. Serve with salsa.
HOMEMADE TACO SEASONING: In a small bowl stir together 2 teaspoons paprika, 1 teaspoon ground cumin, ½ to 1 teaspoon black pepper, ½ teaspoon ground coriander, ⅛ to ¼ teaspoon ground chipotle chile pepper, and ⅛ teaspoon cayenne pepper.

PER SERVING: 291 cal., 11 g total fat (6 g sat. fat), 61 mg chol., 356 mg sodium, 23 g carb. (3 g fiber, 6 g sugars), 24 g pro. Exchanges: 1 vegetable, 1 starch, 3 lean meat, 1 fat.

Turkey and Bean Burritos

Whole wheat bread products are the better option, but if you have white-bread kids, check the nutrition information to select the most healthful plain tortilla.

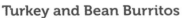

SERVINGS 8 (1 burrito each)
CARB. PER SERVING 27 g
PREP 25 minutes BAKE 10 minutes

  8 8-inch whole wheat flour tortillas
 12 ounces uncooked ground turkey breast
  1 cup chopped onion (1 large)
  2 cloves garlic, minced
  1 15-ounce can no-salt-added black beans or pinto beans, rinsed and drained
$\frac{1}{2}$ cup bottled salsa
  2 teaspoons chili powder
$\frac{1}{2}$ cup shredded reduced-fat cheddar cheese (2 ounces)
$\frac{1}{2}$ cup shredded lettuce
$\frac{1}{2}$ cup light sour cream
  1 tablespoon snipped fresh cilantro

1. Preheat oven to 350°F. Stack tortillas; wrap in foil. Heat in the oven for 10 minutes to soften.
2. Meanwhile, for filling, in a large nonstick skillet cook turkey, onion, and garlic over medium heat until meat is browned and onion is tender, stirring to break up turkey as it cooks. Drain off fat. Stir in beans, salsa, and chili powder. Heat through.

3. Spoon about $\frac{1}{2}$ cup of the filling onto each tortilla and top each with 1 tablespoon cheese and 1 tablespoon lettuce. Fold bottom edge up and over filling, just until covered. Fold in opposite sides. Roll up, tucking in sides.
4. In a small bowl stir together sour cream and cilantro. Serve sour cream mixture with burritos.

PER SERVING: 269 cal., 7 g total fat (3 g sat. fat), 29 mg chol., 524 mg sodium, 27 g carb. (13 g fiber, 3 g sugars), 24 g pro. Exchanges: 2 starch, 3 lean meat, 1 fat.

Corn Pancakes with BBQ Pulled Turkey and Coleslaw

Use up the leftover shredded cabbage and carrot by tossing them into salad or stirring into soup.

SERVINGS 8 (1 pancake, $\frac{1}{2}$ cup turkey-sauce mixture, and a scant $\frac{1}{3}$ cup slaw each)
CARB. PER SERVING 39 g
PREP 40 minutes COOK 5 minutes

$\frac{1}{2}$ of a 14-ounce package shredded cabbage with carrot (coleslaw mix) (about $2\frac{1}{2}$ cups)
  2 tablespoons finely chopped fresh jalapeño chile pepper (see tip, page 20)
  1 tablespoon snipped fresh parsley
$\frac{1}{3}$ cup plain fat-free Greek yogurt
  2 tablespoons creamy salad dressing
  2 teaspoons lime juice
$\frac{1}{2}$ teaspoon ground cumin

1 recipe Mild Red Barbecue Sauce or
  1¼ cups low-sodium barbecue sauce
¾ cup flour
¾ cup yellow cornmeal
2 teaspoons baking powder
⅛ teaspoon salt
1⅓ cups low-fat buttermilk
1 cup fresh or frozen whole kernel corn, thawed
½ cup shredded Parmesan cheese (2 ounces)
½ cup refrigerated or frozen egg product, thawed, or
  2 eggs, beaten
¼ cup thinly sliced green onions (2)
¼ cup chopped red sweet pepper
2 tablespoons canola oil
1 tablespoon snipped fresh parsley
  Nonstick cooking spray
20 ounces shredded cooked turkey breast

1. For coleslaw, in a medium bowl combine coleslaw mix, chile pepper, and 1 tablespoon parsley. In a small bowl whisk together the yogurt, salad dressing, lime juice, and cumin. Pour dressing over cabbage mixture; stir to coat. Cover and chill until serving time.

2. Prepare Mild Red Barbecue Sauce; keep warm. If using other barbecue sauce, heat it in a medium saucepan; keep warm.

3. For corn pancakes, in a large bowl stir together flour, cornmeal, baking powder, and salt. In a medium bowl whisk together buttermilk, corn, Parmesan cheese, egg, green onions, sweet pepper, oil, and 1 tablespoon parsley. Make a well in the flour mixture; pour buttermilk mixture into the well. Stir until well mixed; set aside.

4. Lightly coat an unheated nonstick griddle with cooking spray. Preheat over medium heat. For each pancake, pour a scant ½ cup of the batter (6 to 7 tablespoons) onto the hot griddle. Cook about 4 minutes or until bubbles begin to appear on top of the pancakes. Using a pancake turner or large metal spatula, turn pancakes over. Cook for 1 to 2 minutes more.

5. Add turkey to the barbecue sauce in saucepan. Cook over medium heat until turkey is heated through (165°F), stirring occasionally.

6. To serve, top each pancake with ½ cup of the turkey-sauce mixture. Serve coleslaw on top of turkey.

MILD RED BARBECUE SAUCE: In a medium saucepan combine ⅔ cup water, ½ cup chopped onion, half of a 6-ounce can (⅓ cup) tomato paste, ¼ cup cider vinegar, 2 tablespoons honey, 1 tablespoon molasses, 1 tablespoon yellow mustard, 1 tablespoon Worcestershire sauce, 1 teaspoon chili powder, and ¼ teaspoon salt. Bring to boiling; reduce heat. Simmer, uncovered, about 20 minutes or until onion is tender and sauce is thickened.

PER SERVING: 372 cal., 10 g total fat (3 g sat. fat), 56 mg chol., 593 mg sodium, 39 g carb. (3 g fiber, 13 g sugars), 31 g pro. Exchanges: 2.5 starch, 3 lean meat, 1 fat.

Popover Pizza Casserole

Serve the casserole as soon as it comes out of the oven so the topping doesn't deflate. *Pictured on page 14.*

SERVINGS 6 (1⅓ cups each)
CARB. PER SERVING 31 g
PREP 35 minutes BAKE 30 minutes

- 1¼ pounds ground turkey breast or extra-lean ground beef
- 2 cups sliced fresh mushrooms
- 1½ cups chopped yellow summer squash
- 1 cup chopped onion (1 large)
- 1 cup chopped green sweet pepper (1 large)
- 1 14- to 15.5-ounce can pizza sauce
- 1 teaspoon dried Italian seasoning, crushed
- ½ teaspoon fennel seeds, crushed
- 1 cup fat-free milk
- ½ cup refrigerated or frozen egg product, thawed, or 2 eggs
- 1 tablespoon canola oil
- 1 cup all-purpose flour*
- 1 cup shredded reduced-fat mozzarella cheese (4 ounces)
- 2 tablespoons grated Parmesan cheese

1. Preheat oven to 400°F. In an oven-going large skillet cook turkey, mushrooms, squash, onion, and sweet pepper over medium heat until meat is brown and vegetables are tender, stirring to break up meat as it cooks. Drain off fat. Stir pizza sauce, Italian seasoning, and fennel seeds into meat mixture. Bring to boiling; reduce heat. Simmer, uncovered, for 5 minutes, stirring occasionally. Spread to an even layer.
2. For popover topping, in a medium bowl combine milk, egg, and oil. Beat with an electric mixer on medium speed or whisk for 1 minute. Add flour; beat or whisk about 1 minute more or until smooth.
3. Sprinkle mozzarella cheese over meat mixture in skillet. Pour popover topping evenly over mixture in skillet, covering completely. Sprinkle with Parmesan cheese.
4. Bake, uncovered, for 30 to 35 minutes or until topping is puffed and golden brown. Serve immediately.
*TEST KITCHEN TIP: If desired, substitute ½ cup white whole wheat flour or regular whole wheat flour for ½ cup of the all-purpose flour.

PER SERVING: 327 cal., 7 g total fat (2 g sat. fat), 58 mg chol., 611 mg sodium, 31 g carb. (3 g fiber, 7 g sugars), 34 g pro. Exchanges: 1 vegetable, 1.5 starch, 4 lean meat.

Lime-Marinated Turkey Tenderloin

A turkey tenderloin is quite thick, so cutting it in half horizontally yields two generous steaks.

SERVINGS 4 (4 ounces turkey and 1 cup cantaloupe each)
CARB. PER SERVING 22 g
PREP 10 minutes MARINATE 4 hours GRILL 12 minutes

- 2 turkey breast tenderloins (1 to 1½ pounds total)
- ¼ cup finely snipped fresh mint
- 2 teaspoons finely shredded lime peel
- ¼ cup lime juice
- 3 tablespoons orange juice
- 1 tablespoon olive oil
- 1 tablespoon honey
- ¼ teaspoon salt
- ¼ teaspoon black pepper
- 4 cups cut-up cantaloupe
- Lime wedges
- Fresh mint sprigs

1. Cut each turkey tenderloin in half horizontally to make four steaks. Place turkey steaks in a resealable plastic bag set in a shallow dish. For marinade, in a small bowl whisk together the snipped mint, lime peel, lime juice, orange juice, olive oil, honey, salt, and pepper. Reserve 2 tablespoons marinade; cover and refrigerate. Pour remaining marinade over turkey in bag; seal bag. Marinate in the refrigerator for 4 to 6 hours, turning the bag occasionally.
2. Drain turkey steaks, discarding marinade. For a charcoal grill, place turkey on the grill rack directly over medium coals. Grill, uncovered, for 12 to 15 minutes or until no longer pink (170°F), turning once halfway through grilling. (For a gas grill, preheat grill. Reduce heat to medium. Place turkey on grill rack over heat. Cover and grill as above.)
3. Meanwhile, place cantaloupe in a medium bowl. Drizzle the 2 tablespoons reserved marinade over cantaloupe and toss to coat. Serve turkey with cantaloupe and lime wedges and garnish with mint sprigs.

PER SERVING: 242 cal., 5 g total fat (1 g sat. fat), 70 mg chol., 230 mg sodium, 22 g carb. (2 g fiber, 18 g sugars), 30 g pro. Exchanges: 1 fruit, 0.5 carb., 4 lean meat.

Lime-Marinated
Turkey Tenderloin

QUICK TIP
Skip the task of cleaning and cutting up
a cantaloupe and pick up a container of the
cut-up melon in the produce aisle.

Crispy Chicken Tenders and Savory Waffles with Herb Gravy

Waffle makers vary in size, so the nutrition information is calculated using $1/4$ cup batter, which is half of a $6^{1}/_{2}$-inch round waffle.

SERVINGS 4 ($1/4$ cup batter, 2 chicken tenders, and scant $1/3$ cup gravy each)
CARB. PER SERVING 33 g or 31 g
PREP 40 minutes **BAKE** 15 minutes

- 1 recipe Crispy Chicken Tenders (page 19)
- $1/2$ cup all-purpose flour
- $1/2$ cup whole wheat flour
- $1/4$ cup chopped walnuts, toasted
- 1 tablespoon sugar*
- $3/4$ teaspoon baking powder
- $1/2$ teaspoon dried thyme, crushed
- $1/4$ teaspoon salt
- $3/4$ cup fat-free milk
- $1/4$ cup refrigerated or frozen egg product, thawed, or 1 egg, beaten
- 2 tablespoons water
- Nonstick cooking spray
- 2 garlic, minced
- 2 tablespoons butter
- 2 tablespoons all-purpose flour
- $3/4$ cup reduced-sodium chicken broth
- $1/2$ cup fat-free milk
- 1 teaspoon snipped fresh sage
- 1 teaspoon snipped fresh thyme
- $1/8$ to $1/4$ teaspoon black pepper
- Snipped fresh thyme, sage, or black pepper (optional)

1. Prepare Crispy Chicken Tenders; keep warm.

2. Meanwhile, for the waffle batter, in a large bowl combine the $1/2$ cup all-purpose flour, the whole wheat flour, walnuts, sugar, baking powder, dried thyme, and salt. Make a well in the center of the flour mixture; set aside. In a medium bowl combine the $3/4$ cup milk, the egg, and the water. Add milk mixture all at once to the flour mixture. Stir just until moistened (batter should be slightly lumpy).

3. Lightly coat a waffle baker with cooking spray and preheat. Add batter. Close lid quickly; do not open until done. Bake according to manufacturer's directions. When done, use a fork to lift waffle off of grid. Keep baked waffles warm in a 200°F oven while baking remaining waffles. Repeat with the remaining batter. (Cool, wrap, and freeze any leftover waffles for another meal.)

4. Meanwhile, for herb gravy, in a large saucepan cook garlic in hot butter over medium heat for 30 seconds. Add the 2 tablespoons flour and stir until well mixed. Add broth and the ½ cup milk. Cook and stir over medium heat until thickened and bubbly. Stir in snipped fresh sage, the 1 teaspoon fresh thyme, and the ⅛ teaspoon pepper. Cook and stir for 1 minute more.

5. Serve herb gravy with hot waffles and Crispy Chicken Tenders. If desired, garnish with additional fresh thyme, fresh sage, and/or additional pepper.

CRISPY CHICKEN TENDERS: Preheat oven to 425°F. Lightly coat a 15×10×1-inch baking pan with nonstick cooking spray. In a small bowl whisk together 2 egg whites and 1 tablespoon water. For coating, in a shallow dish combine ¾ cup finely crushed cornflakes, 2 tablespoons grated Parmesan cheese, ¼ teaspoon garlic powder, ¼ teaspoon dried parsley, and ¼ teaspoon black pepper. Using 12 ounces chicken breast tenderloins cut into 8 pieces, dip each tenderloin into the egg white mixture, then coat with the cornflake mixture. Place breaded chicken pieces on the prepared baking pan. Lightly coat breaded chicken pieces with nonstick cooking spray. Bake for 15 to 20 minutes or until crisp and no longer pink.

*SUGAR SUBSTITUTE: Choose Splenda Granular. Follow package directions to use product amount equivalent to 1 tablespoon sugar.

PER SERVING: 354 cal., 12 g total fat (5 g sat. fat), 72 mg chol., 571 mg sodium, 33 g carb. (2 g fiber, 6 g sugars), 29 g pro. Exchanges: 2 starch, 3.5 lean meat, 1 fat.

PER SERVING WITH SUBSTITUTE: Same as above, except 348 cal., 31 g carb. (5 g sugars).

Swiss Chard and Turkey Sausage over Polenta

Use a wire whisk to stir the polenta—it will quickly break up any lumps that form.

SERVINGS 4 (⅔ cup sausage mixture and ¾ cup polenta each)
CARB. PER SERVING 39 g
START TO FINISH 30 minutes

- 4 ounces light smoked turkey sausage, very thinly sliced
- ½ cup chopped onion (1 medium)
- 2 garlic, minced
- 2 teaspoons olive oil
- 1½ pounds green or red Swiss chard, rinsed, trimmed, and cut into 2-inch-thick slices
- ¼ teaspoon crushed red pepper
- ⅛ teaspoon salt
- 3 cups water
- 1 cup cornmeal
- ⅛ teaspoon salt
- 1 cup cold water
- ¼ cup fat-free milk
- 1 ounce Parmesan cheese, shaved (optional)

Swiss Chard and Turkey Sausage over Polenta

1. In a very large skillet cook sausage, onion, and garlic in hot oil for 2 to 3 minutes or just until sausage is browned and onion is softened. Stir in half of the Swiss chard, the crushed red pepper, and ⅛ teaspoon salt. Cook, covered, for 2 minutes. Stir in the remaining Swiss chard. Cook, covered, for 5 minutes more, stirring often.

2. Meanwhile, for polenta, in a large saucepan bring the 3 cups water to boiling. In a medium bowl combine cornmeal and ⅛ teaspoon salt; stir in the 1 cup cold water. Slowly add cornmeal mixture to boiling water in saucepan, stirring constantly. Cook and stir until mixture returns to boiling. Cook, uncovered, over low heat about 5 minutes or until thick, stirring occasionally. Stir in milk.

3. Serve Swiss chard mixture over polenta. If desired, sprinkle with Parmesan cheese.

PER SERVING: 247 cal., 6 g total fat (1 g sat. fat), 22 mg chol., 786 mg sodium, 39 g carb. (4 g fiber, 4 g sugars), 11 g pro. Exchanges: 1 vegetable, 2 starch, 1 lean meat, 0.5 fat.

Sesame Chicken
Noodle Bowls

Chile Peppers

Those little chile peppers that cause a pleasant heat on your tongue can cause a painful burn on your skin when slicing or chopping them. Depending on the amount of capsaicin in the pepper, the volatile oils can linger for hours even if you wash your hands repeatedly.

The best advice: Wear plastic or rubber gloves while handling them to avoid direct contact. If your bare hands do touch the peppers, wash your hands and nails well with soap and warm water. Avoid touching your eyes for as long as possible.

Sesame Chicken Noodle Bowls

If you have regular cabbage on hand, you can substitute it for the napa cabbage.

SERVINGS 4 (2^1/$_2$ cups each)
CARB. PER SERVING 36 g
START TO FINISH 40 minutes

4	ounces thin rice noodles or rice sticks
1	tablespoon vegetable oil
12	ounces skinless, boneless chicken breast, cut into pieces
1	tablespoon toasted sesame oil
2	teaspoons grated fresh ginger
3	garlic, minced
1	cup purchased julienned carrots
1	cup fresh snow pea pods
6	ounces fresh shiitake mushrooms, stemmed and sliced
^{1}/$_2$	cup sliced radishes
1	fresh serrano chile pepper, stemmed, seeded, and thinly sliced (see tip, left)
2	cups unsalted chicken stock
^{1}/$_4$	cup orange juice
2	tablespoons reduced-sodium soy sauce
2	cups shredded napa cabbage
^{1}/$_2$	cup snipped fresh cilantro leaves
1	tablespoon sesame seeds, toasted (optional)

1. Cook rice noodles according to package directions; drain and set aside.

2. Meanwhile, in a large skillet heat the vegetable oil over medium-high heat. Add chicken. Cook and stir for 4 to 5 minutes or until cooked through. Using a slotted spoon, remove chicken from skillet; set aside.

3. Add the sesame oil, ginger, and garlic to skillet; cook and stir for 30 seconds. Add carrots, pea pods, mushrooms, radishes, and chile pepper; cook and stir for 2 minutes.

4. Add chicken stock to mushroom mixture in skillet. Bring to boiling; reduce heat. Simmer, uncovered, for 4 minutes. Stir in orange juice and soy sauce.

5. To serve, divide noodles among four soup bowls. Top with cabbage and chicken. Ladle hot stock mixture over noodles. Sprinkle with cilantro and, if desired, sesame seeds.

PER SERVING: 334 cal., 10 g total fat (2 g sat. fat), 54 mg chol., 612 mg sodium, 36 g carb. (4 g fiber, 5 g sugars), 25 g pro. Exchanges: 3 vegetable, 1.5 starch, 3 lean meat.

Chicken and Sweet Pepper Linguine Alfredo

Make your own chicken stir-fry strips by cutting skinless, boneless chicken breast halves into strips.

SERVINGS 4 (1½ cups each)
CARB. PER SERVING 43 g
START TO FINISH 25 minutes

- 1 9-ounce package refrigerated whole wheat linguine
  Nonstick cooking spray
- 1 red sweet pepper, cut into thin strips
- 2 zucchini and/or yellow summer squash, halved lengthwise and sliced (about 2½ cups)
- 8 ounces packaged chicken stir-fry strips
- 1 10-ounce container refrigerated light Alfredo pasta sauce
- ⅓ cup finely shredded Parmesan cheese (optional)
- 2 teaspoons snipped fresh thyme
- ⅛ teaspoon freshly ground black pepper

1. Using kitchen scissors, cut linguine in half. Cook linguine according to package directions; drain. Return to hot pan; cover and keep warm.

2. Meanwhile, coat a large skillet with cooking spray. Preheat skillet over medium-high heat. Add sweet pepper; cook and stir for 2 minutes. Add squash; cook and stir for 2 to 3 minutes more or until vegetables are crisp-tender. Remove from skillet.

3. Add chicken to skillet. Cook and stir for 2 to 3 minutes or until no longer pink. Return vegetables to skillet. Stir in pasta sauce; heat through.

4. Add chicken-vegetable mixture and, if desired, cheese to cooked linguine; toss gently to coat. Transfer to a serving bowl. Sprinkle with thyme and black pepper.

PER SERVING: 371 cal., 11 g total fat (5 g sat. fat), 66 mg chol., 461 mg sodium, 43 g carb. (7 g fiber, 5 g sugars), 26 g pro. Exchanges: 1.5 vegetable, 2.5 starch, 2 lean meat, 1 fat.

Red Pepper-Basil Raviolettis

For extra heat, sprinkle ⅛ to ¼ teaspoon crushed red pepper over pasta mixture along with the black pepper.

SERVINGS 5 (1¼ cups each)
CARB. PER SERVING 30 g
START TO FINISH 25 minutes

- 1 9-ounce package refrigerated cheese mini ravioli
- 1 medium red sweet pepper, chopped
- 1 cup chopped cooked skinless chicken breast
- ¾ cup chopped fresh basil
- 1 tablespoon extra virgin olive oil
- ¼ to ½ teaspoon coarsely ground black pepper
- ¼ teaspoon salt
- 2 tablespoons grated Parmesan cheese

1. Cook pasta according to package directions, omitting any salt or fat and adding the chopped red sweet pepper the last 1 minute of cooking time.

2. Place the cooked chicken in a colander. Reserve 2 tablespoons of the pasta cooking water; set aside. Drain pasta over the chicken in colander, gently shaking off excess water. Place the pasta mixture on a serving platter or in serving bowls and sprinkle with the reserved pasta water, basil, and olive oil; toss gently. Sprinkle with the pepper and salt and top with the Parmesan cheese.

PER SERVING: 310 cal., 12 g total fat (5 g sat. fat), 68 mg chol., 545 mg sodium, 30 g carb. (3 g fiber, 3 g sugars), 21 g pro. Exchanges: 2 starch, 2 lean meat, 1.5 fat.

Chicken and Sweet Pepper Linguine Alfredo

Red Pepper-Basil Raviolettis

Southwest Chicken Skillet

For an even lower-sodium meal, use fresh deli salsa or homemade salsa rather than purchased bottled salsa.

SERVINGS 4 (1 cup chicken mixture and 1 tortilla each)
CARB. PER SERVING 28 g
START TO FINISH 20 minutes

- 1 pound skinless, boneless chicken breast, cut into bite-size strips
- 1 tablespoon Southwest chipotle-flavored salt-free seasoning (Mrs. Dash)
- 1 tablespoon vegetable oil
- 1 medium yellow sweet pepper, coarsely chopped
- 1 small zucchini, bias-sliced and quartered
- ½ of a medium red onion, cut into thin wedges
- ½ cup bottled salsa
- ½ cup frozen whole kernel corn
- ½ cup no-salt-added canned black beans, rinsed and drained
- 4 small fajita-size low-carb whole wheat tortillas
  Chopped fresh cilantro (optional)

1. Sprinkle chicken with seasoning. In a very large skillet heat oil over medium-high heat. Add chicken; reduce heat to medium. Cook and stir about 2 minutes or until chicken is browned on all sides. Add sweet pepper, zucchini, and onion; cook and stir for 2 to 3 minutes more or until crisp-tender.

2. Add salsa, corn, and beans to skillet. Cook and stir for 1 to 2 minutes more or until heated through and chicken is no longer pink.

3. Serve with warm tortillas. (To heat tortillas, wrap in microwave-safe paper towels; microwave on 100 percent power [high] for 30 seconds.) If desired, sprinkle with cilantro.

PER SERVING: 315 cal., 9 g total fat (1 g sat. fat), 73 mg chol., 572 mg sodium, 28 g carb. (11 g fiber, 4 g sugars), 31 g pro. Exchanges: 1.5 starch, 4 lean meat, 0.5 fat.

Edamame-Chicken Stir-Fry

SERVINGS 4 (1 cup chicken mixture and $1/2$ cup rice each)
CARB. PER SERVING 35 g
START TO FINISH 30 minutes

 8 ounces skinless, boneless chicken breast halves
 3 tablespoons bottled hoisin sauce
 1 tablespoon rice vinegar
 1 tablespoon reduced-sodium soy sauce
 $1/4$ teaspoon crushed red pepper
 3 teaspoons olive oil or canola oil
 2 teaspoons grated fresh ginger
 1 cup bias-sliced carrots (2 medium)
 2 cups broccoli florets
 1 cup ready-to-eat fresh or frozen, thawed, shelled
     sweet soybeans (edamame)
 1 8.75-ounce pouch cooked whole grain brown rice

1. Cut chicken into thin bite-size strips; set aside. For sauce, in a small bowl stir together hoisin sauce, rice vinegar, soy sauce, and crushed red pepper; set aside.
2. Pour 2 teaspoons of the oil into a large nonstick wok or large nonstick skillet. Heat over medium-high heat. Add ginger; cook and stir for 15 seconds. Add carrots and stir-fry for 1 minute. Add broccoli and edamame and stir-fry for 4 to 5 minutes more or until vegetables are crisp-tender. Remove vegetables from wok. Add remaining 1 teaspoon oil to the wok. Add chicken strips and stir-fry for 2 to 4 minutes or until chicken is no longer pink. Return vegetables to the wok. Add sauce to chicken mixture, tossing to coat. Heat through.
3. Meanwhile, heat rice according to package directions. Serve chicken mixture over rice.

PER SERVING: 312 cal., 9 g total fat (1 g sat. fat), 33 mg chol., 299 mg sodium, 35 g carb. (5 g fiber, 8 g sugars), 23 g pro. Exchanges: 1 vegetable, 2 starch, 2 lean meat.

Asian Barbecued Chicken

SERVINGS 4 (1 packet each)
CARB. PER SERVING 21 g
PREP 20 minutes GRILL 35 minutes

 $1/4$ cup bottled plum sauce
 2 tablespoons water
 1 tablespoon bottled hoisin sauce
 1 tablespoon reduced-sodium soy sauce
 1 tablespoon honey
 1 teaspoon sesame seeds
 1 teaspoon grated fresh ginger
 1 clove garlic, minced
 $1/8$ teaspoon five-spice powder
 $1/8$ teaspoon crushed red pepper
 4 medium bone-in chicken breast halves, skin removed
     (about $1 3/4$ pounds total)
 1 medium sweet onion, thinly sliced

Edamame-Chicken Stir-Fry

1. In a small saucepan combine plum sauce, the water, hoisin sauce, soy sauce, honey, sesame seeds, ginger, garlic, five-spice powder, and crushed red pepper. Cook over medium heat until bubbly, stirring frequently. Reduce heat. Cover; simmer for 5 minutes. Remove from heat; set aside.
2. Tear off four 24×18-inch pieces of heavy-duty foil. Fold each in half to make an 18×12-inch rectangle. Place a chicken breast half on each foil rectangle. Top with plum sauce mixture and sweet onion.
3. For each packet, bring up two opposite edges of the foil and seal with a double fold. Fold remaining ends to enclose the food, allowing space for steam to build.
4. For a charcoal grill, place foil packets on the grill rack directly over medium coals. Grill, uncovered, for 35 to 40 minutes or until chicken is done (170°F), turning packets once halfway through cooking and carefully opening packets to check doneness. (For a gas grill, preheat grill. Reduce heat to medium. Place foil packets on grill rack over heat. Cover and grill as above.)

PER SERVING: 242 cal., 4 g total fat (1 g sat. fat), 83 mg chol., 468 mg sodium, 21 g carb. (1 g fiber, 10 g sugars), 29 g pro. Exchanges: 1 vegetable, 1 carb., 4 lean meat.

Jerk-Style Smoked Chicken

If you can't find Pickapeppa sauce, substitute 1 tablespoon Worcestershire sauce mixed with a dash of bottled hot pepper sauce.

SERVINGS 6 (2 drumsticks each)
CARB. PER SERVING 4 g
PREP 15 minutes MARINATE 1 hour SOAK 1 hour
SMOKE 1 hour 30 minutes

- 12 chicken drumsticks (3 pounds), skinned
- ½ cup low-sodium tomato juice
- ⅓ cup finely chopped onion (1 small)
- 2 tablespoons lime juice
- 1 tablespoon vegetable oil
- 1 tablespoon Pickapeppa sauce (optional)
- 4 cloves garlic, minced
- ½ teaspoon salt
- 6 to 8 fruitwood chunks
- 1 to 2 tablespoons Jamaican jerk seasoning
   Lime wedges

1. Place chicken drumsticks in a large resealable plastic bag set in a deep dish. For marinade, in a small bowl stir together tomato juice, onion, lime juice, oil, Pickapeppa sauce (if desired), garlic, and salt. Pour marinade over chicken in bag. Seal bag; turn to coat chicken. Marinate in the refrigerator for 1 to 4 hours, turning bag occasionally.

2. For at least 1 hour before smoke-cooking, soak wood chunks in enough water to cover. Drain before using. Drain chicken, discarding marinade. Sprinkle jerk seasoning evenly over chicken; rub in with your fingers.

Jerk-Style
Smoked Chicken

3. In a smoker arrange preheated coals, wood chunks, and water pan according to the manufacturer's directions. Pour water into pan. Place chicken drumsticks on the grill rack over water pan. Cover and smoke for 1½ to 2 hours or until chicken is tender and juices run clear (180°F). Add additional coals and water as needed to maintain temperature and moisture. Serve chicken with lime wedges. If desired, serve with *corn on the cob* pieces.

PER SERVING: 186 cal., 7 g total fat (1 g sat. fat), 118 mg chol., 477 mg sodium, 4 g carb. (1 g fiber, 1 g sugars), 25 g pro. Exchanges: 3.5 lean meat, 0.5 fat.

Pork and Green Onion Tortilla Pile-Ups

Use a serrated knife to cut romaine into shreds.
SERVINGS 4 (2 tortillas, 3 ounces cooked pork, 1 cup vegetables, and 2 tablespoons sauce each)
CARB. PER SERVING 33 g
START TO FINISH 40 minutes

- 2 teaspoons smoked paprika
- ½ teaspoon coarsely ground black pepper
- ¼ teaspoon salt
- 3 4-ounce boneless pork chops, trimmed of fat
   Nonstick cooking spray
- 8 green onions
- 8 corn tortillas
- ½ cup light sour cream
- ¼ cup snipped fresh cilantro
- 1 tablespoon lime juice
- 1 tablespoon water
- 1 clove garlic, minced
- ¼ teaspoon salt
- 3 cups packed shredded romaine lettuce
- 1 cup quartered grape tomatoes
- 1 medium lime

1. For rub, in a small bowl combine paprika, pepper, and ¼ teaspoon salt. Sprinkle rub evenly over all sides of the pork; press in with your fingers.

2. Coat an unheated grill pan with cooking spray. Heat over medium-high heat. Add pork to hot skillet; cook about 8 minutes or until barely pink in center, turning once halfway through cooking. Transfer pork to a cutting board; thinly slice.

3. Coat green onions with cooking spray; cook on grill pan about 2 minutes or until beginning to lightly brown, turning once halfway through cooking. Transfer green onions to a clean cutting board; when cool enough to handle, cut into 1-inch pieces. Working in batches, cook tortillas on grill pan about 2 minutes or until beginning to lightly brown, turning once halfway through cooking.

4. For sauce, in a small bowl whisk together sour cream, cilantro, lime juice, the water, garlic, and ¼ teaspoon salt.

Pork and Green Onion
Tortilla Pile-Ups

5. To serve, divide romaine and tomatoes among tortillas, placing romaine and tomatoes in the center of each tortilla. Top with sauce, green onions, and pork. Squeeze lime juice over all. Serve open-face with a knife and fork or fold edges over as you would a taco.

PER SERVING: 311 cal., 10 g total fat (4 g sat. fat), 55 mg chol., 383 mg sodium, 33 g carb. (6 g fiber, 3 g sugars), 24 g pro. Exchanges: 1 vegetable, 2 starch, 2 lean meat, 0.5 fat.

Brazilian Pork and Beans

3. If using low-heat setting, turn to high-heat setting. Stir in kale, cooked rice, and vinegar. Cover and cook for 15 minutes more.

PER SERVING: 375 cal., 10 g total fat (3 g sat. fat), 46 mg chol., 311 mg sodium, 43 g carb. (10 g fiber, 5 g sugars), 25 g pro. Exchanges: 1.5 vegetable, 2 starch, 2.5 lean meat, 1 fat.

Sweet-and-Sour Pork

This batter-free version of the restaurant favorite features the same ingredients without all of the fat.

SERVINGS 6 ($^3/4$ cup pork mixture and $^1/3$ cup rice each)
CARB. PER SERVING 29 g or 27 g
START TO FINISH 30 minutes

- $^3/4$ cup reduced-sodium chicken broth
- 3 tablespoons red wine vinegar
- 2 tablespoons reduced-sodium soy sauce
- 4 teaspoons sugar*
- 1 tablespoon cornstarch
- 1 clove garlic, minced
- 4 teaspoons vegetable oil
- 1 cup thinly sliced carrots (2 medium)
- 1 cup red sweet pepper cut into bite-size strips
- 1 cup fresh pea pods, trimmed
- 12 ounces boneless pork loin, trimmed of fat
- 1 8-ounce can pineapple chunks (juice pack), drained
- 2 cups hot cooked brown rice

1. For sauce, in a small bowl stir together broth, vinegar, soy sauce, sugar, cornstarch, and garlic; set aside.

2. In a large nonstick skillet heat 3 teaspoons of the oil over medium-high heat. Add carrots and sweet pepper; cook and stir for 3 minutes. Add pea pods. Cook and stir about 1 minute more or until vegetables are crisp-tender. Remove from skillet; set aside.

3. Add remaining 1 teaspoon oil to skillet. Cut pork into 1-inch pieces. Add pork to skillet. Cook and stir for 4 to 6 minutes or until pork is slightly pink in the center. Push pork from center of skillet. Stir sauce; add to center of skillet. Cook and stir until thickened and bubbly. Add vegetable mixture and pineapple chunks; heat through. Serve with hot cooked rice.

*SUGAR SUBSTITUTE: Choose Splenda Granular. Follow package directions to use product amount equivalent to 4 teaspoons sugar.

PER SERVING: 250 cal., 7 g total fat (2 g sat. fat), 31 mg chol., 306 mg sodium, 29 g carb. (3 g fiber, 11 g sugars), 16 g pro. Exchanges: 1 vegetable, 0.5 fruit, 1 starch, 2 lean meat, 0.5 fat.

PER SERVING WITH SUBSTITUTE: Same as above, except 241 cal, 27 g carb. (8 g sugars).

Brazilian Pork and Black Beans

The classic version of this dish, also known as Feijoada, is made with a combo of beef and pork.

SERVINGS 6 (1$^1/2$ cups each)
CARB. PER SERVING 43 g
PREP 15 minutes SLOW COOK 8 hours (low) or 4 hours (high), plus 15 minutes (high)

- 1 pound boneless pork shoulder roast
- 2 15-ounce cans no-salt-added black beans, rinsed and drained
- 1 14.5-ounce can no-salt-added diced tomatoes, undrained
- 1 cup reduced-sodium chicken broth or water
- $^3/4$ cup chopped onion
- $^3/4$ cup chopped red sweet pepper
- $^1/2$ teaspoon black pepper
- 4 cloves garlic, minced
- 1 teaspoon liquid smoke
- $^1/2$ teaspoon dried oregano, crushed
- $^1/2$ teaspoon ground ancho chile pepper
- $^1/4$ teaspoon salt
- 4 cups shredded fresh kale
- 1 8.8-ounce pouch cooked whole grain brown rice
- 1 tablespoon cider vinegar

1. Trim fat from pork roast and cut pork into 2-inch cubes. In a 3$^1/2$- or 4-quart slow cooker combine pork, beans, tomatoes, broth, onion, sweet pepper, black pepper, garlic, liquid smoke, oregano, ancho chile pepper, and salt.

2. Cover and cook on low-heat setting for 8 to 10 hours or on high-heat setting for 4 to 5 hours.

Grilled Pork and Pineapple

Most grocery stores sell peeled and cored fresh pineapple. Look for it in the produce section by other cut-up fruit.

SERVINGS 4 (1 pork chop, about 2 pineapple slices, and about 3 tablespoons yogurt mixture each)

CARB. PER SERVING 27 g

START TO FINISH 20 minutes

- 4 ¾-inch-thick boneless top loin pork chops (about 1¼ pounds total)
- ¼ teaspoon salt
- ¼ teaspoon black pepper
- 1 fresh pineapple, peeled and cored
- 1 6-ounce carton plain nonfat yogurt
- ⅓ cup low-sugar orange marmalade
- 1 tablespoon snipped fresh thyme

1. Sprinkle both sides of pork with the salt and pepper. Cut pineapple crosswise into ½-inch-thick slices; set aside. Combine yogurt and 2 tablespoons of the marmalade; set aside.

2. For a charcoal grill, place chops on the grill rack directly over medium coals. Grill, uncovered, for 4 minutes. Turn; add pineapple to grill. Brush chops and pineapple with remaining marmalade. Grill for 3 to 5 minutes more or until an instant-read thermometer inserted in pork registers 145°F and pineapple has light grill marks, turning pineapple once. Let pork rest for 3 minutes. (For a gas grill, preheat grill. Reduce heat to medium. Place chops on grill rack. Cover and grill as above.)

3. Arrange pineapple and chops on serving plates. Spoon yogurt mixture over chops and pineapple; sprinkle with fresh thyme.

PER SERVING: 263 cal., 4 g total fat (1 g sat. fat), 78 mg chol., 231 mg sodium, 27 g carb. (2 g fiber, 21 g sugars), 29 g pro. Exchanges: 1 fruit, 1 carb., 4 lean meat.

QUICK TIP

If you are using frozen rhubarb to make this **Pork Rhubarb Skillet**, thaw it and drain off any liquid before cooking it with the apple.

Pork Rhubarb Skillet

Although rhubarb's nickname is "pie plant," its abilities stretch far beyond pies, crisps, and cobblers. The tart, acidic stalks lend themselves to savory preparations that pair perfectly with pork.

SERVINGS 4 (1 cup pork mixture and $^1/_3$ cup couscous each)

CARB. PER SERVING 32 g or 28 g

START TO FINISH 30 minutes

- 1 tablespoon vegetable oil
- 1 pound lean boneless pork, cut into bite-size strips
- 1 medium onion, cut into thin wedges
- $1^1/_2$ cups sliced fresh rhubarb or frozen unsweetened sliced rhubarb, thawed
- 1 medium cooking apple, cored and sliced
- 1 cup chicken broth
- 2 tablespoons packed brown sugar*
- 1 tablespoon cornstarch
- 1 tablespoon snipped fresh sage
- $^1/_2$ teaspoon salt
- $^1/_4$ teaspoon black pepper
- $1^1/_3$ cups hot cooked couscous

1. In a very large skillet heat oil over medium-high heat. Add pork to skillet. Cook and stir for 3 to 4 minutes or until browned. Remove pork from skillet.

2. Add onion to skillet. Cook and stir for 2 to 3 minutes or until tender. Add rhubarb and apple; cook for 3 to 4 minutes or until crisp-tender.

3. For sauce, in a small bowl combine broth, brown sugar, cornstarch, sage, salt, and pepper. Add to skillet; cook and stir until thickened and bubbly. Add pork to skillet; heat through. Serve over hot cooked couscous.

*SUGAR SUBSTITUTE: Choose Splenda Brown Sugar Blend. Follow package directions to use product amount equivalent to 2 tablespoons brown sugar.

PER SERVING: 342 cal., 11 g total fat (3 g sat. fat), 64 mg chol., 565 mg sodium, 32 g carb. (3 g fiber, 13 g sugars), 28 g pro. Exchanges: 1 fruit, 1 starch, 3.5 lean meat, 1 fat.

PER SERVING WITH SUBSTITUTE: Same as above, except 331 cal., 28 g carb. (10 g sugars), 563 mg sodium.

Sicilian Tuna with Capers

This fish and marinade combo is full of flavor yet light on calories and fat. You'll need about an hour from start to finish, including marinating time.

SERVINGS 4 (1 tuna steak and 2 tablespoons tomato mixture each)

CARB. PER SERVING 1 g

PREP 20 minutes **MARINATE** 15 minutes **BROIL** 8 minutes

- 4 fresh or frozen tuna steaks, cut 1 inch thick (about 1 pound total)
- 2 tablespoons red wine vinegar
- 1 tablespoon snipped fresh dill weed or 1 teaspoon dried dill weed
- 2 teaspoons olive oil
- $^1/_4$ teaspoon salt
- $^1/_8$ teaspoon cayenne pepper
- $^1/_2$ cup chopped tomato
- 1 tablespoon capers, drained
- 1 tablespoon chopped pitted ripe olives
- 1 clove garlic, minced

1. Preheat broiler. Thaw fish, if frozen. Rinse fish and pat dry with paper towels. For marinade, in a shallow dish combine vinegar, dill weed, oil, salt, and half of the cayenne pepper. Add fish to marinade in dish, turning to coat. Cover and marinate in the refrigerator for 15 minutes.

2. Meanwhile, in a small bowl stir together tomato, capers, olives, garlic, and the remaining cayenne pepper.

3. Drain fish, reserving marinade. Place fish on the greased unheated rack of a broiler pan. Broil 4 inches from the heat for 4 minutes. Turn fish and brush with all of the reserved marinade. Broil for 4 to 8 minutes more or until fish begins to flake when tested with a fork. Serve tuna topped with tomato mixture. If desired, serve over *hot cooked rice* with *steamed baby bok choy*.

PER SERVING: 192 cal., 8 g total fat (2 g sat. fat), 43 mg chol., 271 mg sodium, 1 g carb. (0 g fiber, 1 g sugars), 27 g pro. Exchanges: 4 lean meat.

Sea Bass with
Fennel Slaw

Sea Bass with Fennel Slaw

This sizzlin' fish dish owes its sensational flavor to a double dose of fennel—fresh strips in the slaw and seeds in the coating for the fish.

SERVINGS 4 (1 fish fillet and about 1$\frac{1}{4}$ cups slaw each)
CARB. PER SERVING 10 g
PREP 40 minutes **CHILL** 2 hours **GRILL** 4 minutes

- 3 tablespoons white wine vinegar
- 1 tablespoon olive oil
- 2 teaspoons chopped fresh tarragon
- 1 teaspoon Dijon-style mustard
- $\frac{1}{8}$ teaspoon salt
- Dash black pepper
- 2 fennel bulbs, thinly sliced and cut into thin strips (about 4 cups)
- 1 cup coarsely shredded carrot
- 4 4- to 5-ounce fresh or frozen sea bass or grouper fillets, $\frac{3}{4}$ to 1 inch thick
- $\frac{1}{2}$ to 1 teaspoon fennel seeds, crushed
- $\frac{1}{2}$ teaspoon salt
- $\frac{1}{4}$ teaspoon black pepper
- Fresh fennel tops (optional)

1. In a screw-top jar combine vinegar, oil, tarragon, mustard, the $\frac{1}{8}$ teaspoon salt, and the dash pepper. Cover and shake well. Set aside 1 tablespoon of the vinegar mixture; cover and chill until serving time. For slaw, in a large bowl combine fennel strips and carrot. Pour the remaining vinegar mixture over fennel mixture. Toss lightly to coat. Cover and chill for 2 to 24 hours.

2. Thaw fish, if frozen. Rinse fish; pat dry with paper towels. Measure thickness of fish. In a small bowl stir together crushed fennel seeds, the $\frac{1}{2}$ teaspoon salt, and the $\frac{1}{4}$ teaspoon pepper; sprinkle evenly over both sides of fish fillets.

3. Place fish in a well-greased grill basket or in a greased grill wok. For a charcoal grill, place grill basket or grill wok on the grill rack directly over medium coals. Grill, uncovered, for 4 to 6 minutes per $\frac{1}{2}$-inch thickness of fish or until fish flakes easily when tested with a fork, turning basket once or carefully turning fish once halfway through grilling. (For a gas grill, preheat grill. Reduce heat to medium. Place fish in well-greased grill basket or in greased grill wok. Place grill basket or grill wok on grill rack over heat. Cover and grill as above.)

4. Drizzle the reserved 1 tablespoon vinegar mixture over grilled fish. Serve fish with slaw. If desired, garnish with fennel tops.

PER SERVING: 185 cal., 6 g total fat (1 g sat. fat), 46 mg chol., 538 mg sodium, 10 g carb. (4 g fiber, 2 g sugars), 22 g pro. Exchanges: 2 vegetable, 3 lean meat.

Scallop and
Asparagus
Alfredo

3. Whisk evaporated milk into the drippings in the skillet. Turn heat to medium-low. Add cream cheese, Parmesan cheese, lemon juice, and lemon-pepper seasoning. Cook and stir until heated through and cheeses are melted.

4. Add cooked pasta and asparagus to the skillet; toss to coat. Divide pasta mixture between two dinner plates. Top with the cooked scallops. If desired, garnish with parsley.

PER SERVING: 398 cal., 11 g total fat (6 g sat. fat), 66 mg chol., 530 mg sodium, 40 g carb. (3 g fiber, 12 g sugars), 36 g pro. Exchanges: 1 milk, 2 vegetable, 1 starch, 3 lean meat, 1 fat.

Grilled Halibut with Blueberry Sauce

Sage and pepper enhance the tantalizing flavor of the blueberries in the easy-fixing topper. Serve it with any grilled or broiled fish. It's great with chicken, too.

SERVINGS 4 (1 fish steak or fillet and $1/3$ cup sauce each)
CARB. PER SERVING 9 g
PREP 25 minutes GRILL 8 minutes

> 4 5- to 6-ounce fresh or frozen halibut steaks, sea bass fillets, or salmon fillets, about 1 inch thick
> $1^{1}/_{2}$ cups fresh blueberries
> 2 teaspoons snipped fresh sage
> $1/_{2}$ teaspoon freshly ground black pepper
> 1 teaspoon finely shredded orange peel
> 2 tablespoons orange juice
> 1 tablespoon olive oil
> Orange wedges (optional)
> Fresh sage leaves (optional)

1. Thaw fish, if frozen. Rinse fish; pat dry with paper towels. For blueberry sauce, in a medium bowl use a potato masher or fork to mash $3/_{4}$ cup of the blueberries. Stir in the remaining $3/_{4}$ cup blueberries, 1 teaspoon of the snipped fresh sage, and $1/_{4}$ teaspoon of the pepper. Cover and chill sauce until ready to serve.

2. In a small bowl combine the orange peel, orange juice, olive oil, remaining 1 teaspoon snipped fresh sage, and remaining $1/_{4}$ teaspoon pepper. Brush half of the orange juice mixture over the fish.

3. Lightly grease the grill rack. For a charcoal grill, place fish on the grill rack directly over medium coals. Grill, covered, for 5 minutes. Turn fish; brush with remaining orange juice mixture. Cover and grill for 3 to 7 minutes more or until fish flakes easily when tested with a fork. (For a gas grill, preheat grill. Reduce heat to medium. Place fish on the greased grill rack over heat. Cover and grill as above.)

4. To serve, place fish on four serving plates. Spoon the blueberry sauce over fish. If desired, garnish with orange wedges and sage leaves.

PER SERVING: 222 cal., 7 g total fat (1 g sat. fat), 45 mg chol., 77 mg sodium, 9 g carb. (1 g fiber, 6 g sugars), 30 g pro. Exchanges: 0.5 fruit, 4 lean meat, 0.5 fat.

Scallop and Asparagus Alfredo

Cut the cream cheese into pieces and sprinkle them into the pan so they melt more quickly.

SERVINGS 2 (2 cups each)
CARB. PER SERVING 40 g
START TO FINISH 30 minutes

> 8 ounces fresh or frozen sea scallops
> 2 ounces dried whole wheat penne pasta
> 1 pound fresh asparagus spears, cut into 1-inch pieces
> 2 teaspoons butter
> 2 cloves garlic, minced
> 1 5-ounce can evaporated fat-free milk
> 2 tablespoons reduced-fat cream cheese (Neufchâtel)
> 2 tablespoons finely shredded Parmesan cheese
> 1 tablespoon lemon juice
> $1/_{4}$ teaspoon lemon-pepper seasoning
> Snipped fresh Italian (flat-leaf) parsley (optional)

1. Thaw scallops, if frozen. Rinse scallops; pat dry with paper towels. Set aside. Cook pasta according to package directions, adding asparagus for the last 3 minutes of cooking time. Drain and keep warm.

2. In a large skillet melt butter over medium-high heat. Add scallops and garlic. Cook for 4 to 5 minutes or until scallops are golden brown, turning once. Remove scallops from skillet and add to the pasta mixture to keep warm.

Pesto Shrimp Pizza

Just a touch of honey sweetens the crispy whole wheat and cornmeal crust.

SERVINGS 6 (2 slices each)
CARB. PER SERVING 26 g
PREP 30 minutes **STAND** 10 minutes
RISE 30 minutes **BAKE** 11 minutes

2	teaspoons active dry yeast
½	cup warm water (105°F to 115°F)
2	teaspoons honey
2	teaspoons olive oil
½	cup whole wheat flour
2	tablespoons yellow cornmeal
¾	to 1 cup all-purpose flour
8	ounces cooked medium shrimp, peeled and deveined, or 1 cup chopped cooked chicken breast
5	tablespoons refrigerated basil pesto
½	cup shredded reduced-fat mozzarella cheese (2 ounces)

1. In a small bowl combine yeast and the warm water. Let stand for 5 minutes. Stir in honey and olive oil. In a medium bowl combine whole wheat flour, cornmeal, and ¼ teaspoon *salt*. Stir in yeast mixture. Using a wooden spoon, stir in as much of the all-purpose flour as you can.

2. Turn dough out onto a lightly floured surface. Knead in enough of the remaining all-purpose flour to make a moderately stiff dough that is smooth and elastic (3 to 4 minutes total). Shape dough in a ball. Cover; let rise in a warm place until nearly double in size (30 to 45 minutes).

3. Preheat oven to 425°F. Grease an extra-large baking sheet or two small baking sheets; set aside. Punch dough down; divide dough in half. Let rest for 10 minutes.

4. On a lightly floured surface roll each dough half into a 10- to 12-inch oval. Transfer to prepared baking sheet(s). Prick dough oval with a fork. Bake for 6 to 8 minutes or until lightly browned.

5. If desired, halve shrimp lengthwise. Toss shrimp with 1 tablespoon of the pesto to coat. Spread the remaining 4 tablespoons pesto over baked crusts. Top with shrimp; sprinkle with mozzarella cheese. Bake for 5 to 8 minutes more or until bubbly. Cut each pizza into six slices.

PER SERVING: 244 cal., 10 g total fat (2 g sat. fat), 70 mg chol., 388 mg sodium, 26 g carb. (2 g fiber, 3 g sugars), 15 g pro. Exchanges: 2 starch, 1.5 lean meat, 1.5 fat.

Sautéed Baby Bok Choy and Shiitake with Shrimp

The stems on shiitake mushrooms are tough, so cut them off and discard. Only use the caps.

SERVINGS 4 (1 cup each)
CARB. PER SERVING 15 g
START TO FINISH 25 minutes

- 1 pound fresh or frozen large shrimp in shells
- 1 tablespoon toasted sesame oil
- 1½ cups sliced shiitake mushrooms
- 2 cloves garlic, minced
- 4 cups halved, trimmed baby bok choy (about 1 pound)
- 2 cups fresh snow pea pods, trimmed
- 1 tablespoon oyster sauce
- 2 teaspoons reduced-sodium soy sauce
- ¼ teaspoon black pepper
- 1 tablespoon sesame seeds, toasted

1. Thaw shrimp, if frozen. Peel and devein shrimp, leaving tails intact. Rinse shrimp; pat dry with paper towels.
2. In a very large skillet heat sesame oil over medium-high heat. Add shrimp, mushrooms, and garlic; cook and stir for 4 to 6 minutes or just until shrimp are opaque. Carefully add baby bok choy; cook for 2 minutes more. Add pea pods, oyster sauce, soy sauce, and pepper to skillet; cook and stir for 1 minute more. Divide among four serving plates or bowls. Sprinkle with sesame seeds.

PER SERVING: 221 cal., 7 g total fat (1 g sat. fat), 172 mg chol., 415 mg sodium, 15 g carb. (3 g fiber, 2 g sugars), 27 g pro. Exchanges: 3 vegetable, 3 lean meat, 1 fat.

Kale-Powered Pasta

When selecting a jar of pasta sauce, read the labels. If there are options, choose one that has no sugar added.

SERVINGS 6 (1¼ cups each)
CARB. PER SERVING 36 g
START TO FINISH 30 minutes

- 6 ounces multigrain rotini pasta
- 8 ounces kale, large stems removed and leaves chopped
- 2 red and/or green sweet peppers, cut into bite-size strips
- 1 24-ounce jar reduced-sodium tomato-flavor pasta sauce
- ¼ cup snipped fresh basil
- ¼ cup crumbled reduced-fat feta cheese (1 ounce)
  Fresh basil leaves (optional)

1. In a large pot cook pasta according to package directions, except omit any salt and add kale and sweet peppers for the last 3 minutes of cooking time. Drain; return to pot.

Sautéed Baby Bok Choy and Shiitake with Shrimp

Two Great Greens

Seeing more green at the grocery store? Try one of these nutrient-loaded garden goodies.

Although **baby bok choy** looks like a leafy green, one taste will tell you it's a member of the cabbage family. The vitamin-packed leaves and fiber-rich stems turn from crisp to creamy when cooked.

Kale is the curly-leaf version of collard greens. Both have a flavor that's earthy and rich and maybe even a little bit sweet. Tear or cut the leaves from the central stalk, which is too tough to eat. Then fully cook the leaves to enjoy this antioxidant-filled food.

2. Stir pasta sauce and snipped basil into pasta and vegetables; heat through.
3. To serve, sprinkle individual servings with feta cheese. If desired, garnish with basil leaves.

PER SERVING: 221 cal., 4 g total fat (1 g sat. fat), 6 mg chol., 443 mg sodium, 36 g carb. (6 g fiber, 12 g sugars), 10 g pro. Exchanges: 1 vegetable, 2 starch, 0.5 lean meat, 0.5 fat.

Lasagna Bella

Spoon another one-third of the tomato mixture over the cheese-stuffed mushroom caps. Place remaining 4 mushroom caps on top of each cheese-stuffed mushroom cap in the baking dish to make stacks. Spoon the remaining tomato mixture evenly over the mushrooms. Sprinkle with the Parmesan cheese. Bake for 20 minutes. Let stand for 10 minutes. Sprinkle with fresh basil.

PER SERVING: 215 cal., 7 g total fat (4 g sat. fat), 19 mg chol., 565 mg sodium, 21 g carb. (6 g fiber, 13 g sugars), 19 g pro. Exchanges: 4 vegetable, 1.5 lean meat, 1 fat.

Caribbean Tofu Skewers

Before cutting, place the tofu blocks on paper towels for a couple minutes so the towels will absorb any liquid.

SERVINGS 4 (2 kabobs each)
CARB. PER SERVING 27 g
PREP 25 minutes MARINATE 8 hours GRILL 8 minutes

    1 peeled and cored fresh pineapple
    1 16- to 18-ounce package extra-firm tofu (fresh bean curd), drained and cut into 1-inch cubes
    3 tablespoons lime juice
    1 tablespoon olive oil
    1 teaspoon Jamaican jerk seasoning
  1/4 teaspoon salt
    1 clove garlic, minced
  1/2 small red onion, cut into thin wedges
    1 cup 1-inch pieces red, yellow, and/or green sweet pepper
       Nonstick cooking spray

1. Drain pineapple, reserving the juice. Cut pineapple into 1-inch cubes; cover and refrigerate until needed. Place tofu in a resealable plastic bag set in a shallow dish. For marinade, in a small bowl combine reserved pineapple juice, lime juice, olive oil, jerk seasoning, salt, and garlic. Pour over tofu. Seal bag; turn to coat tofu. Marinate in the refrigerator for 8 to 24 hours, turning bag occasionally.
2. Drain tofu, reserving marinade. On eight 12-inch skewers,* alternately thread tofu, pineapple chunks, onion wedges, and sweet pepper. Lightly coat assembled skewers with cooking spray.
3. For a charcoal grill, place tofu skewers on the grill rack directly over medium coals. Grill, uncovered, about 8 minutes or until sweet peppers are crisp-tender, turning to brown tofu evenly and brushing occasionally with marinade. (For a gas grill, preheat grill. Reduce heat to medium. Place tofu skewers on grill rack over heat. Cover and grill as above.)
*TEST KITCHEN TIP: If using wooden skewers, soak them in enough water to cover for at least 30 minutes before grilling.

PER SERVING: 231 cal., 10 g total fat (1 g sat. fat), 0 g chol., 234 mg sodium, 27 g carb. (4 g fiber, 16 g sugars), 13 g pro. Exchanges: 1 vegetable, 1 fruit, 0.5 starch, 1.5 lean meat, 1 fat.

Lasagna Bella

Look for portobellos that have medium brown color, a nonwrinkled surface, and no blemishes.

SERVINGS 4 (1 stuffed-mushroom stack each)
CARB. PER SERVING 21 g
PREP 20 minutes ROAST 13 minutes COOK 15 minutes
BAKE 20 minutes STAND 10 minutes

    8 large fresh portobello mushrooms
  1/8 teaspoon salt
    2 14.5-ounce cans no-salt-added diced tomatoes, drained
  1/2 cup chopped onion (1 medium)
    1 teaspoon salt-free tomato-basil-garlic seasoning blend
    1 cup shredded part-skim mozzarella cheese (4 ounces)
  3/4 cup low-fat cottage cheese (1%)
    2 tablespoons grated Parmesan cheese
    5 fresh basil leaves, snipped

1. Preheat oven to 425°F. Remove stems and gills from mushrooms. Place mushroom caps, cap sides down, on an unheated broiler pan; sprinkle with the salt. Roast for 13 to 26 minutes or until tender, turning once halfway through roasting time. Reduce oven temperature to 350°F.
2. Meanwhile, in a large saucepan combine tomatoes, onion, and seasoning blend. Bring to boiling; reduce heat. Simmer, uncovered, over medium heat for 15 minutes, stirring occasionally. In a bowl combine mozzarella cheese and cottage cheese.
3. Spoon one-third of the tomato mixture onto the bottom of a 2-quart square baking dish. Arrange 4 of the mushroom caps, cap sides down, over the tomato mixture. Spoon one-fourth of the cheese mixture over each mushroom cap.

QUICK TIP
Add a lime wedge or two to the grill for the
last few minutes of grilling and then squeeze
the citrusy juices over the sizzling kabobs.

Carribean Tofu Skewers

Four-Cheese
Macaroni and
Cheese

Vegetarian
Citrus-Corn
Tacos

Mexican Rice and
Bean Patties Salad
recipe on page 38

Four-Cheese Macaroni and Cheese

Don't tell! Nutrient-rich butternut squash is hidden within this cheesy kid-pleasing meal.

SERVINGS 8 (³/₄ cup each)
CARB. PER SERVING 31 g
PREP 30 minutes **BAKE** 25 minutes **ROAST** 40 minutes

  Nonstick cooking spray
  1 pound butternut squash, halved and seeded
  8 ounces dried whole grain elbow macaroni (about 2 cups)
  4 teaspoons butter
  2 tablespoons flour
  ½ teaspoon salt
  ⅛ teaspoon ground white pepper
  1 cup fat-free milk
  2 tablespoons semisoft cheese with garlic and fine herbs
  ¾ cup shredded part-skim mozzarella cheese (3 ounces)
  ¾ cup shredded reduced-fat sharp cheddar cheese (3 ounces)
  2 ounces Muenster cheese, very thinly sliced

1. Preheat oven to 375°F. Line a 15×10×1-inch baking pan with parchment paper; set aside. Coat a 2-quart square baking dish with cooking spray; set aside.
2. Coat the cut sides of the butternut squash with cooking spray; place squash halves, cut sides down, on the prepared baking pan. Roast for 40 to 45 minutes or until squash is very tender and cooked through. Remove from oven; let stand until cool enough to handle. Scoop flesh from squash halves; discard skin. Using a potato masher, mash the squash; set aside.
3. Meanwhile, cook pasta according to package directions. Drain well.
4. In a medium saucepan melt butter over medium heat. Whisk in flour, salt, and white pepper until combined. Add milk, whisking until smooth. Cook and stir until thickened and bubbly. Add semisoft cheese; whisk until cheese is melted. Stir in mashed squash. Add cooked pasta; stir until coated.
5. Place half of the pasta mixture in the prepared baking dish. Evenly sprinkle half of the mozzarella cheese and half of the cheddar cheese on top of the pasta. Arrange half of the Muenster cheese over all. Repeat layers. Bake about 25 minutes or until cheese is golden brown.

PER SERVING: 266 cal., 11 g total fat (6 g sat. fat), 26 mg chol., 402 mg sodium, 31 g carb. (4 g fiber, 4 g sugars), 13 g pro. Exchanges: 2 starch, 1 medium-fat meat, 1 fat.

Vegetarian Citrus-Corn Tacos

Along with some sweet peppers and corn, the citrus flavors featured in this tangy sauce transform basic crumbles of ground meat substitute into a tasty taco filling.

SERVINGS 4 (2 tacos each)
CARB. PER SERVING 47 g
START TO FINISH 30 minutes

  ½ cup orange juice
  ¼ cup snipped fresh cilantro
  1 teaspoon finely shredded lime peel
  2 tablespoons lime juice
  1 fresh jalapeño chile pepper, seeded and finely chopped (see tip, page 20)
  3 cloves garlic, minced
  1½ teaspoons cornstarch
  ⅛ teaspoon salt
  ⅛ teaspoon black pepper
  2 teaspoons cooking oil
  1 medium red sweet pepper, cut into thin strips
  1 12-ounce package frozen cooked and crumbled ground meat substitute (soy protein)
  1 cup frozen whole kernel corn
  8 6-inch corn tortillas
  ½ cup light sour cream

1. For sauce, in a small bowl combine orange juice, cilantro, lime peel, lime juice, jalapeño pepper, garlic, cornstarch, salt, and black pepper. Set aside.
2. In a large nonstick skillet heat oil over medium-high heat. Add sweet pepper strips; cook and stir until crisp-tender. Remove sweet pepper strips.
3. Add soy protein crumbles to skillet. Cook, stirring occasionally, for 3 to 4 minutes or until heated through. Stir in corn. Stir sauce; add to skillet. Cook and stir until thickened and bubbly. Reduce heat; cook and stir for 2 minutes more. Return sweet pepper strips to skillet; stir to combine.
4. Wrap tortillas in microwave-safe paper towels. Microwave on 100 percent power (high) for 45 to 60 seconds or until warm. Divide the pepper mixture among tortillas and top with sour cream. Fold the tortillas over the filling.

PER SERVING: 361 cal., 11 g total fat (2 g sat. fat), 8 mg chol., 490 mg sodium, 47 g carb. (10 g fiber, 6 g sugars), 21 g pro. Exchanges: 3 starch, 2 lean meat, 1 fat.

Mexican Rice and Bean Patties Salad

To easily transfer the patties from the platter to the skillet, place each on a square of waxed paper on the platter. Then use the waxed paper edges to pick up the patty and invert it into the skillet. *Pictured on page 36.*

SERVINGS 4 (1 patty, 2 cups greens, and $1/4$ cup sauce each)
CARB. PER SERVING 32 g
PREP 25 minutes **CHILL** 15 minutes **COOK** 6 minutes

　4　teaspoons olive oil
$1/2$　cup chopped red sweet pepper (1 small)
$1/3$　cup chopped red onion (1 small)
　2　tablespoons reduced-sodium taco seasoning
$2/3$　cup cooked brown rice
　1　14.5-ounce can no-salt-added black beans, rinsed and drained
$1/2$　of a 4-ounce can diced green chile peppers
$1/2$　cup light sour cream
$1/2$　cup pico de gallo
　8　cups mixed salad greens
　1　medium tomato, chopped (optional)
　　Snipped fresh cilantro (optional)

1. In a medium skillet heat 1 teaspoon of the oil over medium heat. Add sweet pepper and onion; cook for 4 to 5 minutes or until tender. Stir in 1 tablespoon of the taco seasoning (mixture will be dry). Remove from heat. Stir in rice. Set aside to cool.

2. Use a fork to mash beans slightly. Add rice mixture, chile peppers, and the remaining 1 tablespoon taco seasoning to the beans; stir and mash until the mixture holds together.

3. Divide bean mixture into four equal portions. Shape each portion into a patty about $3^1/2$ inches in diameter. Carefully place patties on a platter. Cover and chill for 15 minutes.

4. In a very large nonstick skillet heat the remaining 3 teaspoons oil over medium-high heat. Fry the patties in hot oil for 6 to 8 minutes or until heated through, turning once halfway through cooking time. (If patties brown too quickly, reduce heat to medium.)

5. In a small bowl stir together sour cream and pico de gallo. Divide greens among four serving plates; place patties on top of greens. Serve sour cream mixture with patties. If desired, garnish with chopped tomato and snipped cilantro.

PER SERVING: 228 cal., 7 g total fat (2 g sat. fat), 8 mg chol., 596 mg sodium, 32 g carb. (5 g fiber, 4 g sugars), 8 g pro. Exchanges: 2 starch, 0.5 lean meat, 1 fat.

Barley-Stuffed Peppers

Precooking the peppers helps to soften them slightly. Set the timer for 3 minutes so you don't overcook them at this point or they will become too soft when baked.

SERVINGS 4 ($1/2$ pepper and $3/4$ cup filling each)
CARB. PER SERVING 35 g
PREP 15 minutes **BAKE** 27 minutes **COOK** 12 minutes

　1　cup sliced fresh mushrooms
　1　cup low-sodium vegetable broth
$2/3$　cup quick-cooking barley
　2　large red, yellow, and/or green sweet peppers
$1/4$　cup refrigerated or frozen egg product, thawed, or 1 egg, lightly beaten
　1　tomato, peeled, seeded, and chopped (about $3/4$ cup)
$3/4$　cup shredded part-skim mozzarella cheese (3 ounces)
$1/2$　cup finely chopped zucchini
$1/3$　cup soft whole wheat bread crumbs
　1　tablespoon snipped fresh basil or $1/2$ teaspoon dried basil, crushed
　1　teaspoon snipped fresh rosemary or $1/8$ teaspoon dried rosemary, crushed
$1/2$　teaspoon onion salt

1. Preheat oven to 350°F. In a medium saucepan combine mushrooms, broth, and barley. Bring to boiling; reduce heat. Simmer, covered, for 12 to 15 minutes or until barley is tender; drain.

2. Meanwhile, halve the sweet peppers lengthwise; remove seeds and membranes. If desired, precook peppers in boiling water for 3 minutes; invert onto paper towels to drain.

3. For filling, in a medium bowl combine egg, tomato, $1/2$ cup of the cheese, the zucchini, bread crumbs, basil, rosemary, and onion salt. Stir in cooked barley mixture. Place peppers, cut sides up, in an ungreased 2-quart baking dish. Spoon barley mixture into peppers.

4. Bake, covered, for 25 to 30 minutes or until barley mixture is heated through. Sprinkle with the remaining $1/4$ cup cheese. Bake, uncovered, about 2 minutes more or until cheese is melted.

PER SERVING: 234 cal., 6 g total fat (3 g sat. fat), 11 mg chol., 451 mg sodium, 35 g carb. (6 g fiber, 7 g sugars), 13 g pro. Exchanges: 1 vegetable, 2 starch, 1 lean meat.

QUICK TIP

If the sweet peppers you use for making **Barley-Stuffed Peppers** have pretty stems, cut through them with a sharp knife so each serving has a stem.

fresh
salad meals

Light and Tangy
Chicken Salad

Whether tossed together in a bowl or carefully arranged on a platter, a bright and colorful salad can serve as a meal's main attraction. When loaded with whole grains, lean meats and seafood, lower-fat cheeses, lots of leafy greens, and plenty of produce, these fresh and tasty combos serve up plenty of nourishment.

Light and Tangy Chicken Salad

If you're cooking for one, eat this as a salad one day and then spoon it into a pita bread half as a sandwich filling the next.

SERVINGS 2 ($^3/_4$ cup each)
CARB. PER SERVING 13 g
START TO FINISH 15 minutes

- 3 tablespoons light mayonnaise
- 2 tablespoons mango chutney, chopped
- 1 cup diced cooked chicken breast
- $^1/_4$ cup halved seedless red grapes
- $^1/_4$ cup finely chopped celery
- 1 tablespoon finely chopped red onion
- $^1/_8$ teaspoon salt
- $^1/_8$ teaspoon black pepper
- 1 tablespoon sliced almonds, toasted

1. In a small bowl combine mayonnaise and mango chutney. Add chicken, grapes, celery, and red onion. Season with the salt and pepper. To serve, if desired, line two serving plates with *leaf lettuce* and spoon chicken mixture over lettuce. Sprinkle chicken salad with almonds.

PER SERVING: 249 cal., 11 g total fat (2 g sat. fat), 67 mg chol., 391 mg sodium, 13 g carb. (1 g fiber, 10 g sugars), 23 g pro. Exchanges: 1 fruit, 3 lean meat, 1.5 fat.

Almond Chicken Salad

If your grill is fired up, toss on a couple skinless, boneless chicken thighs and cook them up instead of purchasing the packaged grilled strips.

SERVINGS 4 ($2^1/_2$ cups each)
CARB. PER SERVING 25 g
START TO FINISH 15 minutes

- 12 ounces refrigerated grilled chicken breast strips, cut up
- 1 11-ounce can mandarin orange sections, drained
- 1 6-ounce package fresh baby spinach
- 1 cup seedless red grapes, halved
- $^1/_4$ cup sliced almonds
- $^1/_2$ cup orange juice
- 2 tablespoons balsamic vinegar
- 1 tablespoon toasted sesame oil
- $^1/_4$ teaspoon black pepper

1. In a very large bowl combine chicken, orange sections, spinach, grapes, and almonds.
2. In a screw-top jar combine orange juice, vinegar, oil, and pepper; cover and shake. Pour mixture over spinach mixture; toss. To serve, divide chicken salad among four plates.

PER SERVING: 249 cal., 8 g total fat (1 g sat. fat), 55 mg chol., 429 mg sodium, 25 g carb. (3 g fiber, 18 g sugars), 22 g pro. Exchanges: 1 vegetable, 1 fruit, 3 lean meat, 1 fat.

Curried Chicken Salad with Melon

Adding a sprinkling of fresh blueberries over a salad is an excellent way to boost fiber and antioxidants in your diet.

SERVINGS 4 ($^{1}/_{2}$ cup chicken salad, 4 melon slices, and $^{1}/_{4}$ cup blueberries each)

CARB. PER SERVING 22 g

START TO FINISH 20 minutes

- $^{1}/_{2}$ cup plain low-fat Greek yogurt
- 1 teaspoon curry powder
- $^{1}/_{2}$ teaspoon finely shredded lemon peel
- 1 teaspoon lemon juice
- $^{1}/_{2}$ teaspoon salt
- $^{1}/_{4}$ teaspoon dry mustard
- 2 cups chopped cooked chicken breast
- $^{1}/_{2}$ cup chopped celery (1 stalk)
- $^{1}/_{4}$ cup chopped walnuts, toasted
- $^{1}/_{4}$ cup snipped fresh cilantro
- $^{1}/_{4}$ cup finely chopped onion
- 8 thin slices cantaloupe
- 8 thin slices honeydew melon
- 1 cup fresh blueberries

1. In a medium bowl combine yogurt, curry powder, lemon peel, lemon juice, salt, and mustard. Add chicken, celery, walnuts, cilantro, and onion. Stir to combine.

2. To serve, arrange 2 cantaloupe slices, 2 honeydew slices, and $^{1}/_{4}$ cup blueberries on each of four serving plates. Divide chicken salad evenly among the plates.

PER SERVING: 266 cal., 9 g total fat (2 g sat. fat), 61 mg chol., 379 mg sodium, 22 g carb. (3 g fiber, 17 g sugars), 27 g pro. Exchanges: 1.5 fruit, 3 lean meat, 1 fat.

QUICK TIP

If purchasing half of a melon is a choice, take it. You should be able to get 16 thin slices from the melon half. If you want, use just one kind of melon instead of two.

Cajun Chicken Pasta Salad

If you have a patch of curly parsley thriving, use it instead of the flat-leaf variety.

SERVINGS 6 ($1^{1}/_{2}$ cups salad each)

CARB. PER SERVING 34 g

PREP 25 minutes **GRILL** 12 minutes

- 1 pound skinless, boneless chicken breast halves
- 1 tablespoon Cajun seasoning or salt-free Cajun seasoning
- 1 small green sweet pepper, halved
- 1 small red sweet pepper, halved
- 1 small onion, cut into $^{1}/_{4}$-inch-thick slices
- 8 ounces dried whole grain penne pasta
- $^{1}/_{2}$ cup sliced celery (1 stalk)
- $^{1}/_{4}$ cup snipped fresh Italian (flat-leaf)parsley
- 3 tablespoons apple juice
- 2 tablespoons cider vinegar
- 2 tablespoons canola oil
- 1 tablespoon snipped fresh thyme
- $^{1}/_{2}$ to 1 teaspoon bottled hot pepper sauce
- 1 clove garlic, minced

1. Sprinkle chicken evenly with Cajun seasoning. For a charcoal grill, place chicken on the greased grill rack directly over medium coals. Grill, uncovered, for 4 minutes. Add green pepper, red sweet pepper, and onion. Continue to grill for 8 to 11 minutes more or until chicken is no longer pink (170°F) and vegetables are slightly charred and tender, turning occasionally. (For a gas grill, preheat grill. Reduce heat to medium. Place chicken on grill rack over heat. Cover and grill as directed.) Transfer to a cutting board. Chop chicken and vegetables into bite-size pieces.

2. Cook pasta according to package directions; drain. Place pasta in a large bowl. Add chicken, grilled vegetables, celery, and parsley; stir to combine.

3. For dressing, in a small bowl whisk together the apple juice, cider vinegar, oil, thyme, hot pepper sauce, and garlic. Pour dressing over pasta mixture; toss to coat. Serve immediately or cover and chill. To serve, spoon salad onto six serving plates.

PER SERVING: 293 cal., 8 g total fat (1 g sat. fat), 48 mg chol., 227 mg sodium, 34 g carb. (1 g fiber, 4 g sugars), 21 g pro. Exchanges: 1 vegetable, 2 starch, 2 lean meat, 1 fat.

Curried Chicken
Salad with Melon

Buffalo Chicken Salad

Read the nutrition labels on the Buffalo wing sauces available at your grocery store and choose the sauce lowest in sodium.

SERVINGS 4 ($^1/_2$ of a romaine heart, $^3/_4$ cup chicken, 1 wedge cheese, 1 tablespoon dressing, 1 stalk celery each)
CARB. PER SERVING 13 g
START TO FINISH 15 minutes

  2 hearts romaine, sliced
  3 cups coarsely chopped cooked chicken breast
$^1/_2$ cup Buffalo wing sauce, such as Wing Time brand
  4 21-gram wedge light blue cheese, such as Laughing Cow brand, crumbled
  1 teaspoon cracked black pepper
$^1/_4$ cup bottled fat-free blue cheese salad dressing
  4 teaspoons fat-free milk
  4 stalks celery, each cut into 4 sticks

1. Divide romaine among four serving plates or bowls. In a medium microwave-safe bowl combine chicken and wing sauce. Microwave on 100 percent power (high) about 60 seconds or until heated through. Evenly divide chicken mixture and spoon over romaine. Top with crumbled cheese and pepper.

2. In a small bowl combine salad dressing and milk; drizzle over salad. Serve with celery sticks.

PER SERVING: 297 cal., 10 g total fat (3 g sat. fat), 99 mg chol., 596 mg sodium, 13 g carb. (3 g fiber, 4 g sugars), 37 g pro. Exchanges: 2.5 vegetable, 4.5 lean meat, 0.5 fat.

Buffalo Chicken Salad

Italian Roasted Chicken and Vegetable Toss

This salad is as tasty served cold as it is warm. Tote leftovers to work in a cooler for a delicious lunch.

SERVINGS 6 (1^1/3 cups greens and 1 cup chicken mixture each)

CARB. PER SERVING 10 g

PREP 25 minutes **ROAST** 50 minutes

  Nonstick cooking spray
2 bone-in chicken breast halves (about 2 pounds total)
1 cup packaged peeled fresh baby carrots
1 medium onion, cut into 8 wedges
2 medium zucchini, cut into 1-inch chunks (about 3 cups)
1 medium red or green sweet pepper, cut into 1-inch chunks (about 1 cup)
8 ounces fresh mushrooms
3 tablespoons olive oil
^{1}/4 teaspoon salt
^{1}/4 teaspoon black pepper
2 tablespoons balsamic vinegar
1 teaspoon dried Italian seasoning, crushed
8 ounces Mediterranean blend salad greens (8 cups)
^{1}/4 cup shredded Parmesan cheese (1 ounce)

1. Preheat oven to 375°F. Coat a shallow roasting pan with cooking spray. Arrange chicken, skin sides up, in one half of the roasting pan. In the other half of the pan arrange the carrots and onion wedges. Roast, uncovered, for 25 minutes.
2. Remove roasting pan from oven. Add zucchini, sweet pepper, and mushrooms to the carrots and onion. Drizzle chicken and vegetables with 2 tablespoons of the oil and sprinkle with the salt and black pepper.
3. Roast, uncovered, about 25 minutes more or until chicken is no longer pink (170°F) and vegetables are tender. Remove and set aside until cool enough to handle (5 to 10 minutes). Transfer vegetables to a large bowl.
4. Remove and discard chicken skin and bones. Using two forks, pull chicken apart into big shreds. Add chicken and any juices in pan to vegetables; toss. In a small bowl whisk together vinegar, the remaining 1 tablespoon olive oil, and the Italian seasoning. Add to chicken mixture; toss to coat.
5. To serve, arrange salad greens on a serving platter or divide among four serving plates. Spoon chicken mixture over greens. Sprinkle with cheese.

PER SERVING: 219 cal., 10 g total fat (2 g sat. fat), 51 mg chol., 217 mg sodium, 10 g carb. (2 g fiber, 5 g sugars), 22 g pro. Exchanges: 2 vegetable, 3 lean meat, 1 fat.

Roast 'em

If getting your family to eat vegetables is difficult, try roasting the veggies. Roasting caramelizes the natural sugars and makes them deliciously sweet.

Roast a large batch of vegetables and eat them as a side dish one night and toss them into a salad of any sort the next—leafy green, pasta, grain, and more. Try different combos: new potatoes, sweet potatoes, carrots, and red onion; and new potatoes, asparagus, sweet onion, and mushrooms.

Greek Pork and Farro Salad

You'll save time cooking if you start with 2 cups packaged cooked farro such as Archer Farms brand.

SERVINGS 5 (1 cup spinach, about 1¼ cups salad mixture, and about 2 tablespoons dressing each)
CARB. PER SERVING 26 g
PREP 20 minutes **COOK** 25 minutes

- ¾ cup farro
- 3 cups water
- 12 ounces pork tenderloin, trimmed
- 1 teaspoon Greek seasoning
- Nonstick cooking spray
- 1 cup chopped tomato (1 large)
- 1 cup chopped cucumber (1 small)
- ¾ cup chopped yellow sweet pepper (1 medium)
- ¼ cup red wine vinegar
- 3 tablespoons olive oil
- 2 tablespoons snipped fresh oregano
- 1 teaspoon Dijon-style mustard
- ¼ teaspoon black pepper
- 1 clove garlic, minced
- 5 cups fresh baby spinach
- 2 ounces reduced-fat feta cheese, crumbled

1. In a medium saucepan combine farro and water. Bring to boiling; reduce heat. Simmer, uncovered, for 15 to 20 minutes or until farro is desired tenderness. Drain. Place farro in a large bowl.

2. Meanwhile, cut tenderloin into 1-inch pieces. Toss pork cubes with Greek seasoning. Coat an unheated large nonstick skillet with cooking spray. Cook tenderloin in hot skillet over medium heat for 5 to 6 minutes or until no longer pink. Add to farro. Cool slightly.

3. Add tomato, cucumber, and sweet pepper to farro mixture.

4. For dressing, in a screw-top jar combine vinegar, olive oil, oregano, mustard, black pepper, and garlic; shake to combine. Toss with farro mixture. Serve farro salad either at room temperature or chilled. To serve, arrange spinach on five serving plates. Spoon farro salad over spinach; sprinkle with feta cheese.

PER SERVING: 299 cal., 11 g total fat (3 g sat. fat), 45 mg chol., 275 mg sodium, 26 g carb. (4 g fiber, 2 g sugars), 22 g pro. Exchanges: 1 vegetable, 1.5 starch, 2.5 lean meat, 1.5 fat.

Watercress and Pancetta-Apple Salad

Keep sweet, crunchy Candied Pecans on hand to sprinkle on any salad. Store them in an airtight container at room temperature for up to 2 weeks or freeze for up to 3 months.

SERVINGS 4 (1$^1/_2$ cups salad mixture with 4 teaspoons dressing, a scant 1$^1/_2$ teaspoons cheese, and 2 teaspoons pecans each)
CARB. PER SERVING 12 g or 11 g
START TO FINISH 40 minutes

Watercress and
Pancetta-Apple Salad

 2 tablespoons apple juice or apple cider
 1 tablespoon olive oil
 1 tablespoon cider vinegar
 2 teaspoons honey
12 ounces pork tenderloin, trimmed
 1 ounce pancetta, chopped
 1 teaspoon olive oil (optional)
 1 medium red apple, cored and thinly sliced into rings
 4 cups watercress, large stems removed
 $^3/_4$ ounce goat cheese (chèvre), crumbled
 8 teaspoons Candied Pecans

1. For dressing, in a screw-top jar combine apple juice, the 1 tablespoon oil, the vinegar, honey, $^1/_8$ teaspoon *salt,* and $^1/_8$ teaspoon *black pepper.* Cover; shake well. Set aside.
2. Cut pork into bite-size strips. Sprinkle pork with $^1/_8$ teaspoon *salt* and $^1/_8$ teaspoon *black pepper.* In a very large skillet cook pancetta over medium-high heat until crisp. Remove from skillet with a slotted spoon; transfer pancetta to paper towels. In the same skillet cook and stir pork for 3 to 4 minutes or just until done. Remove pork with a slotted spoon. If necessary, add the 1 teaspoon olive oil to skillet. Add apples; cook for 2 to 3 minutes or until apples are crisp-tender, turning occasionally.
3. To serve, arrange watercress on four serving plates; top with pork and apples. Sprinkle with pancetta and goat cheese. Sprinkle each salad with 2 teaspoons Candied Pecans. Drizzle salads with dressing.
CANDIED PECANS: Preheat oven to 300°F. In a small bowl beat 1 egg white until frothy. Add 2 cups pecans; toss to coat. Let stand for 5 minutes. Place 2 tablespoons packed brown sugar* in a large resealable plastic bag. Add the pecans; shake to coat. Spread pecans evenly in an ungreased 15x10x1-inch baking pan. Bake 20 minutes or until pecans are toasted and dry, stirring twice. Transfer to a large sheet of foil. Cool.
***SUGAR SUBSTITUTES:** Choose from Sweet'N Low Brown or Sugar Twin Granulated Brown. Follow package directions to use product amount equivalent to 2 tablespoons brown sugar.

PER SERVING: 236 cal., 12 g total fat (3 g sat. fat), 59 mg chol., 271 mg sodium, 12 g carb. (2 g fiber, 9 g sugars), 21 g pro. Exchanges: 1 vegetable, 0.5 fruit, 3 lean meat, 1 fat.

PER SERVING WITH SUBSTITUTE: Same as above, except 243 cal., 11 g carb.

Pork and Cabbage Salad

Keep nuts fresher longer by storing them in freezer bags or air-tight containers in the freezer.

SERVINGS 4 (1$^1/_2$ cups each)
CARB. PER SERVING 8 g
PREP 25 minutes **COOK** 5 minutes

 2 tablespoons reduced-sodium soy sauce
 1 tablespoon Asian chili sauce (Sriracha sauce)
 1 tablespoon canola oil
 4 cups shredded napa cabbage or savoy cabbage
 $^3/_4$ cup sliced red sweet pepper (1 medium)
 $^1/_2$ cup shredded carrot (1 medium)
 1 pound pork tenderloin, trimmed
 $^1/_4$ cup bias-sliced green onions (2)
 2 tablespoons chopped unsalted cashews

1. In a small bowl stir together soy sauce, chili sauce, and oil; set aside. In a large bowl combine the cabbage, sweet pepper strips, and carrot; set aside.
2. Cut the pork tenderloin crosswise into 2x$^1/_4$-inch strips. Toss with 1 tablespoon of the soy sauce mixture. In a large nonstick skillet cook and stir half of the pork mixture at a time over medium-high heat about 5 to 7 minutes or until pork is no longer pink. Add cooked pork and remaining soy sauce mixture to cabbage mixture in bowl. Toss to combine. To serve, divide salad among four serving plates and sprinkle with the green onions and cashews.

PER SERVING: 203 cal., 8 g total fat (1 g sat. fat), 70 mg chol., 438 mg sodium, 8 g carb. (2 g fiber, 4 g sugars), 26 g pro. Exchanges: 1 vegetable, 3.5 lean meat, 0.5 fat.

Cherry, Turkey,
and Wild Rice Salad

Beef and Arugula with
Raspberry-Chipotle
Dressing

Cherry, Turkey, and Wild Rice Salad

For a healthful dose of antioxidants, substitute fresh
spinach for the butterhead lettuce.

SERVINGS 6 (1 cup rice mixture and 1 cup greens each)
CARB. PER SERVING 30 g or 29 g
PREP 25 minutes **CHILL** up to 24 hours **COOK** 45 minutes

  4 cups water
  1 cup uncooked wild rice
  2 cups chopped cooked turkey breast
1½ cups halved, pitted fresh sweet cherries
 ½ cup sliced celery (1 stalk)
  1 teaspoon finely shredded orange peel
  3 tablespoons orange juice
  2 tablespoons canola oil
  2 tablespoons white wine vinegar
  1 teaspoon sugar*
  6 cups torn butterhead (Boston or Bibb) lettuce
 ¼ cup chopped pecans, toasted

1. In a medium saucepan combine water and rice. Bring to
boiling; reduce heat. Simmer, covered, for 45 to 50 minutes
or until rice is tender. Drain. Place rice in a large mixing bowl;
cool. Add turkey, cherries, and celery to cooled rice.
2. For dressing, in a small bowl whisk together orange peel,
orange juice, oil, vinegar, sugar, ¼ teaspoon each *salt* and
black pepper. Pour over rice mixture. Toss to combine.
Cover; chill for up to 24 hours.
3. To serve, arrange lettuce or spinach on a serving platter.
Spoon rice mixture over lettuce. Sprinkle with pecans.

*SUGAR SUBSTITUTES: Choose from Splenda Granular, Equal
Spoonful or packets, Truvia Spoonable or packets, or Sweet'N
Low bulk or packets. Follow package directions to use
product amount equivalent to 1 teaspoon sugar.

PER SERVING: 287 cal., 11 g total fat (1 g sat. fat), 35 mg chol.,
141 mg sodium, 30 g carb. (4 g fiber, 8 g sugars), 19 g pro.
Exchanges: 0.5 fruit, 1.5 starch, 2 lean meat, 1 fat.

PER SERVING WITH SUBSTITUTE: Same as above, except 285 cal.,
29 g carb. (7 g sugars).

Beef and Arugula with Raspberry-Chipotle Dressing

Slip a piece of foil over the cooked steak and let it stand
about 10 minutes before slicing.

SERVINGS 4 (2½ cups salad, about 4 ounces steak,
and 2 tablespoons dressing each)
CARB. PER SERVING 17 g
PREP 15 minutes **GRILL** 8 minutes

  1 pound lean boneless beef sirloin steak, cut 1 inch thick
  6 cups arugula leaves
  2 cups halved red and/or yellow cherry tomatoes
  2 cups fresh raspberries
  2 tablespoons soft goat cheese (chèvre)
  1 recipe Raspberry-Chipotle Dressing (page 49)

1. Sprinkle steak with ¼ teaspoon each *salt* and *black
pepper*. For a gas or charcoal grill, place steak on the grill rack
directly over medium heat. Grill, covered, to desired
doneness, turning steak once halfway through grilling. (Allow

Southwestern Beef, Rice, and Black Bean Salad

8 to 12 minutes for medium rare and 12 to 15 minutes for medium.) Slice steak.

2. To serve, place arugula on a serving platter. Arrange cherry tomatoes, steak, and raspberries on arugula. Dot with goat cheese. Drizzle with Raspberry-Chipotle Dressing.

RASPBERRY-CHIPOTLE DRESSING: Mash $\frac{1}{2}$ cup fresh raspberries. In a screw-top jar combine mashed berries, 2 tablespoons white wine vinegar, 1 tablespoon canola oil, 2 teaspoons honey, and 1 teaspoon chopped canned chipotle peppers in adobo sauce (see tip, page 20). Cover and shake.

PER SERVING: 249 cal., 10 g total fat (3 g sat. fat), 61 mg chol., 246 mg sodium, 17 g carb. (7 g fiber, 9 g sugars), 23 g pro. Exchanges: 2 vegetable, 0.5 fruit, 3 lean meat, 1 fat.

Southwestern Beef, Rice, and Black Bean Salad

If using wooden skewers, soak them in enough water to cover for 30 minutes before using.

SERVINGS 6 (2 skewers and $\frac{2}{3}$ cup rice mixture each)
CARB. PER SERVING 32 g
PREP 45 minutes **GRILL** 4 minutes

  1 pound beef top sirloin steak, cut 1 inch thick
  2 teaspoons salt-free Southwest seasoning blend
  1 teaspoon olive oil
  4 green onions, cut into 1-inch lengths
  12 6- to 8-inch skewers
  1$\frac{1}{2}$ cups cooked brown rice
  1 15-ounce can no-salt-added black beans, rinsed and drained
  $\frac{1}{2}$ cup chopped, seeded tomato (1 medium)
  $\frac{1}{4}$ cup snipped fresh cilantro
  1 cup frozen whole kernel corn
  $\frac{3}{4}$ cup chopped green sweet pepper (1 medium)
  $\frac{1}{2}$ cup chopped sweet onion (1 small)
  2 teaspoons olive oil
  $\frac{1}{2}$ cup bottled salsa
  $\frac{1}{4}$ cup lime juice
  $\frac{1}{2}$ teaspoon ground cumin

1. Cut steak into 2x$\frac{1}{4}$-inch strips. In a medium bowl toss steak, seasoning blend, and 1 teaspoon olive oil. Thread steak strips and green onions evenly onto skewers; set aside.

2. In a large bowl combine rice, black beans, tomato, and cilantro; set aside. In a large nonstick skillet cook corn, sweet pepper, and sweet onion in 2 teaspoons olive oil over medium-high heat for 5 minutes or until corn is slightly blackened, stirring frequently. Add to rice mixture. In a small bowl stir together salsa, lime juice, and cumin. Add to rice mixture; toss to combine. Set salad aside.

3. For a charcoal grill, place skewers on the grill rack directly over medium coals. Grill, uncovered, for 4 to 6 minutes or until meat is just pink in the center, turning once. (For a gas grill, preheat grill. Reduce heat to medium. Place skewers on grill rack over heat. Cover and grill as above.) To serve, spoon rice salad onto six serving plates and top with beef skewers.

PER SERVING: 271 cal., 6 g total fat (2 g sat. fat), 45 mg chol., 185 mg sodium, 32 g carb. (6 g fiber, 3 g sugars), 23 g pro. Exchanges: 2 starch, 3 lean meat.

Berries and Beef Summer Salad

You can substitute milder white (button) mushrooms for the cremini mushrooms if you wish.

SERVINGS 4 (1 cup fruit, 1 cup arugula, 2 ounces beef, and 2 tablespoons dressing each)
CARB. PER SERVING 20 g
PREP 20 minutes **MARINATE** 4 hours **GRILL** 17 minutes
STAND 5 minutes

12	ounces beef flank steak
1	recipe Orange-Balsamic Vinaigrette
12	cremini mushrooms
4	6- to 8-inch skewers (see tip, page 49)
4	cups arugula and/or baby spinach leaves
2	cups quartered or sliced strawberries and/or whole blueberries
2	kiwifruits, peeled and sliced
1	orange, peeled and sliced crosswise
1/4	cup loosely packed fresh Italian (flat-leaf) parsley, snipped

1. Place steak in a large resealable plastic bag set in a large bowl; pour half of the Orange-Balsamic Vinaigrette over steak. Seal bag; turn to coat steak. Marinate in the refrigerator for 4 to 24 hours, turning bag occasionally. Cover and chill the remaining vinaigrette to use for brushing the mushrooms and for the dressing.

2. Remove steak from marinade; discard marinade. Thread the mushrooms onto skewers. Brush mushrooms with 1 to 2 teaspoons of the reserved vinaigrette; set aside.

3. For a charcoal or gas grill, place steak on the grill rack directly over medium heat. Grill, covered, to desired doneness, turning steak once halfway through grilling. Allow 17 to 21 minutes for medium-rare to medium doneness (145°F to 160°F). Place skewers with mushrooms on the grill rack after turning the steak; turn skewers occasionally. Let steak stand for 5 minutes; thinly slice across the grain.

4. To serve, place arugula on a large serving platter. Arrange sliced steak, strawberries, kiwifruit slices, orange slices, and mushrooms on arugula. Top with parsley. Shake remaining Orange-Balsamic Vinaigrette and drizzle over salad.

ORANGE-BALSAMIC VINAIGRETTE: In a screw-top jar combine 3 tablespoons olive oil, 3 tablespoons white balsamic vinegar or white wine vinegar, 2 teaspoons finely shredded orange peel, 3 tablespoons orange juice, 2 tablespoons snipped fresh Italian (flat-leaf) parsley, 2 cloves minced garlic, and 1/4 teaspoon salt. Cover and shake well to mix. Serve immediately or cover and store in the refrigerator for up to 1 week.

PER SERVING: 263 cal., 12 g total fat (3 g sat. fat), 25 mg chol., 143 mg sodium, 20 g carb. (4 g fiber, 13 g sugars), 21 g pro. Exchanges: 1 vegetable, 1 fruit, 3 lean meat, 1 fat.

Sesame Scallop Salad

Cooking sesame seeds for a few minutes in a dry skillet turns them extra nutty, crunchy, and golden. If there's an Asian market nearby, you can save a step by buying them already toasted.

SERVINGS 2 (2 1/2 cups salad and 2 scallops each)
CARB. PER SERVING 35 g
START TO FINISH 30 minutes

4	fresh or frozen sea scallops or peeled and deveined large shrimp
2	ounces dried multigrain spaghetti
3	cups shredded napa cabbage and/or shredded romaine lettuce
1/2	cup coarsely shredded carrot
1/4	cup quartered and thinly sliced red onion
2	tablespoons rice vinegar or white wine vinegar
1	tablespoon reduced-sodium soy sauce
2	teaspoons canola oil
1 1/2	teaspoons honey
1/4	teaspoon crushed red pepper
2	teaspoons canola oil
1	teaspoon sesame seeds, toasted

1. Thaw scallops or shrimp, if frozen. Rinse and pat dry with paper towels. Cut scallops in half and set aside.

2. Cook spaghetti according to package directions; drain. Rinse with cold water; drain again. In a medium bowl toss together spaghetti, cabbage, carrot, and red onion. Transfer mixture to a serving bowl.

3. For dressing, in a small bowl whisk together vinegar, soy sauce, 2 teaspoons oil, the honey, and crushed red pepper. Set aside.

4. In a medium skillet heat the 2 teaspoons oil over medium heat. Add scallops or shrimp; cook for 3 to 4 minutes or until opaque, turning once to brown evenly. Place scallops or shrimp over the cabbage mixture. Drizzle dressing over all; sprinkle with sesame seeds. Gently toss to coat. To serve, divide salad between two serving plates.

PER SERVING: 355 cal., 12 g total fat (1 g sat. fat), 37 mg chol., 514 mg sodium, 35 g carb. (5 g fiber, 9 g sugars), 27 g pro. Exchanges: 2 vegetable, 1.5 starch, 3 lean meat, 1 fat.

Maple Mahi Mahi Salad

Mahi mahi, also known as dolphinfish, is a firm saltwater fish with a mild flavor. If you need a substitute, try grouper or red snapper.

SERVINGS 2 (3 ounces cooked fish and $2^{1}/_{2}$ cups cabbage mixture each)

CARB. PER SERVING 37 g

START TO FINISH 30 minutes

- $^{1}/_{2}$ cup frozen shelled sweet soybeans (edamame)
- 8 ounces fresh or frozen skinless mahi mahi fillets
- 2 tablespoons pure maple syrup
- 1 tablespoon balsamic vinegar
- 1 tablespoon finely chopped onion
- 1 tablespoon honey mustard
- 2 teaspoons olive oil
- $^{1}/_{8}$ teaspoon salt
- $^{1}/_{8}$ teaspoon black pepper
- 4 cups coarsely shredded napa cabbage
- $^{1}/_{2}$ cup fresh snow peas pods, trimmed and halved crosswise
- 2 tablespoons snipped dried cherries
- 2 tablespoons sliced almonds, toasted

Maple Mahi Mahi Salad

1. Cook edamame according to package directions; drain. Set aside to cool.

2. Preheat broiler. Thaw fish, if frozen. Rinse fish; pat dry with paper towels. Cut fish into two portions. Measure thickness of fish; set aside.

3. For dressing, in a small bowl whisk together maple syrup, vinegar, onion, honey mustard, oil, salt, and pepper.

4. Remove 2 tablespoons of the dressing and brush on all sides of the fish pieces.

5. Place fish on the unheated greased rack of a broiler pan. Broil 4 inches from heat until fish flakes easily when tested with a fork. Allow 4 to 6 minutes per $\frac{1}{2}$-inch thickness of fish.

6. Meanwhile, in a large bowl combine napa cabbage, snow pea pods, and cooked edamame. Pour the remaining dressing over cabbage mixture; toss to coat. To serve, divide cabbage mixture between two serving plates. Sprinkle with cherries and almonds. Top with fish.

PER SERVING: 359 cal., 11 g total fat (1 g sat. fat), 83 mg chol., 313 mg sodium, 37 g carb. (6 g fiber, 24 g sugars), 30 g pro. Exchanges: 2 vegetable, 0.5 fruit, 1 carb., 3.5 lean meat, 1 fat.

Green Bean and Tuna Salad

The beans are beautiful when left whole, but for easier eating, cut them into 1-inch pieces.

SERVINGS 4
CARB. PER SERVING 12 g
PREP 15 minutes COOK 6 minutes

1 pound fresh green beans, trimmed
2 6-ounce cans chunk white tuna (water pack), drained and broken into chunks
$\frac{1}{2}$ cup slivered red onion
$\frac{1}{4}$ cup chopped walnuts, toasted
$\frac{1}{3}$ cup light sour cream
2 teaspoons Dijon-style mustard
2 teaspoons balsamic vinegar
2 teaspoons cider vinegar
1 teaspoon snipped fresh dill weed
$\frac{1}{4}$ teaspoon black pepper

1. In a medium saucepan cook beans, covered, in a small amount of boiling water for 6 to 8 minutes or until crisp-tender; drain. Rinse beans with cold water; drain again. Transfer to a bowl.

2. Add tuna, red onion, and walnuts to beans. Toss gently to combine. For dressing, in a small bowl whisk together sour cream, mustard, balsamic and cider vinegars, dill weed, and pepper. Drizzle dressing over bean mixture. To serve, divide salad among four serving plates.

PER SERVING: 226 cal., 9 g total fat (2 g sat. fat), 41 mg chol., 400 mg sodium, 12 g carb. (4 g fiber, 5 g sugars), 24 g pro. Exchanges: 2 vegetable, 3 lean meat, 1 fat.

Green Bean and Tuna Salad

Go Green

Many salads start with a lettuce—iceberg, romaine, mixed baby, or butterhead, for example. But other fresh and flavorful greens loaded with good-for-you vitamins, nutrients, and antioxidants are tasty options.

Get a nutrition boost by substituting half of one of these greens for half of the lettuce you typically use. Try spinach—it is very high in iron and folate, as well as antioxidants such as vitamins A, C, and B complex. Or experiment with kale—it is rich in fiber; vitamins A, K, C, and B_6; as well as copper, calcium, magnesium, manganese, zinc, and selenium.

Asparagus and Shrimp Salad

Showcase fresh spring asparagus in this citrus- and tarragon-accented salad. The tender green stalks are nutrition powerhouses. They're excellent sources of many nutrients, including vitamins A, C, and K.

SERVINGS 4 (2$\frac{1}{2}$ cups each)
CARB. PER SERVING 17 g
START TO FINISH 30 minutes

- 12 ounces fresh or frozen medium shrimp in shells
- $\frac{1}{2}$ teaspoon finely shredded orange peel
- 2 tablespoons orange juice
- 1 pound fresh asparagus, trimmed
- 3 oranges

Orange juice (optional)
- 1 tablespoon olive oil or salad oil
- 1 tablespoon white wine vinegar
- 1 clove garlic, minced
- 1 teaspoon chopped fresh tarragon
- $\frac{1}{4}$ teaspoon black pepper
- $\frac{1}{8}$ teaspoon salt
- 6 cups torn mixed salad greens
- $\frac{1}{4}$ cup sliced green onions (2)

1. Thaw shrimp, if frozen. Peel and devein shrimp, leaving tails intact if desired. Rinse shrimp; pat dry with paper towels. In a large saucepan bring 4 cups water to boiling. Add shrimp; reduce heat. Simmer, uncovered, for 1 to 3 minutes or until shrimp are opaque. Drain in a colander. Rinse with cold water; drain again. Transfer shrimp to a bowl. Add orange peel and the 2 tablespoons orange juice; toss gently to coat.

2. In a medium saucepan cook asparagus, covered, in a small amount of boiling water for 4 to 6 minutes or until crisp-tender. Drain in a colander. Rinse with cold water; drain again.

3. Peel oranges. Working over a bowl, cut oranges into sections; reserve $\frac{1}{3}$ cup of the juice. (If necessary, add additional orange juice to make $\frac{1}{3}$ cup.) For dressing, in a small bowl whisk together the $\frac{1}{3}$ cup orange juice, the oil, vinegar, garlic, tarragon, pepper, and salt.

4. In a large bowl combine shrimp, asparagus, orange sections, greens, and green onions. Pour dressing over all; toss gently to coat. To serve, divide salad among four serving plates.

PER SERVING: 174 cal., 5 g total fat (1 g sat. fat), 107 mg chol., 504 mg sodium, 17 g carb. (5 g fiber, 12 g sugars), 16 g pro. Exchanges: 1 vegetable, 1 fruit, 2 lean meat.

Zesty Shrimp Row Salad

Bottled cayenne pepper sauce, such as Frank's RedHot, kicks up the heat in the shrimp and the dressing.

SERVINGS 4 ($\frac{3}{4}$ cup lettuce, $\frac{1}{2}$ cup couscous, 10 to 12 shrimp, $\frac{1}{4}$ cup tomato mixture, and 3 tablespoons dressing each)
CARB. PER SERVING 34 g
PREP 30 minutes MARINATE 1 hour COOK 2 minutes

- 3 tablespoons lime juice
- 2 tablespoons finely chopped green onion (1)
- 2 tablespoons olive oil
- 2 teaspoons honey
- 2 teaspoons prepared horseradish
- 1 teaspoon bottled cayenne pepper sauce
- 12 ounces fresh peeled, deveined medium shrimp
- $\frac{3}{4}$ cup Israeli (large pearl) couscous
- $\frac{1}{4}$ cup sliced green onions (2)
- 1 cup coarsely chopped, seeded tomato (2 medium)
- $\frac{1}{4}$ cup slivered red onion
- 2 tablespoons snipped fresh cilantro
- 3 cups mixed baby lettuces or baby spinach
- $\frac{1}{4}$ cup dehydrated corn
- 1 recipe Cilantro Buttermilk Dressing

1. In a large resealable plastic bag combine lime juice, 2 tablespoons green onion, 1 tablespoon of the olive oil, the honey, horseradish, and 1 teaspoon cayenne pepper sauce.

Rinse shrimp well and pat dry with paper towels. Add shrimp to the bag and seal. Turn to coat. Marinate in the refrigerator for 1 to 2 hours. Drain and discard marinade.

2. In a large skillet heat the remaining 1 tablespoon oil over medium-high heat. Add shrimp; cook and stir for 2 to 3 minutes or until shrimp are opaque. Set aside.

3. Prepare couscous according to package directions. Toss with $\frac{1}{4}$ cup green onions. Set aside and let cool. In a small bowl stir together the tomato, red onion, and cilantro.

4. To serve, arrange rows of ingredients evenly on a serving platter in the following order: lettuce, couscous mixture, shrimp, and tomato mixture. Sprinkle corn over the top. Serve with Cilantro Buttermilk Dressing.

CILANTRO BUTTERMILK DRESSING: In a small bowl whisk together $\frac{1}{3}$ cup low-fat buttermilk; $\frac{1}{4}$ cup plain low-fat Greek yogurt; 2 tablespoons snipped fresh cilantro; 1 tablespoon lime juice; $\frac{1}{4}$ to $\frac{1}{2}$ teaspoon bottled cayenne pepper sauce; 1 clove garlic, minced; and $\frac{1}{8}$ teaspoon salt.

PER SERVING: 287 cal., 9 g total fat (2 g sat. fat), 110 mg chol., 589 mg sodium, 34 g carb. (3 g fiber, 8 g sugars), 18 g pro. Exchanges: 1 vegetable, 2 starch, 4 lean meat, 1 fat.

Zesty Shrimp Row Salad

Cucumber-Radish Barley Salad

Regular barley should not be mistaken for quick-cooking—it takes a lot longer to cook.

SERVINGS 5 (1¼ cups barley and ¾ cup spinach each)
CARB. PER SERVING 34 g
PREP 15 minutes **COOK** 10 minutes

- 1½ cups water
- ¾ cup uncooked quick-cooking barley
- 1 15-ounce can no-salt-added garbanzo beans (chickpeas), rinsed and drained
- 2 cups chopped, peeled cucumber (1 medium)
- 1 cup thinly sliced radishes
- ½ cup sliced green onions (4)
- 3 tablespoons cider vinegar
- 2 tablespoons olive oil
- 2 tablespoons apple juice or orange juice
- 2 tablespoons snipped fresh oregano
- ½ teaspoon black pepper
- ¼ teaspoon salt
- 4 cups torn fresh spinach
- 2 ounces feta cheese, crumbled

1. In a medium saucepan bring water to boiling. Add barley; reduce heat. Simmer, covered, for 10 to 12 minutes or until barley is tender and water is absorbed. Transfer barley to a colander and rinse with cold water; drain well.

2. In a large bowl combine barley, garbanzo beans, cucumber, radishes, and green onions; set aside.

3. For dressing, in a small bowl stir together the vinegar, olive oil, apple juice, oregano, pepper, and salt. Add to barley mixture; toss to coat. To serve, arrange spinach on a platter or five serving plates. Spoon barley mixture over spinach and sprinkle with feta cheese.

PER SERVING: 251 cal., 9 g total fat (2 g sat. fat), 10 mg chol., 283 mg sodium, 34 g carb. (7 g fiber, 3 g sugars), 10 g pro. Exchanges: 2 starch, 1 lean meat, 1 fat.

QUICK TIP
Make use of the extra black beans. Eat them as a snack or toss them into an omelet, soup, or salad.

Mexican Edamame and Couscous Salad

Present this colorful arranged salad and then give it a toss with tongs or two forks before serving.

SERVINGS 4 (2 cups romaine, ½ cup couscous, 2 tablespoons edamame, 2 tablespoons beans, ½ cup vegetables, ½ tablespoon queso fresco, and 2 tablespoons dressing each)
CARB. PER SERVING 37 g
START TO FINISH 30 minutes

- ¼ cup cider vinegar
- 3 tablespoons snipped fresh cilantro
- 3 tablespoons olive oil
- 1 to 2 teaspoons chopped canned chipotle chile pepper in adobo sauce (see tip, page 20)
- 1 clove garlic, minced
- ¼ teaspoon salt
- ¼ teaspoon black pepper
- 8 cups coarsely shredded romaine lettuce
- 2 cups cooked Israeli (large pearl) couscous,* whole grain small pasta, or whole grain penne pasta
- 10 grape tomatoes, halved
- 1 medium yellow sweet pepper, cut into bite-size pieces
- ½ cup frozen shelled sweet soybeans (edamame), cooked according to package directions
- ½ cup canned no-salt-added black beans, rinsed and drained
- 1 lime, cut into thin wedges
- 2 tablespoons crumbled queso fresco

1. For dressing, in a screw-top jar combine vinegar, cilantro, oil, chile pepper, garlic, salt, and black pepper. Cover and shake well to combine; set aside.

2. Cover a large serving platter with romaine. Toss couscous with 1 tablespoon of the dressing. In a small bowl combine tomatoes and sweet pepper. Arrange tomato mixture, couscous, edamame, black beans, and lime wedges on romaine on the platter. To serve, drizzle with the remaining dressing; sprinkle with queso fresco..

*TEST KITCHEN TIP: To cook the couscous, in a small saucepan combine 1 cup water and ¾ cup Israeli (large pearl) couscous. Bring to boiling; reduce heat. Simmer, covered, for 8 minutes. Remove from heat. Let stand, covered, for 5 minutes.

PER SERVING: 290 cal., 12 g total fat (2 g sat. fat), 3 mg chol., 184 mg sodium, 37 g carb. (7 g fiber, 4 g sugars), 10 g pro. Exchanges: 1 vegetable, 2 starch, 0.5 lean meat, 2 fat.

comforting
soups and stews

Beef Fajita Soup

It's easy to indulge in a hearty amount of good-for-you ingredients with spoon after spoon of these meals in a bowl. Each simmering soup is chock-full of lean protein, vitamin-rich vegetables, and just-right spices that make it fresh and flavorful. Along with one-bowl meals, you'll find soups—both hot and cold—to serve as a side.

Beef Fajita Soup

To make slicing the beef into strips easier, partially freeze it for 30 minutes before slicing.

SERVINGS 4 (2 cups each)
CARB. PER SERVING 16 g
START TO FINISH 40 minutes

- $\frac{1}{2}$ teaspoon garlic powder
- $\frac{1}{2}$ teaspoon ground cumin
- $\frac{1}{2}$ teaspoon paprika
- $\frac{1}{8}$ teaspoon cayenne pepper
- 12 ounces boneless beef sirloin steak, trimmed and cut into very thin bite-size strips
- Nonstick cooking spray
- 2 teaspoons canola oil
- 2 cups yellow or green sweet peppers cut into thin bite-size strips (2 medium)
- 1 medium onion, halved and thinly sliced
- 2 14.5-ounce cans lower-sodium beef broth
- 1 14.5-ounce can no-salt-added diced tomatoes, undrained
- $\frac{1}{4}$ cup light sour cream
- $\frac{1}{2}$ teaspoon finely shredded lime peel
- 1 ounce baked tortilla chips, coarsely crushed ($\frac{2}{3}$ cup) (optional)
- $\frac{1}{2}$ of an avocado, seeded, peeled, and chopped or sliced (optional)
- $\frac{1}{4}$ cup snipped fresh cilantro (optional)

1. In a medium bowl combine garlic powder, cumin, paprika, and cayenne pepper. Add steak strips and toss to coat.

2. Coat an unheated 4-quart nonstick Dutch oven with cooking spray. Heat over medium-high heat. Add half of the steak strips; cook for 2 to 4 minutes or until browned, stirring occasionally. Remove meat from the pan and repeat with remaining steak strips.

3. Add the oil to the Dutch oven. Add sweet peppers and onion. Cook over medium heat about 5 minutes or until lightly browned and just tender, stirring occasionally. Add broth and tomatoes. Bring to boiling. Stir in steak strips and heat through.

4. To serve, ladle soup into bowls. Add a spoonful of sour cream to individual servings and sprinkle with lime peel. If desired, top with tortilla chips, avocado, and cilantro.

PER SERVING: 221 cal., 7 g total fat (2 g sat. fat), 55 mg chol., 443 mg sodium, 16 g carb. (3 g fiber, 8 g sugars), 24 g pro. Exchanges: 3 vegetable, 1 starch, 3 lean meat, 1 fat.

Barley-Beef Soup

Either regular or clear balsamic vinegar will serve the same purpose—rounding out the flavor—in this full-of-veggies bowl.

SERVINGS 8 (1$\frac{1}{2}$ cups each)

CARB. PER SERVING 21 g

PREP 25 minutes **SLOW COOK** 8 hours (low) or 4 hours (high)

  12 ounces lean beef or lean lamb stew meat
   1 tablespoon vegetable oil
   4 14.5-ounce cans lower-sodium beef broth
   1 14.5-ounce diced tomatoes, undrained
   1 cup chopped onion (1 large)
   1 cup peeled parsnips or potato cut into $\frac{1}{2}$-inch pieces
   1 cup frozen mixed vegetables
  $\frac{2}{3}$ cup regular pearled barley
  $\frac{1}{2}$ cup chopped celery (1 stalk)
   1 bay leaf
   2 cloves garlic, minced
   1 teaspoon dried oregano or basil, crushed
  $\frac{1}{4}$ teaspoon black pepper
   1 tablespoon balsamic vinegar

1. Trim fat from meat. Cut meat into $\frac{3}{4}$- to 1-inch pieces. In a large skillet brown meat in hot oil over medium-high heat; drain off fat.

2. Transfer meat to a 5- to 6-quart slow cooker. Stir in broth, tomatoes, onion, parsnips, frozen vegetables, barley, celery, bay leaf, garlic, oregano, and pepper.

3. Cover and cook on low-heat setting for 8 to 10 hours or on high-heat setting for 4 to 5 hours. Remove and discard bay leaf. Stir in vinegar. To serve, ladle soup into bowls.

PER SERVING: 177 cal., 4 g total fat (1 g sat. fat), 20 mg chol., 517 mg sodium, 21 g carb. (4 g fiber, 4 g sugars), 15 g pro. Exchanges: 1 vegetable, 1 starch, 1.5 lean meat.

Creole Beef Stew

If beef chuck roast is cheaper than lean stew meat, purchase a 2$\frac{1}{2}$- to 2$\frac{3}{4}$-pound roast, trim the fat, and cut the meat into $\frac{3}{4}$-inch cubes to use instead of the stew meat.

SERVINGS 6 (1$\frac{1}{4}$ cups stew and $\frac{1}{3}$ cup rice each)

CARB. PER SERVING 27 g

PREP 20 minutes **SLOW COOK** 8 hours (low) or 4 hours high

   1 cup chopped onion (1 large)
   1 cup chopped green sweet pepper
   1 cup sliced celery (2 stalks)
   1 cup fresh or frozen sliced okra
   2 bay leaves
 1$\frac{1}{2}$ pounds cubed lean beef stew meat
  $\frac{1}{4}$ teaspoon black pepper

   1 14.5-ounce can diced tomatoes, undrained
   1 cup reduced-sodium chicken broth
   3 tablespoons tomato paste
   2 tablespoons quick-cooking tapioca, crushed
   1 teaspoon dried thyme leaves, crushed
  $\frac{1}{2}$ teaspoon sugar (optional)
  $\frac{1}{2}$ teaspoon salt
  $\frac{1}{4}$ to $\frac{1}{2}$ teaspoon cayenne pepper
   1 10-ounce bag frozen whole grain brown rice
   3 tablespoons snipped fresh parsley (optional)

1. Place onion, sweet pepper, celery, okra, and bay leaves in a 4- to 5-quart slow cooker. Top with beef; sprinkle with black pepper. Combine tomatoes, broth, tomato paste, tapioca, thyme, sugar (if using), salt, and cayenne pepper; pour over meat. Cover and cook on low-heat setting for 8 to 10 hours or on high heat setting for 4 to 5 hours. Remove and discard bay leaves.

2. Five minutes before serving, cook frozen brown rice according to package directions. To serve, ladle stew into bowls and add a mound of rice. If desired, garnish individual servings with parsley.

PER SERVING: 289 cal., 7 g total fat (2 g sat. fat), 73 mg chol., 576 mg sodium, 27 g carb. (3 g fiber, 6 g sugars), 29 g pro. Exchanges: 1 vegetable, 1.5 starch, 3 lean meat.

Wagon Wheel Chili

Kids love wagon wheel pasta, but if you cannot find it, use any shape of medium-size pasta such as shells or rotini.

SERVINGS 6 (1$\frac{1}{8}$ cups each)

CARB. PER SERVING 36 g

PREP 20 minutes **COOK** 25 minutes

   8 ounces lean ground beef
  $\frac{3}{4}$ cup chopped green sweet pepper (1 medium)
  $\frac{1}{2}$ cup chopped onion (1 medium)
   1 tablespoon chili powder
 1$\frac{1}{2}$ teaspoons ground cumin
  $\frac{1}{2}$ teaspoon dried oregano, crushed
  $\frac{1}{4}$ teaspoon salt
   1 15-ounce can no-salt-added red kidney beans, rinsed and drained
   1 14.5-ounce can no-salt-added stewed tomatoes, snipped and undrained
   1 14.5-ounce can no-salt-added diced tomatoes, undrained
   2 tablespoons no-salt-added tomato paste
   4 ounces dried wagon wheel pasta (about 1$\frac{3}{4}$ cups)
   6 tablespoons shredded reduced-fat cheddar cheese
    Chopped red onion (optional)

1. In large saucepan cook ground beef, sweet pepper, and onion over medium heat until browned; drain off fat.

Wagon Wheel Chili

2. Stir in chili powder, cumin, oregano, and salt; cook for 1 minute more. Add beans, stewed tomatoes, diced tomatoes, and tomato paste. Bring to boiling; reduce heat. Simmer, covered, for 20 minutes.

3. Meanwhile, in a medium saucepan cook pasta in boiling water until just tender. Drain. Add pasta to chili mixture in the large saucepan. Return to boiling.

4. To serve, ladle chili into bowls. Top individual servings with cheese. If desired, sprinkle with chopped red onion.

PER SERVING: 257 cal., 5 g total fat (2 g sat. fat), 28 mg chol., 260 mg sodium, 36 g carb. (9 g fiber, 9 g sugars), 18 g pro. Exchanges: 2 starch, 2 lean meat.

Save Time

Make soup prep swift by chopping or slicing carrots, onions, sweet peppers, and other veggies a day or two ahead. Place each in a separate container or resealable plasic bag and refrigerate portions.

Or instead of purchasing produce that needs prepping, look for precut vegetables in the produce aisle or on the salad bar. You may not find all of the vegetables there, but having one or two ready to go saves time.

Lamb and Eggplant Stew

Summer Corn Tortilla Soup

Lamb and Eggplant Stew

If you prefer, make this hearty stew with lean beef stew meat instead of lamb.

SERVINGS 4 (1³/4 cups each)
CARB. PER SERVING 27 g
PREP 20 minutes SLOW COOK 8 hours (low) or
4 hours (high), plus 30 minutes (high)

    Nonstick cooking spray
1½ pounds lamb stew meat, trimmed
  1 14.5-ounce can diced tomatoes, undrained
  1 14.5-ounce can lower-sodium beef broth
  1 large onion, cut into wedges
  2 large carrots, coarsely chopped
 ⅓ cup snipped dried apricots
  4 cloves garlic, minced
  2 teaspoons dried oregano, crushed
  1 teaspoon ground turmeric
 ¼ teaspoon ground cinnamon
 ¼ teaspoon cayenne pepper
  1 pound eggplant, cut into 1-inch cubes
 ¼ cup snipped fresh parsley

1. Coat an unheated very large nonstick skillet with cooking spray. Add lamb and brown lamb on all sides.
2. In a 3½- or 4-quart slow cooker stir together the lamb, tomatoes, broth, onion, carrots, apricots, garlic, oregano, turmeric, cinnamon, and cayenne pepper.
3. Cover and cook on low-heat setting for 8 to 10 hours or on high-heat setting for 4 to 5 hours. If using low-heat setting, turn to high-heat setting. Stir in the eggplant. Cover and cook for 30 minutes more. Stir in parsley just before serving. To serve, ladle stew into bowls.

PER SERVING: 349 cal., 10 g total fat (3 g sat. fat), 111 mg chol., 513 mg sodium, 27 g carb. (8 g fiber, 15 g sugars), 39 g pro. Exchanges: 2 vegetable, 1 starch, 4 lean meat, 0.5 fat.

Summer Corn Tortilla Soup

When fresh sweet corn is out of season, use frozen whole kernel corn instead.

SERVINGS 8 (1½ cups each)
CARB. PER SERVING 27 g
START TO FINISH 40 minutes

 ½ cup chopped onion (1 medium)
 12 cloves garlic, minced
  1 tablespoon olive oil
  2 cups fresh sweet corn kernels (4 ears of corn)
  2 cups chopped tomatoes
  2 cups diced yellow summer squash or zucchini
  1 15-ounce can no-salt-added black beans,
    rinsed and drained
  8 ounces coarsely chopped boneless pork loin
  4 6-inch corn tortillas
  8 cups reduced-sodium chicken broth
 ½ teaspoon chili powder
 ½ teaspoon ground cumin
 ¼ cup snipped fresh cilantro
    Nonstick cooking spray
  1 ripe avocado, halved, seeded, peeled, and thinly sliced

1. In a 4-quart Dutch oven cook onion and garlic in hot oil about 5 minutes or until tender. Stir in corn, tomatoes, squash, beans, and pork. Cook and stir until heated through. Chop 2 of the corn tortillas. Stir chopped tortillas, broth, chili powder, and cumin into mixture in Dutch oven. Cook and stir about 5 minutes or until tortillas dissolve and meat is done. Stir in cilantro.
2. Meanwhile, preheat broiler. Place the remaining 2 tortillas on a baking sheet. Coat both sides of each tortilla with cooking spray. Broil 4 to 5 inches from the heat for 2 to 3 minutes or until crisp and golden brown, turning once halfway through broiling time. Using a long knife, cut tortillas into thin strips. While still warm, gently "scrunch" the strips to create wavy tortilla strips. Carefully place on a paper towel; cool.
3. To serve, ladle soup into bowls. Top individual servings with tortilla strips and avocado slices.

PER SERVING: 224 cal., 7 g total fat (1 g sat. fat), 17 mg chol., 595 mg sodium, 27 g carb. (7 g fiber, 4 g sugars), 15 g pro. Exchanges: 1 vegetable, 1.5 starch, 1.5 lean meat, 1 fat.

Gingered Sweet Potato and Pork Soup

You can substitute thinly sliced green onion tops for the snipped chives.

SERVINGS 6 (1 cup each)
CARB. PER SERVING 19 g
PREP 25 minutes COOK 13 minutes

　1　tablespoon butter or vegetable oil
　12　ounces lean pork loin, cut into 3/4-inch pieces
　1/2　cup sliced shallots
　2　teaspoons minced, peeled fresh ginger
　1　teaspoon minced garlic
　2　14.5-ounce cans reduced-sodium chicken broth
　1/4　teaspoon black pepper
　1　pound sweet potatoes, peeled and cut into 3/4-inch chunks
　1　tablespoon lime juice
　1　tablespoon snipped fresh chives

1. In a 4- to 5-quart Dutch oven heat butter over medium-high heat. Cook pork, shallots, ginger, and garlic in hot butter, turning occasionally, until pork is browned on all sides and shallot is tender. Transfer pork mixture to a bowl; set aside.

2. Carefully add broth and pepper to Dutch oven, scraping up any browned bits left on the bottom of the pan. Add sweet potatoes to pan. Bring to boiling; reduce heat. Simmer, covered, for 8 minutes. Add pork mixture to pan. Return to boiling. Simmer, covered, for 5 to 8 minutes more or until pork is done and sweet potatoes are tender.

3. Before serving, stir in lime juice. To serve, ladle soup into bowls and garnish individual servings with snipped chives.

PER SERVING: 178 cal., 4 g total fat (2 g sat. fat), 41 mg chol., 405 mg sodium, 19 g carb. (3 g fiber, 5 g sugars), 16 g pro. Exchanges: 1 starch, 2 lean meat.

Sausage Albondigas Soup

Chorizo adds a little heat to the meatballs (albondigas) in this classic Mexican soup.

SERVINGS 6 (1 1/3 cups each)
CARB. PER SERVING 12 g
PREP 20 minutes BAKE 15 minutes COOK 12 minutes

　12　ounces lean ground pork
　4　ounces uncooked chorizo sausage, casing removed
　1/2　cup cooked brown rice
　1/4　cup finely shredded carrot
　1/4　cup snipped fresh cilantro
　2　cloves garlic, minced
　1　teaspoon ground cumin
　1/4　teaspoon black pepper
　1　egg, beaten, or 1/4 cup refrigerated or frozen egg product, thawed
　1/2　cup chopped onion (1 medium)
　2　teaspoons canola oil
　2　14.5-ounce cans reduced-sodium chicken broth
　1　14.5-ounce can no-salt-added diced tomatoes, undrained
　1　teaspoon dried oregano, crushed
　1/2　teaspoon ground cumin
　2　cups coarsely chopped zucchini
　1/4　cup fresh cilantro leaves

1. Preheat oven to 350°F. Line a 15×10×1-inch baking pan with foil; set aside.

2. In a medium bowl combine pork, chorizo, rice, carrot, 1/4 cup snipped cilantro, garlic, 1 teaspoon cumin, and the black pepper. Mix to combine thoroughly. Add egg and stir to combine. Shape into 24 meatballs. Place meatballs on prepared baking pan. Bake about 15 to 20 minutes or until browned and cooked through (160°F). Remove from baking sheet with a slotted spoon.

3. Meanwhile, in a 4-quart Dutch oven, cook onion in hot oil over medium heat for 5 minutes or until just tender. Add broth, tomatoes, oregano, and 1/2 teaspoon cumin. Bring to boiling. Stir in zucchini; return to boiling. Cook about 2 minutes or until zucchini is just tender. Remove from heat. Stir in 1/4 cup cilantro leaves and the cooked meatballs. To serve, ladle soup into bowls.

PER SERVING: 241 cal., 12 g total fat (4 g sat. fat), 81 mg chol., 635 mg sodium, 12 g carb. (2 g fiber, 4 g sugars), 21 g pro. Exchanges: 2 vegetable, 2.5 lean meat, 1.5 fat.

Sausage
Albondigas
Soup

Chicken Pot Pie Stew

Dried herbs may be substituted for the fresh herbs. Use ¹/₂ teaspoon dried thyme leaves, crushed, and ¹/₄ teaspoon dried oregano, crushed, and add them with the chicken broth.

SERVINGS 6 (1¹/₈ cups stew and about 3 piecrust leaves each)

CARB. PER SERVING 30 g

PREP 25 minutes **BAKE** 6 minutes **COOK** 25 minutes

- 4 teaspoons canola oil
- 1 pound skinless, boneless chicken thighs, cut into ³/₄-inch pieces
- 1 cup chopped celery (2 stalks)
- 1 cup chopped carrots (2 medium)
- ¹/₂ cup chopped onion (1 medium)
- 2 cloves garlic, minced
- 2¹/₂ cups reduced-sodium chicken broth
- 2 cups fresh mushrooms, sliced
- 1 cup fresh sweet corn kernels or frozen whole kernel corn, thawed
- ¹/₂ cup frozen peas, thawed
- 1 12-ounce can evaporated fat-free milk
- ¹/₄ cup flour
- 1 teaspoon snipped fresh thyme
- ¹/₂ teaspoon snipped fresh oregano
- ¹/₄ teaspoon salt
- ¹/₄ teaspoon black pepper
- 1 recipe Piecrust Leaves (use about ¹/₄ of the recipe)

1. In a 4-to 5-quart nonstick Dutch oven heat 2 teaspoons of the oil over medium heat. Add chicken. Cook and stir about 4 to 5 minutes until chicken pieces are browned on all sides. Remove from Dutch oven and transfer to a bowl; set aside.

Chicken Pot Pie Stew

2. In the same Dutch oven heat the remaining 2 teaspoons oil over medium heat. Add celery, carrots, onion, and garlic. Cook and stir for 8 to 10 minutes or until vegetables are just tender.

3. Add chicken broth to pot; bring to boiling. Add chicken, mushrooms, corn, and peas. Return to boiling; reduce heat. Simmer, uncovered, about 8 minutes or until chicken is done and vegetables are just tender.

4. In a small bowl whisk together evaporated milk and flour. Add flour mixture to soup mixture. Cook and stir until mixture thickens and bubbles. Cook and stir for 2 minutes more to thicken soup mixture. Stir in fresh thyme, fresh oregano, salt, and pepper. To serve, ladle soup into bowls and garnish individual servings with about 3 Piecrust Leaves.

PIECRUST LEAVES: Preheat oven to 400°F. Let $^1/_2$ of a 15-ounce package rolled refrigerated unbaked piecrust (1 crust) stand according to package directions. Unroll piecrust onto a lightly floured surface. In a small bowl whisk 1 tablespoon refrigerated or frozen egg product, thawed, and $^1/_4$ teaspoon water together. Lightly brush mixture over piecrust. Sprinkle piecrust with 1 teaspoon fresh thyme leaves. Using a 1- to $1^1/_4$-inch floured cutter, cut piecrust into leaves or desired shapes. Place piecrust shapes on a baking sheet. Bake for 6 to 8 minutes or until golden brown. Cool completely on the baking sheet. To store extra piecrust leaves, place them in an airtight container and freeze for up to 1 month. Use as soup toppers, salad toppers, or mix into your favorite snack mix.

PER SERVING: 295 cal., 9 g total fat (2 g sat. fat), 72 mg chol., 557 mg sodium, 30 g carb. (3 g fiber, 12 g sugars), 24 g pro. Exchanges: 1 vegetable, 1.5 starch, 3 lean meat.

Farro and Vegetable Chicken Chili

Read the labels to identify the tomato paste with the lowest sodium.

SERVINGS 8 ($1^1/_2$ cups chili and 2 tablespoons cheese each)
CARB. PER SERVING 31 g
PREP 50 minutes **COOK** 20 minutes

- 1   cup semipearled farro
- $1^1/_4$ pounds skinless, boneless chicken breast halves
- 2   cups chopped onions (2 large)
- 2   cups chopped zucchini (2 small)
- 1   cup chopped carrots (2 medium)
- 1   fresh jalapeño chile pepper, stemmed, seeded (if desired), and finely chopped (see tip, page 20)
- 2   teaspoons olive oil
- 2   tablespoons chili powder
- 2   teaspoons ground cumin
- $^1/_2$ teaspoon crushed red pepper
- 2   14.5-ounce cans reduced-sodium chicken broth
- 1   14.5-ounce can no-salt-added diced tomatoes, undrained
- 1   6-ounce can tomato paste
- 1   cup shredded cheddar cheese (4 ounces)

1. Rinse farro. In a medium saucepan bring 2 cups water to boiling. Stir in farro. Return to boiling; reduce heat. Simmer, covered, for 20 to 25 minutes or until farro is tender. Drain off any excess water.

2. In a large skillet bring 2 cups water to boiling. Add chicken breasts. Reduce heat. Simmer, covered, for 12 to 15 minutes or until chicken is no longer pink (170°F). Using a slotted spoon, transfer chicken to a cutting board. Cool slightly. Coarsely chop or shred chicken. Set aside.

3. Meanwhile, in a 4-quart Dutch oven cook onions, zucchini, carrots, and chile pepper in hot oil about 5 minutes or until tender. Stir in chili powder, cumin, and crushed red pepper. Stir in broth, tomatoes, tomato paste, and another 2 cups water. Bring to boiling; reduce heat. Simmer, covered, for 20 minutes. Stir in cooked farro and chopped or shredded chicken. Cook and stir until heated through.

4. To serve, ladle chili into bowls. Top individual servings with 2 tablespoons of the cheddar cheese each.

PER SERVING: 305 cal., 8 g total fat (4 g sat. fat), 60 mg chol., 504 mg sodium, 31 g carb. (5 g fiber, 7 g sugars), 26 g pro. Exchanges: 2 vegetable, 1.5 starch, 3 lean meat, 0.5 fat.

Vietnamese Chicken Noodle Soup

If some at your table like spicy, pass the crushed red pepper and they can add more.

SERVINGS 6 (1 cup each)

CARB. PER SERVING 14 g

PREP 20 minutes COOK 10 minutes

- 1 pound skinless, boneless chicken thighs, cut into 3/4-inch pieces
- 1/2 cup sliced shallots
- 2 teaspoons minced, peeled fresh ginger
- 2 teaspoons minced garlic
- 2 teaspoons canola oil
- 2 14.25-ounce cans no-salt-added, fat-free chicken broth
- 1 cup snow pea pods, trimmed and thinly sliced lengthwise
- 1 tablespoon fish sauce
- 1/4 teaspoon black pepper
- 1/8 teaspoon crushed red pepper
- 2 ounces thin rice noodles
- 1 cup fresh bean sprouts or canned bean sprouts, rinsed and drained
- 2 tablespoons thinly sliced green onions
- 2 tablespoons snipped fresh cilantro
- 2 tablespoons thinly sliced fresh basil
- 6 lime wedges

1. In a 4-quart Dutch oven cook and stir chicken, shallots, ginger, and garlic in hot oil until chicken is browned and shallots are just tender. Add broth, pea pods, fish sauce, black pepper, and crushed red pepper. Bring to boiling; reduce heat. Simmer, covered, for 8 minutes. Add rice noodles and bean sprouts and cook 2 minutes more or until chicken is no longer pink.

2. Stir in green onions and cilantro just before serving. To serve, ladle soup into bowls. Sprinkle individual servings with basil. Serve with lime wedges.

PER SERVING: 176 cal., 5 g total fat (1 g sat. fat), 72 mg chol., 376 mg sodium, 14 g carb. (1 g fiber, 3 g sugars), 19 g pro. Exchanges: 1 starch, 2.5 lean meat.

Turkey and Cranberry Roasted Squash Soup

Special enough serve for the holidays yet easy enough to dish up every day, this soup warms the taste buds with a touch of cinnamon.

SERVINGS 6 (1 cup each)

CARB. PER SERVING 23 g

PREP 30 minutes COOK 20 minutes ROAST 20 minutes

- 3 cups 3/4-inch pieces peeled butternut or acorn squash or pumpkin
- 1 medium sweet onion, cut into thin wedges
- 2 tablespoons canola oil
- 1 pound skinless, boneless turkey breast tenderloin, cut into 3/4-inch pieces
- 2 14.5-ounce cans reduced-sodium chicken broth
- 3/4 cup thinly sliced carrot
- 1/2 cup dried cranberries
- 1/4 teaspoon ground cinnamon
- 2 teaspoons snipped fresh sage
- 1 teaspoon snipped fresh thyme
- 6 tablespoons chopped pecans, toasted (optional)

1. Preheat oven to 400°F. Line a 15x10x1-inch baking pan with foil. Toss squash or pumpkin and onion with 1 tablespoon of the oil in the prepared baking pan. Roast, uncovered, for 20 to 25 minutes or until squash is tender and lightly browned, gently tossing once. Remove from oven.

2. Meanwhile, in a 4-quart Dutch oven heat remaining 1 tablespoon oil over medium heat. Add turkey pieces. Cook and stir to brown turkey on all sides. Carefully add broth, carrot, cranberries, and cinnamon to pan. Bring to boiling; reduce heat. Simmer, covered, about 10 minutes or until turkey is done and carrot is tender. Stir in roasted squash mixture, sage, and thyme. Heat through.

3. To serve, ladle soup into bowls. If desired, garnish individual servings with toasted pecans.

PER SERVING: 203 cal., 5 g total fat (1 g sat. fat), 33 mg chol., 588 mg sodium, 23 g carb. (3 g fiber, 12 g sugars), 17 g pro. Exchanges: 0.5 fruit, 1 starch, 2 lean meat, 1 fat.

QUICK TIP
To keep the numbers in your meal plan in line, it's important to stick with the suggested serving size. Use a measuring cup to ladle the soup into bowls.

Turkey and Cranberry
Roasted Squash Soup

Fish and Potato Chowder

Place the cooked bacon on paper towels to drain. Use an additional paper towel to blot the fat from the bacon.

SERVINGS 6 (1⅓ cups each)
CARB. PER SERVING 27 g
PREP 15 minutes **COOK** 25 minutes

2	slices bacon
1	cup chopped onion (1 large)
2	cloves garlic, minced
3	cups reduced-sodium chicken broth
1	pound Yukon gold potatoes, peeled and cut into ¾-inch pieces
1	pound cod fillets, cut into ¾-inch pieces
1	12-ounce can evaporated fat-free milk
1	tablespoon butter
½	teaspoon black pepper

1. In a 4-quart Dutch oven cook bacon over medium-high heat until crisp. Remove bacon, reserving bacon drippings in pan. Add onion and garlic to bacon drippings. Cook and stir for 5 minutes or until onion is just tender.

2. Add broth and potatoes to Dutch oven. Bring to boiling; reduce heat. Simmer, covered, about 10 minutes or until potatoes are almost tender. Add fish pieces, evaporated milk, butter, and pepper. Return to boiling; reduce heat. Simmer, covered, about 10 minutes more or until potatoes are very tender.

3. To serve, ladle chowder into bowls. Top individual servings with crumbled bacon pieces.

PER SERVING: 274 cal., 8 g total fat (3 g sat. fat), 46 mg chol., 513 mg sodium, 27 g carb. (2 g fiber, 10 g sugars), 22 g pro. Exchanges: 1 milk, 1 starch, 2 lean meat, 1 fat.

Lemon-Sesame Shrimp Soup

Water plays an essential role in nearly all body functions, including maintaining a good energy level. One way to get enough water is to eat foods that have a high water content, such as this soup, which is loaded with flavorful broth from the vegetables.

SERVINGS 6 (1$\frac{1}{2}$ cups each)
CARB. PER SERVING 12 g
PREP 40 minutes COOK 10 minutes

Lemon-Sesame
Shrimp Soup

12	ounces fresh or frozen large shrimp in shells
4	green onions
2$\frac{1}{2}$	cups coarsely chopped yellow, red, orange, and/or green sweet peppers (2 large)
1	tablespoon canola oil
1	tablespoon grated fresh ginger or 1 teaspoon ground ginger
3	cloves garlic, minced
6	cups water
1	cup small fresh broccoli florets
2	tablespoons reduced-sodium soy sauce
$\frac{1}{4}$	teaspoon crushed red pepper
4	cups coarsely chopped fresh kale or spinach
2	teaspoons finely shredded lemon peel
2	tablespoons lemon juice
1	tablespoon toasted sesame oil
	Sesame seeds, toasted (optional)

1. Thaw shrimp, if frozen. Peel and devein shrimp. Cut tails off shrimp. Rinse shrimp; pat dry with paper towels. Set aside. Cut green onions into $\frac{1}{2}$-inch slices, keeping white parts separate from green tops. Set green tops aside. In a large saucepan cook white parts of the green onions and sweet peppers in hot oil for 5 minutes, stirring occasionally. Add ginger and garlic; cook and stir for 1 minute more.
2. Add the water, broccoli, soy sauce, and crushed red pepper. Bring to boiling; reduce heat. Simmer, uncovered, for 2 minutes.
3. Add shrimp and kale (if using). Return to boiling; reduce heat. Simmer, uncovered, for 2 to 3 minutes or until shrimp are opaque. Stir spinach (if using), green onion tops, lemon peel, lemon juice, and sesame oil into hot soup just before serving.
4. To serve, ladle soup into bowls. If desired, sprinkle individual servings with sesame seeds.

PER SERVING: 136 cal., 6 g total fat (1 g sat. fat), 71 mg chol., 547 mg sodium, 12 g carb. (3 g fiber, 4 g sugars), 11 g pro. Exchanges: 2 vegetable, 1 lean meat, 1 fat.

Italian Shrimp Soup

This tasty soup is best when made fresh. To feed a family of four to six, double or triple the amounts.

SERVINGS 2 (1 cup each)
CARB. PER SERVING 10 g
START TO FINISH 30 minutes

$\frac{1}{2}$	cup chopped green sweet pepper
$\frac{1}{2}$	cup chopped onion (1 medium)
1	clove garlic, minced
2	teaspoons olive oil
1	medium roma tomato, seeded and chopped
$\frac{1}{2}$	cup reduced-sodium chicken broth
1	tablespoon lemon juice
$\frac{1}{4}$	teaspoon black pepper
8	ounces peeled and deveined fresh shrimp and/or fresh sea scallops
1	teaspoon chopped fresh basil or $\frac{1}{4}$ teaspoon dried basil, crushed
1	teaspoon chopped fresh thyme or $\frac{1}{4}$ teaspoon dried thyme leaves, crushed

1. In a medium saucepan cook sweet pepper, onion, and garlic in hot oil until tender. Stir in tomato, broth, lemon juice, and black pepper. Bring to boiling.
2. Stir in shrimp and/or scallops. Return to boiling; reduce heat. Simmer, covered, for 2 to 3 minutes or until the shrimp and/or scallops are opaque. Stir in the basil and thyme. To serve, ladle soup into bowls.

PER SERVING: 200 cal., 7 g total fat (1 g sat. fat), 172 mg chol., 316 mg sodium, 10 g carb. (2 g fiber, 4 g sugars), 25 g pro. Exchanges: 1 vegetable, 3 lean meat, 1 fat.

Egg Drop Soup

To make curly strips from egg roll wrappers, shape foil into small logs and place on a baking sheet. Drape the egg roll wrappers over the foil logs and coat and bake as directed.

SERVINGS 4 (1³/₄ cups soup and 1 tablespoon crispy strips each)

CARB. PER SERVING 18 g

PREP 25 minutes BAKE 6 minutes

    Nonstick cooking spray
 1 egg roll wrapper, cut into thin 1- to 1¹/₂-inch-long strips
 6 cups low-sodium chicken broth
 4 teaspoons reduced-sodium soy sauce
 1 clove garlic, minced
 ¼ teaspoon ground white pepper
 2 medium carrots
 ½ cup frozen baby sweet peas
 8 teaspoons cornstarch
 4 eggs
 2 green onions, bias-sliced

1. Preheat oven to 375°F. Lightly coat a baking sheet with cooking spray. Place egg roll wrapper strips on prepared baking sheet. Lightly coat strips with cooking spray. Bake for 6 to 7 minutes or until lightly browned and crisp, stirring once after 3 minutes; set aside.

2. In a large saucepan combine 5 cups of the broth, the soy sauce, garlic, and pepper. Bring to boiling.

3. To make carrot flowers, using a paring knife or channel knife,* make four or five shallow lengthwise notches around each carrot; thinly slice carrots. (Or thinly slice carrots; cut each slice with a 1-inch or smaller flower-shape cutter.) Add carrots and peas to boiling broth; return to boiling.

4. Stir cornstarch into the remaining 1 cup broth; stir into soup. Reduce heat. Cook and stir until slightly thickened and bubbly; cook and stir for 2 minutes more. Remove from heat. Place eggs in a liquid measuring cup; use a fork to beat eggs. While gently stirring the broth, pour eggs in a thin stream into soup (eggs will form fine shreds).

5. To serve, ladle soup into bowls. Garnish individual servings with green onions. Serve with crisp egg roll wrapper strips.

*TEST KITCHEN TIP: A channel knife is a garnishing tool used to make thin strips of citrus peel and other garnishes.

PER SERVING: 186 cal., 5 g total fat (2 g sat. fat), 212 mg chol., 559 mg sodium, 18 g carb. (2 g fiber, 4 g sugars), 15 g pro. Exchanges: 0.5 vegetable, 1 starch, 1.5 lean meat, 0.5 fat.

Roasted Tomato Soup and Grilled Cheese Sandwiches

Roasting the tomatoes intensifies their flavor in this creamy blended soup. Pair it with toasty cheese sandwiches for a classic combo.

SERVINGS 4 (1¹/₃ cups soup and 2 sandwich quarters each)

CARB. PER SERVING 29 g

PREP 40 minutes ROAST 30 minutes

3½ pounds roma tomatoes, halved
 ½ cup chopped onion (1 medium)
 ¼ cup finely chopped celery
 ¼ cup shredded carrot
 1 clove garlic, minced
 2 teaspoons olive oil
 1 cup unsalted chicken stock or reduced-sodium chicken broth
 1 tablespoon snipped fresh thyme
 1 teaspoon snipped fresh rosemary
 1 tablespoon snipped fresh basil
 ¼ teaspoon salt
 ¼ teaspoon black pepper
 2 tablespoons plain fat-free Greek yogurt
    Plain fat-free Greek yogurt
    Snipped fresh basil (optional)
 1 recipe Grilled Cheese Sandwiches

1. Preheat oven to 350°F. Arrange tomatoes, cut sides down, in two shallow baking pans. Roast on separate oven racks for 30 minutes, rearranging pans halfway through roasting time. Remove from oven; let stand until cool enough to handle. Using your fingers, lift skins from tomatoes and discard skins (some skins may remain on tomatoes); set tomatoes aside.

2. In a large saucepan cook onion, carrot, celery, and garlic in hot oil about 4 minutes or until onion is tender, stirring

Egg Drop Soup

QUICK TIP
Use kitchen scissors to snip basil over each bowl. The cut edges will brown if snipped too early.

Roasted Tomato Soup and Grilled Cheese Sandwiches

occasionally. Add tomatoes and any liquid from baking pans, the chicken stock, thyme, and rosemary. Bring to boiling; reduce heat. Simmer, covered, for 5 minutes. Remove from heat; cool slightly.

3. Transfer half of the tomato mixture to a food processor or blender. Cover and process or blend until smooth. Repeat with the remaining tomato mixture. Return all to the saucepan. Stir in the 1 tablespoon basil, the salt, and pepper. Stir in the 2 tablespoons yogurt. Heat through.

4. To serve, ladle soup into bowls. Spoon additional yogurt onto individual servings. If desired, sprinkle with additional fresh basil. Serve soup with Grilled Cheese Sandwiches.

GRILLED CHEESE SANDWICHES: Coat one side of each of 4 slices reduced-calorie whole wheat bread with nonstick cooking spray. Lay slices of the bread, coated sides down, on a sheet of waxed paper. Sprinkle 2 of the bread slices with ¼ cup shredded reduced-fat cheddar cheese (1 ounce) and ¼ cup shredded American cheese (1 ounce), dividing cheeses evenly. Top with the remaining 2 bread slices, coated sides up. Heat a griddle or large skillet over medium heat. Place sandwiches on hot griddle or skillet; cook about 6 minutes or until bread is golden brown and cheese is melted, turning once halfway through cooking time. Cut sandwiches into quarters to serve.

PER SERVING: 213 cal., 8 g total fat (3 g sat. fat), 12 mg chol., 466 mg sodium, 29 g carb. (8 g fiber, 13 g sugars), 12 g pro. Exchanges: 3 vegetable, 0.5 starch, 1 medium-fat meat, 0.5 fat.

Chunky Minestrone

Minestrone is Italian for "big soup." Beans, zucchini, onion, carrot, and tomatoes makes this version big indeed.

SERVINGS 4 (1^2/3 cups each)
CARB. PER SERVING 36 g
PREP 20 minutes COOK 40 minutes

- 1 cup chopped onion (1 large)
- 1 medium carrot, halved lengthwise and thinly sliced
- 2 cloves garlic, minced
- 1 tablespoon olive oil
- 1 14.5-ounce can no-salt-added diced tomatoes, undrained
- 1 14.5-ounce can reduced-sodium chicken broth
- 1 cup water
- ¼ cup uncooked brown rice
- 1 teaspoon dried Italian seasoning, crushed
- 3 cups fresh baby spinach
- 1 15-ounce can no-salt-added navy beans, rinsed and drained
- 1 medium zucchini, quartered lengthwise and sliced (about 1½ cups)
- ¼ teaspoon black pepper
- ⅛ teaspoon salt
- Shredded Parmesan cheese (optional)

1. In a 4-quart Dutch oven cook onion, carrot, and garlic in hot oil about 5 minutes or until onion is tender, stirring occasionally.

2. Stir in tomatoes, broth, the water, rice, and Italian seasoning. Bring to boiling; reduce heat. Cover and simmer for 35 to 40 minutes or until rice is tender.

3. Stir in spinach, beans, zucchini, pepper, and salt. Return to boiling; reduce heat. Cover and simmer for 5 minutes more.

4. To serve, ladle soup into bowls. If desired, sprinkle individual servings with Parmesan cheese.

PER SERVING: 215 cal., 4 g total fat (1 g sat. fat), 0 mg chol., 399 mg sodium, 36 g carb. (12 g fiber, 7 g sugars), 11 g pro. Exchanges: 2 vegetable, 1.5 starch, 1 lean meat, 1 fat.

Chunky
Minestrone

Red Lentil Soup

To save the remaining tomato paste for another use, spoon it in 1-tablespoon portions on a waxed paper-lined baking sheet and freeze. Transfer the portions to a freezer bag and store in the freezer until needed.

SERVINGS 6 (1 cup each)
CARB. PER SERVING 43 g
PREP 20 minutes **COOK** 30 minutes

- 1 tablespoon butter
- 1/2 cup chopped onion (1 medium)
- 1/2 cup chopped carrot (1 medium)
- 2 cloves garlic, minced
- 1 teaspoon ground cumin
- 1/2 teaspoon salt
- 1/4 teaspoon crushed red pepper
- 1 32-ounce carton no-salt-added or low-sodium vegetable broth (4 cups)
- 3 tablespoons no-salt-added tomato paste
- 8 ounces dried red lentils, rinsed and drained (1 cup plus 2 tablespoons)
- 8 ounces peeled russet potato, cut into 1/2-inch pieces (1 1/2 cups)
- 1 to 2 cups hot water
- 1 tablespoon lemon juice
- 1 recipe Pita Croutons

1. In a 4-quart Dutch oven heat butter over medium heat. Add onion, carrot, and garlic. Cook and stir for 5 to 8 minutes or until onion starts to brown. Stir in cumin, salt, and crushed red pepper. Carefully add vegetable broth and tomato paste; bring to boiling. Add lentils and potato. Return to boiling; reduce heat. Simmer, uncovered, for 25 to 30 minutes or until lentils are tender, stirring frequently and adding hot water as needed to keep mixture from going dry.
2. Transfer one-third of the lentil mixture to a bowl; set aside. Transfer remaining mixture, half at a time, to a food processor or blender. Cover; process or blend until smooth. Return pureed mixture, chunky lentil mixture, and lemon juice to the Dutch oven and heat through.
3. To serve, ladle soup into bowls. Garnish individual servings with Pita Croutons.
PITA CROUTONS: Preheat oven to 350°F. Split 1 whole wheat pita bread round horizontally. Coat the cut sides of the pita rounds with nonstick olive oil cooking spray; sprinkle with 1/8 teaspoon paprika. Cut each pita half into four wedges. Spread wedges in a single layer in a 15×10×1-inch baking pan. Bake for 8 to 10 minutes or until crisp. When cool enough to handle, break into bite-size pieces.

PER SERVING: 244 cal., 3 g total fat (1 g sat. fat), 5 mg chol., 379 mg sodium, 43 g carb. (15 g fiber, 5 g sugars), 12 g pro. Exchanges: 1 vegetable, 2 starch, 1 lean meat, 0.5 fat.

Avocado Soup

Avocado Soup

This first-course chilled soup made with two ripe avocados is sublime.

SERVINGS 6 (3/4 cup each)
CARB. PER SERVING 5 g
PREP 20 minutes **CHILL** 1 hour

- 2 small ripe avocados, halved, seeded, peeled, and cut up
- 1/2 cup peeled, seeded, and chopped cucumber
- 1/3 cup chopped onion
- 1/4 cup shredded carrot
- 1 clove garlic, minced
- 1 14.5-ounce can reduced-sodium chicken broth
- 1 1/2 cups water
  Several dashes bottled hot pepper sauce
- 1/8 teaspoon salt
- 1/2 teaspoon paprika
- 1/3 cup refrigerated fresh salsa
  Snipped fresh cilantro

1. In a blender or food processor combine avocados, cucumber, onion, carrot, garlic, and the broth. Cover; process until almost smooth.
2. Add the water, hot pepper sauce, and salt. Cover; process until smooth. Pour into a bowl. Cover surface of the soup with plastic wrap. Chill for 1 to 24 hours.
3. To serve, ladle soup into chilled bowls or cups. Sprinkle individual servings with paprika and top with salsa and snipped cilantro.

PER SERVING: 64 cal., 5 g total fat (1 g sat. fat), 0 mg chol., 217 mg sodium, 5 g carb. (2 g fiber, 1 g sugars), 2 g pro. Exchanges: 1 vegetable, 1 carb., 1 fat.

Butternut Squash
Corn Chowder

Butternut Squash Corn Chowder

Use a chef's knife to cut the firm squash. One small squash will yield the 4 cups you need.

SERVINGS 8 (3/4 cup each)
CARB. PER SERVING 19 g
PREP 30 minutes **ROAST** 25 minutes

  4 ears fresh sweet corn or 2 cups frozen
     whole kernel corn
    Nonstick cooking spray
  4 cups diced, peeled butternut squash (about
     1 small squash)
  1 tablespoon butter, melted
  1/2 cup chopped onion (1 medium)
  1/3 cup chopped leek (1 medium)
  2 14.5-ounce cans reduced-sodium chicken broth
  1/4 cup half-and-half or milk
  2 teaspoons snipped fresh sage
  1/4 teaspoon ground white pepper
  2 tablespoons honey (optional)
    Fresh sage leaves

1. If using fresh corn, use a sharp knife to cut the kernels off the cobs (you should have about 2 cups corn kernels). Set aside.
2. Preheat oven to 425°F. Coat the bottom and sides of a roasting pan with cooking spray. Arrange squash in the bottom of the pan. Drizzle with melted butter; toss to coat. Roast for 10 minutes, stirring once. Remove from oven. Add corn, onion, and leek to pan. Toss to combine. Return to oven and roast about 15 minutes more or until vegetables are tender, stirring once.
3. Place one-third of the squash mixture and one-third of the broth in a food processor or blender. Cover and process or blend until almost smooth. Repeat with half of the remaining squash mixture and remaining broth at a time. Transfer processed mixture to a 4-quart Dutch oven. Add the half-and-half, snipped sage, and white pepper. Heat through.
4. To serve, ladle chowder into bowls. If desired, drizzle a little honey over individual servings. Garnish with fresh sage leaves.

PER SERVING: 107 cal., 3 g total fat (2 g sat. fat), 7 mg chol., 264 mg sodium, 19 g carb. (3 g fiber, 5 g sugars), 4 g pro. Exchanges: 1 starch, 0.5 fat.

Super Squash

For a big nutrient boost, work the veggie powerhouse butternut squash into your diet—roast it and eat it as a side dish or puree it in soup.

Butternut squash is very high in vitamins A, C, and E and also a good source of B complex vitamins and folate.

Green Tea and Honeyed Cantaloupe Soup

This refreshing soup is best served cold. For a quicker chill, start with cold cantaloupe.

SERVINGS 6 ($^3/_4$ cup each)
CARB. PER SERVING 22 g
PREP 25 minutes **CHILL** 2 hours

- $^3/_4$ cup cold water
- 1 green tea bag
- 6 cups cubed cantaloupe (about 1 medium)
- $^3/_4$ cup plain fat-free yogurt
- $^1/_4$ cup apricot nectar
- 1 tablespoon grated fresh ginger
- 1 tablespoon honey
- 1 teaspoon lime juice
- 6 tablespoons plain fat-free yogurt
- Finely shredded lime peel

1. In a small saucepan bring the water just to boiling. Remove from heat. Add tea bag to hot liquid. Steep tea for 2 minutes. Remove and discard tea bag.

2. In a food processor or blender combine half of the cantaloupe, half of the $^3/_4$ cup yogurt, and half each of the apricot nectar, ginger, honey, lime juice, and brewed tea. Cover and process or blend until smooth. Transfer to a large bowl. Repeat with the remaining half of the ingredients. Stir into processed mixture in bowl. Cover and chill soup in the refrigerator for at least 2 hours.

3. To serve, ladle soup into chilled bowls. Garnish individual servings with 1 tablespoon yogurt and lime peel each.

PER SERVING: 99 cal., 0 g total fat, 1 mg chol., 63 mg sodium, 22 g carb. (2 g fiber, 21 g sugars), 4 g pro. Exchanges: 1.5 fruit, 0.5 lean meat.

Green Tea
and Honeyed
Cantaloupe Soup

sensational
sandwiches

Grilled Veggie
Sandwiches

When a sandwich is exactly

what you want for lunch

or dinner, go for it! Stacked

on a bun, rolled in a wrap,

or stuffed in a pita, each

sandwich here presents

itself on a healthful base and

is decked with slimmed-

down condiments, colorful

vegetables, and lean proteins.

Try them all! Each is designed

to fit a diabetes meal plan.

Grilled Veggie Sandwiches

Make a mock aïoli by stirring fresh garlic into light mayonnaise. The zesty spread complements hot-off-the-grill vegetables perfectly.

SERVINGS 4 (1 sandwich each)
CARB. PER SERVING 39 g
START TO FINISH 25 minutes

- 1 small eggplant, sliced 1 inch thick
- 1 4-inch portobello mushroom, stem removed
- 1 medium yellow or green sweet pepper, halved
- 1 tablespoon olive oil
- 1/4 teaspoon black pepper
- 1/8 teaspoon salt
- 2 tablespoons light mayonnaise
- 2 cloves garlic, minced
- 4 2-ounce whole wheat rolls, split and toasted

1. Brush eggplant, mushroom, and sweet pepper with olive oil and sprinkle with black pepper and salt. For a charcoal grill, place the vegetables on the grill rack directly over medium coals. Grill, uncovered, for 10 to 12 minutes or until vegetables are just tender, turning once halfway through grilling. Transfer vegetables to a cutting board and cut into 1/2-inch slices. (For a gas grill, preheat grill. Reduce heat to medium. Place vegetables on grill rack over heat. Cover and grill as above.)
2. Meanwhile, in a small bowl combine mayonnaise and garlic. Spread mayonnaise mixture over cut sides of rolls. Fill rolls with grilled vegetables.

PER SERVING: 247 cal., 9 g total fat (1 g sat. fat), 3 mg chol., 353 mg sodium, 39 g carb. (8 g fiber, 9 g sugars), 7 g pro. Exchanges: 1 vegetable, 2 starch, 1.5 fat.

Crunch-Time Veggie Wrap

Skip high-calorie fast food for lunch—pack this filling, delicious wrap instead.

SERVINGS 1
CARB. PER SERVING 28 g
START TO FINISH 15 minutes

 1 original-flavor light flatbread wrap
 1/4 of a medium avocado, peeled
 1/8 teaspoon lime juice
 1 medium carrot, cut into thin bite-size strips
 1/4 of a small red sweet pepper, cut into thin bite-size strips
 1/4 of a small cucumber, cut into thin bite-size strips
 1 tablespoon crumbled feta cheese

Crunch-Time Veggie Wrap

1. Place the wrap on a work surface. In a small bowl mash together avocado and lime juice. Spread mixture evenly over the wrap.
2. Arrange carrot, cucumber, and sweet pepper strips on top of the avocado mixture, leaving about 2 inches of space at each end of the wrap.
3. Sprinkle with feta cheese; roll up into a spiral. Serve immediately or cover and chill for up to 4 hours. If desired, cut in half diagonally.

PER SERVING: 211 cal., 10 g total fat (2 g sat. fat), 8 mg chol., 471 mg sodium, 28 g carb. (14 g fiber, 5 g sugars), 12 g pro. Exchanges: 2 vegetable, 1 starch, 1 lean meat, 1 fat.

Fresh Tomato Sandwiches

If you are a fan of colorful heirloom tomatoes, pick some up at the market and use in place of the romas.

SERVINGS 2 (2 bagel halves each)
CARB. PER SERVING 27 g
PREP 15 minutes **BAKE** 10 minutes

 2 whole wheat bagel thins
 1/3 cup shredded part-skim mozzarella cheese
 1/4 cup part-skim ricotta cheese
 1 tablespoon light mayonnaise
 1 teaspoon snipped fresh dill or 1/4 teaspoon dried dill weed
 2 to 3 roma tomatoes, sliced
 1/4 cup red onion cut into thin wedges and separated into pieces
   Dash garlic powder
 2 teaspoons grated Parmesan cheese
   Fresh dill (optional)

1. Split and lightly toast bagel thins. Place bagel thins, cut sides up, on a baking sheet. Preheat oven to 350°F.
2. In a small bowl combine mozzarella, ricotta, mayonnaise, and dill. Spread mixture on bagel thins.
3. Layer tomato slices and onion pieces on bagel thins. Sprinkle lightly with garlic powder. Sprinkle 1/2 teaspoon of the Parmesan cheese over each bagel thin half.
4. Bake for 10 to 15 minutes or until mayonnaise mixture is melted and Parmesan is lightly browned. If desired, garnish with additional fresh dill.

PER SERVING: 248 cal., 11 g total fat (5 g sat. fat), 27 mg chol., 423 mg sodium, 27 g carb. (6 g fiber, 6 g sugars), 16 g pro. Exchanges: 1 vegetable, 1.5 starch, 1.5 lean meat, 1 fat.

Sandwich Swaps

Think of a sandwich recipe as a guide—it's a great place to start, but you can easily add or subtract. To fit your diabetes meal plan, remember to swap ingredients that are equal or better in nutritional value. For instance, try another whole grain bread product, use spinach instead of leaf lettuce, vary the lean meat, add crunchy vegetables, and/or go lightly on the condiment. Make a note of your concoction—you may have created a recipe worth keeping!

Fresh Tomato
Sandwiches

Lentil Sloppy Joes

Asian Tuna Wraps

Lentil Sloppy Joes

This makes a big batch, so if you wish to store some, place it in an airtight container and refrigerate for up to 1 week or freeze for up to 3 months.

SERVINGS 16 ($^1/_2$ cup lentil mixture and 1 bun each)
CARB. PER SERVING 43 g or 42 g
PREP 15 minutes **SLOW COOK** 8 hours (low) or 5 hours (high)

    2 cups lentils, rinsed and drained
    1 large green sweet pepper, chopped (1$^1/_4$ cups)
    2 medium carrots, shredded (1 cup)
  $^3/_4$ cup chopped onion
    1 cup reduced-sodium hot-style vegetable juice
  $^1/_4$ cup no-salt-added tomato paste
    1 4-ounce can diced green chiles, undrained
    1 tablespoon reduced-sodium Worcestershire sauce
    2 teaspoons chili powder
    1 teaspoon cider vinegar
    2 cloves garlic, minced
    3 cups water
  $^1/_2$ cup reduced-sodium ketchup
    2 tablespoons packed brown sugar*
   16 whole wheat hamburger buns, split and toasted

1. In a 3$^1/_2$- or 4-quart slow cooker combine lentils, sweet pepper, carrots, onion, vegetable juice, tomato paste, chiles, Worcestershire sauce, chili powder, vinegar, garlic, and water.
2. Cover and cook on low-heat setting for 8 to 10 hours or on high-heat setting for 4 to 5 hours.

3. Before serving, stir in ketchup and brown sugar. Serve lentil mixture on toasted buns. If desired, top each serving with *shredded carrot*.
***SUGAR SUBSTITUTE:** Choose from Sweet'N Low Brown or Sugar Twin Granulated Brown. Follow package directions to use product amount equivalent to 2 tablespoons brown sugar.

PER SERVING: 228 cal., 1 g total fat (0 g sat. fat), 265 mg sodium, 43 g carb. (10 g fiber, 10 g sugars), 11 g pro. Exchanges: 2.5 starch, 0.5 lean meat.

PER SERVING WITH SUBSTITUTE: Same as above, except 221 cal., 42 g carb. (9 g sugars).

Asian Tuna Wraps

To store fresh ginger, wrap the unpeeled piece in freezer wrap and place it in the freezer—it will keep indefinitely.

SERVINGS 4 (1 wrap each)
CARB. PER SERVING 20 g
START TO FINISH 15 minutes

    2 6-ounce cans very low-sodium solid white tuna (water pack), drained and broken into chunks
    3 tablespoons bottled sesame-ginger salad dressing
  $^1/_4$ cup light mayonnaise
    1 teaspoon minced garlic
  $^1/_2$ teaspoon minced fresh ginger
    4 8-inch whole wheat low-carb flour tortillas
    2 cups shredded bok choy
    1 medium red sweet pepper, thinly sliced
  $^1/_2$ cup jicama, cut into matchstick-size pieces

Fish Tacos with Jalepeño Slaw

1. In a large bowl stir together tuna, salad dressing, 2 tablespoons of the mayonnaise, the garlic, and ginger. Spread remaining mayonnaise over one side of each of the tortillas. Divide bok choy, sweet pepper, and jicama among wraps. Top with tuna mixture and roll up.

PER SERVING: 267 cal., 11 g total fat (1 g sat. fat), 43 mg chol., 525 mg sodium, 20 g carb. (10 g fiber, 5 g sugars), 22 g pro. Exchanges: 1 vegetable, 1 starch, 3 lean meat, 0.5 fat.

Fish Tacos with Jalapeño Slaw

To keep the fish from sticking, be sure to grease the grill rack with vegetable oil before placing it over the hot coals.

SERVINGS 4 (1 taco and $^2/_3$ cup slaw each)
CARB. PER SERVING 20 g
PREP 20 minutes **GRILL** 4 minutes

- 1 pound fresh or frozen skinless cod, tilapia, or other fish fillets, about $^1/_2$ inch thick
- 1 recipe Jalapeño Slaw
- $^1/_2$ teaspoon ground cumin
- $^1/_4$ teaspoon ground ancho chile pepper or cayenne pepper
- Dash salt
- 4 8-inch whole grain flour tortillas
- Peach or mango salsa (optional)
- Lime wedges (optional)

1. Thaw fish, if frozen. Rinse fish; pat dry with paper towels. Set aside. Prepare Jalapeño Slaw; cover and chill.

2. In a small bowl combine cumin, ground ancho chile pepper, and salt; sprinkle evenly over one side of each fish fillet.

3. Stack tortillas and wrap in heavy foil. For a charcoal grill, place fish and tortilla stack on the greased grill rack directly over medium coals. Grill, uncovered, for 4 to 6 minutes or until fish flakes easily when tested with a fork and tortillas are heated through, turning fish and tortilla stack once. (For a gas grill, preheat grill. Reduce heat to medium. Place fish and tortilla stack on greased grill rack over heat. Cover and grill as above.)

4. To serve, cut fish into four serving-size pieces. Divide Jalapeño Slaw among tortillas and top with fish. If desired, serve with salsa and lime wedges.

JALAPEÑO SLAW: In a bowl combine $2^1/_2$ cups packaged shredded cabbage with carrot (coleslaw mix); $^1/_4$ cup thinly sliced, halved red onion; and 1 small fresh jalapeño chile pepper, seeded and finely chopped (see tip, page 20); set aside. In a small bowl whisk together 2 tablespoons lime juice, 2 tablespoons orange juice, 2 tablespoons olive oil, $^1/_2$ teaspoon ground cumin, and dash salt. Pour lime juice mixture over cabbage mixture. Toss to coat. Cover and chill for up to 6 hours.

PER SERVING: 304 cal., 11 g total fat (2 g sat. fat), 48 mg chol., 467 mg sodium, 20 g carb. (11 g fiber, 3 g sugars), 29 g pro. Exchanges: 1 vegetable, 1 starch, 3.5 lean meat, 1 fat.

QUICK TIP
This toasted stack is super tasty with the flavored fish fillets, but this combo is equally good with any simply-seasoned cooked fish.

Cheesy Tilapia Panini with Apple-Carrot Slaw

Cheesy Tilapia Panini with Apple-Carrot Slaw

There is not any cabbage in this slaw. Shredded sweet apple and carrot combine to mimic the classic tag-along for fish.

SERVINGS 2 (1 sandwich and $1/2$ cup slaw each)
CARB. PER SERVING 30 g
START TO FINISH 20 minutes

  1 6.3-ounce package grilled tilapia fillets with roasted garlic and butter (2 fillets)
     Nonstick cooking spray
  4 slices very thin 100% whole wheat bread
$1/2$ cup baby spinach
  2 slices tomato
  2 ounce slices reduced-fat Monterey Jack or part-skim mozzarella cheese
  1 recipe Apple-Carrot Slaw

1. Cook tilapia in the microwave according to package directions. Break cooked fish into pieces. Lightly coat a panini sandwich maker or a griddle with cooking spray. Preheat panini sandwich maker or a griddle over medium heat.

2. On 2 slices of the bread, layer spinach, tomato, fish, and cheese. Top with the remaining 2 bread slices.

3. Cook sandwiches about 3 minutes in the panini sandwich maker or about 5 minutes on the griddle or until browned on both sides. If using a griddle, weight sandwich down with a skillet and turn once halfway through cooking time. Serve with Apple-Carrot Slaw.

APPLE-CARROT SLAW: In a small bowl stir together 1 small apple, cored and coarsely shredded; 1 carrot, coarsely shredded; $1/4$ cup honey-flavor fat-free Greek yogurt; and $1/4$ teaspoon poppy seeds.

PER SERVING: 288 cal., 9 g total fat (4 g sat. fat), 67 mg chol., 533 mg sodium, 30 g carb. (5 g fiber, 13 g sugars), 25 g pro. Exchanges: 0.5 vegetable, 0.5 fruit, 1.5 starch, 2.5 lean meat, 1 fat.

Coffee-Rubbed Salmon Sandwiches

This trendy sandwich, all decked out with a crunchy coffee-spice coating would be a hit at an upscale restaurant.

SERVINGS 4 (1 sandwich each)
CARB. PER SERVING 33 g
PREP 20 minutes **COOK** 5 minutes

$1/4$ cup light sour cream
  1 tablespoon snipped fresh parsley
  2 teaspoons cider vinegar
  1 teaspoon prepared horseradish
  1 teaspoon instant espresso coffee powder
  1 teaspoon dried ancho chile powder
$1/2$ teaspoon packed brown sugar*
$1/4$ teaspoon dry mustard
$1/4$ teaspoon ground cumin
$1/8$ teaspoon cayenne pepper
  1 pound skinless salmon fillets
  2 teaspoons olive oil
  4 whole wheat hamburger buns, toasted
  2 cups baby salad greens
  8 thin red onion rings

Coffee-Rubbed
Salmon Sandwiches

1. In a small bowl stir together the sour cream, parsley, vinegar, and horseradish. Set aside.

2. In another small bowl stir together espresso powder, chile powder, brown sugar, mustard, cumin, and cayenne pepper. Cut salmon into four equal pieces. Sprinkle evenly with spice mixture; rub mixture into salmon with your fingers.

3. In a large nonstick skillet heat oil over medium heat. Cook salmon in hot oil for 5 to 7 minutes or until fish begins to flake when tested with a fork.

4. Top bottom halves of toasted buns with salad greens, salmon pieces, and onion rings. Spoon sauce over salmon and onion rings. Add top halves of buns.

*SUGAR SUBSTITUTE: We do not recommend using a sugar substitute for this recipe.

PER SERVING: 363 cal., 12 g total fat (2 g sat. fat), 67 mg chol., 347 mg sodium, 33 g carb. (4 g fiber, 8 g sugars), 29 g pro. Exchanges: 2 starch, 3.5 lean meat, 1 fat.

Indian-Spiced
Turkey Kabob Pitas

Indian-Spiced Turkey Kabob Pitas

To evenly toast the cumin seeds, gently shake the skillet to keep them moving while over the heat.

SERVINGS 4 (1 pita round, 1 tablespoon yogurt, $^1/_2$ cup cucumber mixture, and about 3 ounces turkey each)
CARB. PER SERVING 35 g
PREP 25 minutes **GRILL** 8 minutes

- 4   8- to 10-inch bamboo skewers
- 1   teaspoon whole cumin seeds
- 1   cup shredded cucumber (1 small)
- $^1/_3$ cup seeded and chopped roma tomato (1 small)
- $^1/_4$ cup slivered red onion
- $^1/_4$ cup shredded radishes
- $^1/_4$ cup snipped fresh cilantro
- $^1/_4$ teaspoon black pepper
- 1   pound turkey breast, cut into 1-inch cubes
- 1   recipe Curry Blend
- $^1/_4$ cup plain fat-free Greek yogurt
- 4   2-ounce whole-wheat pita bread rounds

1. Soak bamboo skewers in water for at least 30 minutes before using on the grill.
2. In a small dry skillet toast cumin seeds over medium heat for 1 minute or until fragrant. Transfer to a medium bowl. Add cucumber, tomato, red onion, radishes, cilantro, and black pepper. Stir to combine. Set aside.
3. In another medium bowl combine turkey breast cubes and Curry Blend. Stir to coat turkey cubes with seasonings. Thread turkey cubes evenly onto skewers. For a charcoal grill, grill kabobs on the grill rack directly over medium coals. Grill, uncovered, for 8 to 12 minutes or until turkey is no longer pink (170°F), turning kabobs occasionally while grilling. (For a gas grill, preheat grill. Reduce heat to medium. Place kabobs on grill rack over heat. Cover and grill as directed.)
4. Remove turkey from skewers. To serve, spread Greek yogurt evenly on pita rounds. Using a slotted spoon, place cucumber mixture on top of yogurt. Top with grilled turkey.
CURRY BLEND: In a small bowl stir together 2 teaspoons olive oil, 1 teaspoon curry powder, $^1/_2$ teaspoon ground cumin, $^1/_2$ teaspoon ground turmeric, $^1/_2$ teaspoon ground coriander, $^1/_4$ teaspoon ground ginger, $^1/_8$ teaspoon salt, and $^1/_8$ teaspoon cayenne pepper.

PER SERVING: 322 cal., 5 g total fat (1 g sat. fat), 70 mg chol., 442 mg sodium, 35 g carb. (5 g fiber, 2 g sugars), 35 g pro. Exchanges: 2 starch, 4 lean meat.

Turkey Pizza Burgers

Turkey Pizza Burgers

Get a serving or two of vegetables in with this plump and juicy burger by adding a salad of mixed greens, cucumbers, and tomatoes alongside.

SERVINGS 4 (1 sandwich each)
CARB. PER SERVING 28 g
PREP 25 minutes **GRILL** 14 minutes

- 1   egg, beaten, or $^1/_4$ cup refrigerated or frozen egg product, thawed
- $^1/_4$ cup quick-cooking rolled oats
- 4   teaspoons snipped fresh oregano
- $^1/_8$ teaspoon salt
- $^1/_8$ teaspoon black pepper
- 1   pound uncooked ground turkey breast
- 4   0.5-ounce slices provolone cheese
- $^1/_2$ cup organic low-sodium tomato pasta sauce
- 4   whole wheat hamburger buns, toasted

1. In a medium bowl combine egg, rolled oats, half of the oregano, the salt, and pepper. Add ground turkey breast; mix well. Shape turkey mixture into four $^3/_4$-inch-thick patties.
2. For a charcoal grill, place patties on the grill rack directly over medium coals. Grill, uncovered, for 14 to 18 minutes or until no longer pink (165°F), turning once halfway through grilling and topping each burger with a cheese slice for the last minute of grilling. (For a gas grill, preheat grill. Reduce heat to medium. Place patties on grill rack over heat. Cover and grill as above.)
3. Meanwhile, in a small saucepan cook pasta sauce over medium heat until heated though.
4. Place burgers on the bottom halves of buns. Top with pasta sauce, the remaining oregano, and bun tops.

PER SERVING: 351 cal., 9 g total fat (3 g sat. fat), 127 mg chol., 487 mg sodium, 28 g carb. (3 g fiber, 5 g sugars), 38 g pro. Exchanges: 2 starch, 4.5 lean meat.

Mediterranean Chicken Pita Sandwiches

These wedges are too stuffed to pick up and eat, so serve them with knives and forks.

SERVINGS 4 (1 sandwich each)
CARB. PER SERVING 32 g
START TO FINISH 30 minutes

- 1 cup chopped cooked chicken breast
- 1/2 of a 15-ounce can no-salt-added organic garbanzo beans (chickpeas), rinsed and drained (about 3/4 cup)
- 1/2 cup diced tomato
- 1/4 cup thinly sliced red onion
- 1/4 cup crumbled reduced-fat feta cheese
- 1/3 cup plain low-fat yogurt
- 1 tablespoon snipped fresh mint
- 1 clove garlic, minced
- 1/4 teaspoon ground cumin
- 1/4 teaspoon cracked black pepper
- 1/8 teaspoon salt
- 2 whole wheat pita bread rounds
- 1/2 of a medium cucumber, thinly sliced

1. In a large bowl toss together chicken, beans, tomato, red onion, and feta cheese. In a small bowl combine yogurt, mint, garlic, cumin, pepper, and salt. Spoon yogurt mixture over chicken mixture; toss to combine evenly.

2. To serve, spoon chicken mixture over 1 pita bread round. Top with cucumber slices and the other pita bread round. Cut into four wedge-shape sandwiches.

PER SERVING: 242 cal., 4 g total fat (1 g sat. fat), 33 mg chol., 416 mg sodium, 32 g carb. (5 g fiber, 3 g sugars), 20 g pro. Exchanges: 2 starch, 2 lean meat.

Peanut-Ginger Lettuce Wraps

Tender butterhead lettuce leaves are just right to use for wraps. Their natural cupped shape cradles the filling.

SERVINGS 4 (3 wraps each)
CARB. PER SERVING 12 g
START TO FINISH 20 minutes

- 2 cups chopped cooked chicken breast
- 2 cups shredded cabbage with carrot (coleslaw mix)
- 1 medium carrot, cut up
- 2 green onions, cut up
- 2 tablespoons unsalted peanuts
- 1 teaspoon minced fresh ginger
- 1/3 cup bottled light Asian salad dressing
- 1/3 cup drained canned crushed pineapple
- 12 leaves butterhead (Boston or Bibb) or green leaf lettuce

1. In a food processor combine about half of the chicken, coleslaw mix, carrot, green onions, peanuts, and ginger;

cover and process with several on/off turns until finely chopped. Transfer to a large bowl. Repeat with remaining chicken, coleslaw mix, carrot, green onions, peanuts, and ginger. Add salad dressing and pineapple to mixture; stir to combine well.

2. Spoon about 1/4 cup of the chicken mixture onto each lettuce leaf; roll up.

PER SERVING: 221 cal., 8 g total fat (2 g sat. fat), 60 mg chol., 267 mg sodium, 12 g carb. (2 g fiber, 8 g sugars), 24 g pro. Exchanges: 1 vegetable, 0.5 carb., 3 lean meat, 0.5 fat.

Chicken and Black Bean Pesto Wraps

Look for oval-shape flatbread wraps in the bread section or near the deli meats in the grocery store.

SERVINGS 4 (1 wrap each)
CARB. PER SERVING 35 g
PREP 20 minutes **COOK** 4 minutes

- 1 15-ounce can no-salt-added black beans, rinsed and drained
- 1/2 cup loosely packed cilantro leaves
- 1/4 cup chopped onion
- 3 tablespoons lime juice
- 1 teaspoon chili powder
- 2 cloves garlic, minced
- 1/4 teaspoon crushed red pepper
- 1/8 teaspoon salt
- 12 ounces skinless, boneless chicken breast halves, cut into strips
- 1/2 teaspoon dried oregano, crushed
- 1/8 teaspoon salt
- 2 teaspoons olive oil
- 4 multigrain flatbread wraps
- 2 cups shredded fresh spinach
- 1 small red sweet pepper, cut into bite-size strips

1. In a medium bowl combine beans, cilantro, onion, 1 tablespoon of the lime juice, 1/2 teaspoon of the chili powder, the garlic, crushed red pepper, and 1/8 teaspoon salt. Mash with a potato masher until almost smooth. Set aside.

2. In a medium bowl toss chicken breast strips with the remaining chili powder, the oregano, and remaining 1/8 teaspoon salt to coat. In a large nonstick skillet cook chicken in hot oil over medium-high heat for 4 to 5 minutes or until chicken is no longer pink. Remove from heat and stir in the remaining 2 tablespoons lime juice.

3. To assemble wraps, spread bean mixture evenly on wraps. Top with spinach, sweet pepper strips, and chicken. Roll up. Serve immediately.

PER SERVING: 311 cal., 7 g total fat (1 g sat. fat), 54 mg chol., 561 mg sodium, 35 g carb. (14 g fiber, 2 g sugars), 33 g pro. Exchanges: 1 vegetable, 1.5 starch, 4 lean meat.

Build It Better

Consider the process of building a sandwich similar to that of building a house. You must have a solid foundation before you can add to it.

The best foundation for a sandwich is a fiber-rich bread (or lettuce leaves for a carb-free option). Look for bread products that are labeled whole grain, such as bread slices, sandwich thins, bagel thins, a pita, a flatbread wrap, or a tortilla. Check labels for those with less than 150 calories, 2 g total fat, 1 g saturated fat, 30 g carbohydrate, 300 mg sodium, and at least 2 g fiber per serving.

Mediterranean Chicken
Pita Sandwiches

Peanut-Ginger
Lettuce Wraps

Orange-Soy Chicken Sandwiches

When cooked, a spiced-up orange juice and soy mixture creates an amber glaze on the chicken.

SERVINGS 4 (1 sandwich each)
CARB. PER SERVING 30 g
START TO FINISH 30 minutes

- ½ teaspoon finely shredded orange peel
- ⅓ cup orange juice
- 1 tablespoon low-sodium soy sauce
- 1 clove garlic, minced
- 1 teaspoon snipped fresh thyme
- ½ teaspoon paprika
- ¼ teaspoon black pepper
- ¼ teaspoon crushed red pepper
- 2 8-ounce skinless, boneless chicken breast halves
- 2 teaspoons olive oil
- 1 tablespoon mango chutney
- 3 tablespoons light mayonnaise
- 4 multigrain sandwich thins, toasted
- 2 cups loosely packed watercress

1. In a small bowl stir together orange peel, orange juice, soy sauce, garlic, thyme, paprika, black pepper, and crushed red pepper; set aside.

2. Cut each chicken breast half crosswise in half. Place each piece between two pieces or plastic wrap. Using the flat side of a meat mallet, pound the chicken lightly to about ¼ inch thick. Remove plastic wrap.

3. In a very large nonstick skillet heat the oil over medium-high heat. Cook chicken in hot oil for 4 minutes, turning once. Carefully add orange juice mixture to skillet. Simmer for 3 minutes or until liquid reduces to a glaze, turning to coat chicken.

4. Place chutney in a small bowl; snip any large pieces of fruit. Stir in mayonnaise. To assemble sandwiches, spread mayonnaise mixture on cut sides of toasted sandwich thins. For each sandwich, place ½ cup of the watercress and a chicken portion on bottom half of sandwich thin. Add sandwich thin top, spread side down.

PER SERVING: 272 cal., 9 g total fat (1 g sat. fat), 51 mg chol., 564 mg sodium, 30 g carb. (5 g fiber, 7 g sugars), 21 g pro. Exchanges: 0.5 fruit, 1.5 starch, 3 lean meat.

QUICK TIP

Watercress leaves are small in size, but they pack a pungent, almost peppery bite. Use baby arugula or spinach if you prefer.

Garlic-Mustard Steak Sandwiches

Honey mustard gives these sandwiches a lighter flavor than the classic Dijon-style mustard.

SERVINGS 4 (1 sandwich each)
CARB. PER SERVING 33 g
PREP 25 minutes **BROIL** 18 minutes

> 8 ¾-ounce slices French bread
> 1 tablespoon honey mustard
> 2 cloves garlic, minced
> ½ teaspoon dried marjoram or thyme, crushed
> ¼ teaspoon coarsely ground black pepper
> 12 ounces beef flank steak
> 1 large red onion, cut into ½-inch-thick slices
> 2 tablespoons fat-free or light sour cream
> 2 ounces thinly sliced reduced-fat Swiss cheese

1. Preheat broiler. Place bread on the unheated rack of a broiler pan. Broil 4 to 5 inches from heat for 2 to 4 minutes or until toasted, turning once. Transfer to a wire rack; set aside. In a small bowl stir together honey mustard, garlic, marjoram or thyme, and pepper; set aside.

2. Trim fat from the steak. Score both sides of steak in a diamond pattern by making shallow diagonal cuts at 1-inch intervals. Place steak on one side of the broiler pan. Spoon half of the mustard mixture onto steak; spread evenly.

3. Place onion slices beside steak on broiler pan. Broil 4 to 5 inches from heat for 15 to 18 minutes or until steak is medium doneness (160°F) and onion is crisp-tender, turning onion slices once (do not turn steak).

4. In a small bowl stir together sour cream and the remaining mustard mixture. Spread sour cream-mustard mixture on one side of half of the bread slices; set aside. Transfer steak to a cutting board; thinly slice steak across the grain. Separate onion slices into rings. Arrange steak strips, onion rings, and cheese on the bread slices spread with the sour cream-mustard mixture. Place on the broiler pan. Broil about 1 minute or until cheese is melted. Top with the remaining bread slices.

GRILL METHOD: For a charcoal grill, place bread on the grill rack directly over medium coals. Grill, uncovered, for 2 to 4 minutes or until toasted, turning once halfway through grilling. Place steak and onion slices on the grill rack directly over medium coals. Grill, uncovered, for 17 to 21 minutes or until steak is medium doneness (160°F) and onion is tender, turning steak and onion slices once halfway through grilling. (For a gas grill, preheat grill. Reduce heat to medium. Place steak and onion slices on grill rack over heat. Cover and grill as above.)

PER SERVING: 327 cal., 9 g total fat (4 g sat. fat), 63 mg chol., 400 mg sodium, 33 g carb. (2 g fiber, 4 g sugars), 29 g pro. Exchanges: 2 starch, 3.5 lean meat, 0.5 fat.

Goat Cheese and Prosciutto Panini

Some goat cheese is creamier than others, so if it doesn't crumble very well, use a spoon to drop small bits of cheese over the bread.

SERVINGS 4 (1 sandwich each)
CARB. PER SERVING 30 g
PREP 15 minutes **COOK** 4 minutes

> 1 12-ounce loaf whole grain Italian bread
> Nonstick cooking spray
> 2 ounces goat cheese (chèvre), crumbled
> ½ cup fresh basil leaves
> 2 medium tomatoes, sliced
> 2 ounces thinly sliced prosciutto
> 2 cups arugula leaves
> 1 tablespoon balsamic vinegar (optional)

1. Cut the bread in half lengthwise. Hollow out top and bottom halves of bread, leaving a ½-inch-thick shell. Reserve removed bread for another use. (There should be about 4 ounces of bread removed.)

2. Lightly coat outsides of the bread halves with cooking spray. Sprinkle goat cheese over the cut side of the bread bottom. Top evenly with the basil, tomatoes, prosciutto, and arugula. If desired, drizzle with balsamic vinegar. Cover with loaf top.

3. Coat a large nonstick skillet with cooking spray; preheat over medium heat. Place loaf in skillet. Place another skillet on top of the loaf, pressing gently to flatten loaf slightly. Cook for 2½ minutes on one side; turn and cook for 2 to 2½ minutes more or until bread is beginning to brown.

4. Remove from skillet. Let stand on cutting board for 5 minutes. Use a serrated knife to slice loaf into four equal sandwiches. Serve sandwiches warm or at room temperature. If desired, serve with grapes.

PER SERVING: 253 cal., 10 g total fat (3 g sat. fat), 11 mg chol., 606 mg sodium, 30 g carb. (5 g fiber, 8 g sugars), 13 g pro. Exchanges: 2 starch, 1 medium-fat meat, 0.5 fat.

Goat Cheese and Prosciutto Panini

Philly Steak Sandwiches

Philly Steak Sandwiches

If you do not have a very large nonstick skillet, use a large nonstick skillet and cook the sweet peppers and onions separately.

SERVINGS 4 (1 sandwich each)
CARB. PER SERVING 29 g
PREP 20 minutes **BROIL** 17 minutes

- 1 12-ounce boneless beef top sirloin steak, cut 1 inch thick
- ½ teaspoon garlic-pepper seasoning
  Nonstick cooking spray
- 2 medium red and/or green sweet peppers, cut into thin strips
- 1 large onion, thinly sliced and separated into rings
- 4 whole wheat frankfurter buns, split
- ½ cup shredded reduced-fat cheddar or reduced-fat Monterey Jack cheese (2 ounces)

1. Preheat broiler. Trim fat from steak. Sprinkle steak with garlic-pepper seasoning. Place seasoned steak on the unheated rack of a broiler pan. Broil 3 to 4 inches from heat to desired doneness. Allow 15 to 17 minutes for medium rare (145°F) or 20 to 22 minutes for medium (160°F).
2. Meanwhile, coat an unheated very large nonstick skillet with cooking spray. Preheat skillet over medium heat. Add sweet peppers and onion. Cover; cook 5 minutes. Uncover; cook 5 minutes more or just until tender, stirring occasionally.
3. Place split buns on a large baking sheet. Broil 4 to 5 inches from heat for 1 to 2 minutes or until lightly toasted. Remove bun tops from baking sheet; set aside. Slice steak into bite-size strips. To assemble sandwiches, divide steak strips and sweet pepper mixture among bun bottoms. Sprinkle with cheese. Broil 4 to 5 inches from the heat for 1 to 2 minutes or until cheese is melted. Add bun tops.

PER SERVING: 295 cal., 8 g total fat (3 g sat. fat), 61 mg chol., 381 mg sodium, 29 g carb. (4 g fiber, 8 g sugars), 27 g pro. Exchanges: 1 vegetable, 2 starch, 3 lean meat, 1 fat.

Pork Tenderloin Sandwich with Chimichurri Sauce

Use the back of a heavy skillet to pound the pork if you don't have a meat mallet on hand.

SERVINGS 4 (1 sandwich each)
CARB. PER SERVING 30 g
PREP 25 minutes **COOK** 5 minutes

- 1 cup packed fresh Italian (flat-leaf) parsley
- 2 tablespoons snipped fresh oregano
- 2 tablespoons finely chopped shallot
- 2 tablespoons red wine vinegar
- 2 tablespoons lime juice
- 1 tablespoon olive oil
- 3 cloves garlic, minced
- ½ teaspoon crushed red pepper
- 1 pound pork tenderloin, trimmed
- ¼ teaspoon salt
- ¼ teaspoon black pepper
- 2 teaspoons olive oil
- 4 leaves lettuce
- 8 slices whole grain bread, toasted
- 4 slices tomato

1. For Chimichurri Sauce, in a food processor or blender combine the parsley, oregano, shallot, vinegar, lime juice, 1 tablespoon olive oil, the garlic, and crushed red pepper. Cover and blend or process until finely chopped, scraping sides as necessary; set aside.
2. Cut tenderloin into four equal pieces. Place each piece between two pieces of plastic wrap. Using the flat side of a meat mallet, pound the tenderloin lightly to about ¼ inch thick. Remove plastic wrap. Sprinkle evenly with the salt and pepper.
3. In a very large nonstick skillet heat the 2 teaspoons olive oil over medium-high heat. Reduce heat to medium. Cook tenderloin in hot oil for 5 to 7 minutes or until just pink inside. Remove from heat.
4. To assemble sandwiches, place a lettuce leaf on each of 4 slices toast. Top each with a tenderloin piece, a scant 3 tablespoons Chimichurri Sauce, a tomato slice, and another toast slice. Serve immediately.

PER SERVING: 343 cal., 10 g total fat (2 g sat. fat), 70 mg chol., 506 mg sodium, 30 g carb. (6 g fiber, 4 g sugars), 32 g pro. Exchanges: 2 starch, 4 lean meat, 1 fat.

Pork Tenderloin Sandwich
with Chimichurri Sauce

simple
sides and salads

Asparagus and
Wild Mushrooms

A main dish comprised of lean protein such as meat, poultry, fish, or legumes usually gets the oohs and aahs at mealtime, but the side dishes brimming with nutrient-rich fruits, vegetables, and grains round out the menu. Based on the guidelines for carb and fat in your daily meal plan, choose one of these healthful sides to add some wow to your plate.

Asparagus and Wild Mushrooms

Mushrooms absorb water like a sponge, so clean them by gently wiping them off with a slightly damp paper towel.

SERVINGS 4 (5 asparagus spears and $^1/3$ cup mushrooms each)
CARB. PER SERVING 5 g
PREP 20 minutes **ROAST** 15 minutes

- 3 cups halved cremini, shiitake, and/or button mushrooms
- 2 tablespoons white wine
- 2 teaspoons snipped fresh tarragon
- 1 pound fresh asparagus spears
- 1 tablespoon olive oil
- $^1/4$ teaspoon salt
- $^1/4$ teaspoon black pepper
- Snipped fresh tarragon (optional)

1. Preheat oven to 400°F. In a medium bowl toss together mushrooms, wine, and 2 teaspoons tarragon; set aside.
2. Snap off and discard woody bases from asparagus. Place asparagus in a 15×10×1-inch baking pan. Drizzle with oil and sprinkle with the salt and pepper. Toss to coat.
3. Roast, uncovered, for 5 minutes. Add mushroom mixture to the pan; toss gently to combine. Return to oven; roast about 10 minutes more or until asparagus is crisp-tender. If desired, garnish with additional fresh tarragon.

PER SERVING: 64 cal., 4 g total fat (1 g sat. fat), 0 mg chol., 151 mg sodium, 5 g carb. (2 g fiber, 2 g sugars), 4 g pro. Exchanges: 1 vegetable, 1 fat.

Lemon-Dill Cauliflower and Broccoli

If you don't have a fine-toothed Microplane or grater to remove the lemon peel, remove a strip with a vegetable peeler and then finely chop using a chef's knife.

SERVINGS 4 (1 cup each)
CARB. PER SERVING 6 g
PREP 25 minutes **GRILL** 20 minutes

> 2 cups cauliflower florets
> 2 cups broccoli florets
> 1 tablespoon olive oil
> 2 teaspoons snipped fresh dill weed or
> ½ teaspoon dried dill weed
> ¼ teaspoon finely shredded lemon peel
> 2 teaspoons lemon juice
> 1 small clove garlic, minced
> ⅛ teaspoon salt
> ⅛ teaspoon dry mustard
> ⅛ teaspoon black pepper

Lemon-Dill Cauliflower and Broccoli

1. Fold a 36×18-inch piece of heavy-duty foil in half to make an 18-inch square. Place cauliflower and broccoli in center of the foil square.
2. In a small bowl combine oil, dill, lemon peel, lemon juice, garlic, salt, mustard, and pepper; drizzle over vegetables. Bring up two opposite edges of the foil and seal with a double fold. Fold remaining ends to completely enclose the food, allowing space for steam to build.
3. For a charcoal grill, place foil packet on the grill rack directly over medium coals. Grill, uncovered, about 20 minutes or until vegetables are tender, turning packet once halfway through cooking and carefully opening packet to check doneness. (For a gas grill, preheat grill. Reduce heat to medium. Place foil packet on grill rack over heat. Cover and grill as above.) Remove from foil packet. If desired, garnish with *fresh dill sprigs*.
OVEN METHOD: Preheat oven to 350°F. Prepare as directed through Step 2. Bake packet directly on the oven rack about 35 minutes or until vegetables are tender, turning packet once halfway through cooking and carefully opening packet to check doneness.

PER SERVING: 60 cal., 4 g total fat (1 g sat. fat), 0 mg chol., 103 mg sodium, 6 g carb. (2 g fiber, 2 g sugars), 2 g pro. Exchanges: 1 vegetable, 0.5 fat.

Broccoli with Roasted Red Pepper

Once opened, a jar of roasted red peppers will keep for only a week. Add them to salads, sandwiches, omelets, and more.

SERVINGS 6 (¾ cup each)
CARB. PER SERVING 9 g
PREP 15 minutes **COOK** 8 minutes

> 8 cups large broccoli florets
> 2 tablespoons slivered almonds, toasted (see tip, page 100)
> 2 tablespoons chopped bottled roasted red sweet pepper
> 1 tablespoon toasted sesame oil
> 2 teaspoons reduced-sodium soy sauce
> 1 teaspoon finely chopped fresh ginger
> ⅛ teaspoon crushed red pepper

1. Place a steamer basket in a Dutch oven with a tight-fitting lid. Add water to just below the basket. Bring water to boiling. Place broccoli in the steamer basket. Cover and steam about 8 minutes or until broccoli is tender. Remove steamer basket with broccoli, allowing excess water to drain off.
2. Meanwhile, in a large bowl combine almonds, roasted red sweet pepper, sesame oil, soy sauce, ginger, and crushed red pepper. Add broccoli; toss well to coat.

PER SERVING: 75 cal., 4 g total fat (0 g sat. fat), 0 mg chol., 104 mg sodium, 9 g carb. (4 g fiber, 2 g sugars), 4 g pro. Exchanges: 1.5 vegetable, 1 fat.

Summer Corn
and Tomatoes

Summer Corn and Tomatoes

Tote this delicious saladlike vegetable dish to a picnic and
serve at room temperature.

SERVINGS 6 (1/2 cup each)

CARB. PER SERVING 15 g

PREP 15 minutes **COOK** 5 minutes

4 ears fresh sweet corn or 2 cups frozen
   whole kernel corn, thawed
1 tablespoon butter
1/2 cup sliced green onions (4)
2 cloves garlic, minced
2 cups grape tomatoes or cherry tomatoes, halved

1 tablespoon red wine vinegar
1/4 teaspoon salt
1/4 teaspoon black pepper

1. If using fresh corn, cut corn from cobs; set aside. In a
large skillet heat butter over medium heat. Add green onions
and garlic; cook and stir about 1 minute or until onions and
garlic are slightly softened. Add corn and tomatoes; cook
and stir for 4 to 5 minutes or until vegetables are crisp-
tender. Drizzle with vinegar and sprinkle with the salt
and pepper.

PER SERVING: 81 cal., 2 g total fat (1 g sat. fat), 5 mg chol.,
120 mg sodium, 15 g carb. (2 g fiber, 3 g sugars), 2 g pro.
Exchanges: 1 starch.

Tri-Color
Summer
Veggies

Tri-Color Summer Veggies

Showcase this peak-season combo alongside grilled meat, poultry, or fish.

SERVINGS 6 (^{2}/$_3$ cup each)

CARB. PER SERVING 6 g

PREP 25 minutes **COOK** 8 minutes

- 1 tablespoon butter
- 1¼ cups coarsely chopped yellow summer squash
- 1¼ cups coarsely chopped zucchini
- 1 cup frozen shelled sweet soybeans (edamame)
- ¾ cup coarsely chopped red sweet pepper
- ¾ cup thinly sliced red onion
- 2 cloves garlic, minced
- 1 tablespoon champagne vinegar or white wine vinegar
- 1½ teaspoons snipped fresh oregano
- 1 teaspoon snipped fresh thyme
- ¼ teaspoon salt
- ¼ teaspoon black pepper

1. In a large skillet heat butter over medium heat. Add yellow squash, zucchini, soybeans, sweet pepper, red onion, and garlic to butter. Cook and stir about 8 minutes or until vegetables are crisp-tender.

2. Stir in vinegar, oregano, thyme, salt, and black pepper. Serve immediately.

PER SERVING: 61 cal., 3 g total fat (1 g sat. fat), 5 mg chol., 119 mg sodium, 6 g carb. (2 g fiber, 3 g sugars), 3 g pro. Exchanges: 1 vegetable, 0.5 fat.

Sweet Onion and Butternut Squash Curry

Peeling a butternut squash can be a bit tricky. First cut the squash in half and then use a vegetable peeler or knife to remove the skin.

SERVINGS 6 (½ cup each)

CARB. PER SERVING 14 g

PREP 20 minutes **COOK** 5 minutes **ROAST** 20 minutes

- 1 small butternut squash (about 1¼ pounds)
- 1 small sweet onion, cut into wedges (1 to 1½ cups)
- 4 teaspoons canola oil
- ¼ teaspoon salt
- ¼ teaspoon black pepper
- 2 cloves garlic, minced
- 1 teaspoon grated fresh ginger
- ¼ cup dry white wine or reduced-sodium chicken broth
- ½ cup unsweetened light coconut milk
- 1 teaspoon curry powder
- 2 tablespoons snipped fresh basil
- Fresh basil leaves

1. Preheat oven to 425°F. Peel squash and remove the seeds. Cut into 1-inch pieces. Arrange squash pieces and onion in a 15x10x1-inch baking pan. Drizzle with 3 teaspoons of the oil and sprinkle with the salt and pepper; toss to coat. Roast, uncovered, for 20 to 25 minutes or until squash is tender, stirring once or twice.

2. Meanwhile, in a large skillet heat remaining 1 teaspoon oil over medium heat. Add garlic and ginger. Cook and stir about 30 seconds or until just tender. Carefully add wine to skillet and stir to combine. Add coconut milk and curry powder. Bring to boiling; reduce heat. Simmer for 3 to 5 minutes until slightly reduced. Stir in snipped basil and the roasted squash and onion. Heat through. To serve, garnish with additional fresh basil leaves.

PER SERVING: 122 cal., 7 g total fat (4 g sat. fat), 0 mg chol., 109 mg sodium, 14 g carb. (2 g fiber, 4 g sugars), 2 g pro. Exchanges: 1 starch, 1 fat.

Coriander Rice with Zucchini

Coriander is a spice ground from the tiny dried fruit of the cilantro plant. Its light, lemony flavor is less pungent than that of fresh cilantro.

SERVINGS 5 (^{2}/$_3$ cup each)

CARB. PER SERVING 16 g

PREP 25 minutes **COOK** 25 minutes **STAND** 5 minutes

- 1 14.5-ounce can reduced-sodium chicken broth
- ½ cup uncooked basmati rice or brown basmati rice
- 1 clove garlic, minced
- 1 medium zucchini, quartered lengthwise, then cut crosswise into ½-inch slices (1¼ cups)
- ½ cup julienned carrots
- 2 tablespoons snipped fresh parsley
- 1 tablespoon snipped fresh mint
- 1½ teaspoons finely shredded lemon peel
- 1 tablespoon lemon juice
- ¼ teaspoon ground coriander
- ⅛ teaspoon black pepper

1. In a medium saucepan combine broth, rice, and garlic. Bring to boiling; reduce heat. Simmer, covered, for 15 minutes for white rice or 35 minutes for brown rice. Stir in zucchini and carrots. Cook, covered, about 10 minutes more or until rice is tender and liquid is absorbed. Remove from heat.

2. Let stand, covered, for 5 minutes. Stir in parsley, mint, lemon peel, lemon juice, coriander, and pepper.

PER SERVING: 82 cal., 0 g total fat, 0 mg chol., 202 mg sodium, 16 g carb. (1 g fiber, 2 g sugars), 3 g pro. Exchanges: 1 starch.

Coconut Rice
with Snow Peas

Indian Basmati Rice

Coconut Rice with Snow Peas

When toasting a small quantity of nuts, toast them in a small skillet on the stove top rather than in the oven. Heat and stir the nuts over medium heat until golden.

SERVINGS 6 (^{2}/3 cup each)
CARB. PER SERVING 22 g
PREP 15 minutes **COOK** 20 minutes **STAND** 5 minutes

- 1 cup water
- 1 cup unsweetened lite coconut milk
- ^{3}/4 cup uncooked long grain rice
- ^{1}/2 teaspoon salt
- 2^1/4 cups 1^1/2- to 2-inch bias-sliced fresh snow pea pods
- 2 tablespoons sliced or slivered almonds, toasted

1. In a medium saucepan combine the water, coconut milk, rice, and salt. Bring to boiling; reduce heat. Simmer, covered, for 15 minutes.
2. Place pea pods on top of rice. Cover and cook about 5 minutes more or until rice and vegetables are nearly tender; there may still be some liquid. Remove from heat; let stand, covered, for 5 minutes.
3. Gently stir to combine and sprinkle with toasted nuts.

PER SERVING: 130 cal., 3 g total fat (2 g sat. fat), 0 mg chol., 205 mg sodium, 22 g carb. (1 g fiber, 2 g sugars), 3 g pro. Exchanges: 1 vegetable, 1 starch, 0.5 fat.

Indian Basmati Rice

Lightly coat your kitchen scissor blades with nonstick cooking spray to keep the sticky apricots from clinging to them.

SERVINGS 12 (^{1}/2 cup each)
CARB. PER SERVING 20 g
PREP 30 minutes **COOK** 18 minutes

- ^{1}/2 cup chopped onion (1 medium)
- 1 tablespoon butter
- 1 cup basmati rice
- ^{2}/3 cup snipped dried apricots
- 1 medium carrot, bias-sliced
- 1 teaspoon ground turmeric
- ^{1}/2 teaspoon ground cumin
- ^{1}/8 teaspoon crushed red pepper
- 1 14.5-ounce can reduced-sodium chicken broth
- ^{1}/4 cup water
- 1 6-ounce package frozen snow pea pods, thawed
- 2 tablespoons snipped fresh parsley
- 2 tablespoons slivered almonds, toasted (see tip, left)

1. In a medium saucepan cook onion in hot butter over medium heat about 5 minutes or until onion is tender. Stir in uncooked rice. Cook and stir for 4 minutes. Stir in apricots, carrot, turmeric, cumin, and crushed red pepper.
2. Carefully stir broth and the water into rice mixture in saucepan. Bring to boiling; reduce heat. Cover and simmer for 18 to 20 minutes or until liquid is absorbed and rice is tender. Stir in pea pods and parsley. Sprinkle individual servings with almonds.

PER SERVING: 100 cal., 2 g total fat (1 g sat. fat), 3 mg chol., 94 mg sodium, 20 g carb. (2 g fiber, 5 g sugars), 2 g pro. Exchanges: 0.5 fruit, 1 starch.

Lemon-Cilantro Slaw

Sweet and Tangy Broccoli Slaw

Take your pick—either slaw mix makes a crunchy and delicious serve-along.

SERVINGS 4 (³/4 cup each)
CARB. PER SERVING 14 g
PREP 10 minutes

- ¼ cup plain fat-free Greek yogurt
- 3 tablespoons light mayonnaise
- 1 tablespoon honey
- 2 teaspoons cider vinegar
- 3 cups packaged shredded broccoli (broccoli slaw mix) or packaged shredded cabbage with carrot (coleslaw mix)
- 2 tablespoons raisins
- 2 tablespoons finely chopped red onion
- 2 tablespoons slivered almonds, toasted (see tip, page 100)

1. In a medium bowl combine the yogurt, mayonnaise, honey, and vinegar. Stir until combined. Add the slaw, raisins, red onion, and almonds. Stir until well combined. Cover and chill for up to 2 hours. Toss before serving.

PER SERVING: 115 cal., 5 g total fat (1 g sat. fat), 4 mg chol., 96 mg sodium, 14 g carb. (2 g fiber, 10 g sugars), 4 g pro. Exchanges: 1 vegetable, 0.5 fruit, 1 fat.

Lemon-Cilantro Slaw

The lemon and Dijon-style mustard dressing and a sprinkling of cilantro give coleslaw an enchanting flavor twist.

SERVINGS 4 (1 cup each)
CARB. PER SERVING 6 g
PREP 20 minutes **CHILL** 2 hours

- 2 tablespoons lemon juice
- 1 tablespoon olive oil
- ½ teaspoon sugar*
- ½ teaspoon Dijon-style mustard
- ⅛ teaspoon black pepper
- 4 cups packaged shredded cabbage with carrot (coleslaw mix)
- ½ cup coarsely shredded carrot
- 2 tablespoons snipped fresh cilantro
- 2 tablespoons chopped green onion

1. In a large bowl whisk together lemon juice, oil, sugar, mustard, and pepper. Add coleslaw mix, carrot, cilantro, and green onion; toss gently to coat. Cover and chill for 2 to 24 hours before serving.

***SUGAR SUBSTITUTES:** Choose from Splenda Granular, Sweet'N Low bulk or packets, or Equal Spoonful or packets. Follow package directions to use product amount equivalent to ½ teaspoon sugar.

PER SERVING: 59 cal., 3 g total fat (0 g sat. fat), 0 mg chol., 43 mg sodium, 6 g carb. (2 g fiber, 4 g sugars), 1 g pro. Exchanges: 1 vegetable, 0.5 fat.

PER SERVING WITH SUBSTITUTE: Same as above, except 57 cal.

QUICK TIP
Tender Bibb or butterhead lettuce serves as a bed for **Basil Quinoa Salad,** but torn romaine, leaf lettuce, or spinach makes a good base, too.

Basil Quinoa Salad

Turn this side salad into a main dish by adding some shredded cooked chicken or turkey breast.

SERVINGS 8 ($^2/_3$ cup quinoa mixture and $^1/_2$ cup lettuce each)

CARB. PER SERVING 21 g

START TO FINISH 30 minutes

- 1 cup fresh basil leaves
- 2 tablespoons grated Parmesan cheese
- 2 tablespoons lemon juice
- 2 tablespoons olive oil
- 4 cloves garlic, minced
- $^1/_4$ teaspoon salt
- $^1/_4$ teaspoon black pepper
- 2 cups cooked quinoa*
- 1 15-ounce can no-salt-added red kidney beans, rinsed and drained, or 1$^3/_4$ cups cooked red kidney beans
- 1 cup chopped yellow sweet pepper
- $^1/_2$ cup chopped, seeded tomato
- $^1/_2$ cup sliced green onions (4)
- 4 cups torn Bibb lettuce

1. Place basil in a food processor. Add Parmesan cheese, lemon juice, olive oil, garlic, salt, and black pepper. Cover and process until nearly smooth, stopping to scrape down sides as needed; set aside.

2. In a large bowl stir together cooked quinoa, beans, sweet pepper, tomato, and green onions. Add basil mixture; stir to coat.

3. Serve quinoa mixture over torn lettuce.

***TEST KITCHEN TIP:** To make 2 cups cooked quinoa, in a fine strainer rinse $^1/_2$ cup quinoa under cold running water; drain. In a small saucepan combine 1$^1/_4$ cups water, the quinoa, and $^1/_4$ teaspoon salt. Bring to boiling; reduce heat. Cover and simmer for 15 minutes. Let stand to cool slightly. Drain off any remaining liquid.

PER SERVING: 148 cal., 5 g total fat (1 g sat. fat), 1 mg chol., 178 mg sodium, 21 g carb. (6 g fiber, 1 g sugars), 7 g pro. Exchanges: 1 vegetable, 1 starch, 1 fat.

Potato Salad

This version of the classic side gets its creaminess from light sour cream rather than the traditional mayonnaise.

SERVINGS 8 ($^1/_2$ cup each)

CARB. PER SERVING 12 g

PREP 30 minutes **COOK** 20 minutes

- 3 medium white, red, or Yukon gold potatoes (1 pound), rinsed and scrubbed but not peeled
- 1 tablespoon olive oil
- 1 tablespoon cider vinegar
- 1 clove garlic, minced

Autumn Fruit Salad

- $^1/_4$ teaspoon black pepper
- 2 hard-cooked eggs, chopped
- $^1/_2$ cup light sour cream
- $^1/_2$ cup chopped celery
- $^1/_3$ cup chopped sweet onion

1. In a medium saucepan place unpeeled potatoes in enough water to cover. Bring to boiling; reduce heat. Simmer, covered, for 20 to 25 minutes or just until tender. Drain well; cool slightly. Cut the potatoes into 1-inch cubes.

2. Meanwhile, in medium bowl whisk together olive oil, vinegar, garlic, and pepper. Fold in eggs, sour cream, celery, and onion. Add the potatoes. Toss lightly to coat.

PER SERVING: 99 cal., 4 g total fat (1 g sat. fat), 51 mg chol., 33 mg sodium, 12 g carb. (1 g fiber, 1 g sugars), 3 g pro. Exchanges: 1 starch, 0.5 fat.

Autumn Fruit Salad

Look for agave nectar near the sugar and other sweeteners in the grocery store.

SERVINGS 4 ($^3/_4$ cup salad and 1 tablespoon yogurt mixture each)

CARB. PER SERVING 20 g

START TO FINISH 15 minutes

- 2 ripe pears, cubed
- 2 tablespoons lemon juice
- $^1/_3$ cup chopped pecans, toasted
- $^1/_4$ cup plain low-fat Greek yogurt
- 1 tablespoon honey or agave nectar
- Ground cinnamon (optional)

1. In a medium bowl combine pears and lemon juice. Stir in pecans. Divide pear mixture among four bowls.

2. In a small bowl combine yogurt and honey. Top each serving of the pear mixture with a spoonful of the yogurt mixture. If desired, sprinkle with cinnamon.

PER SERVING: 140 cal., 7 g total fat (1 g sat. fat), 1 mg chol., 7 mg sodium, 20 g carb. (3 g fiber, 14 g sugars), 3 g pro. Exchanges: 0.5 milk, 0.5 fruit, 1 fat.

Coucous
Salad Platter

Get Fresh

Fresh herbs add life to food. Choose herbs
that have fresh-looking leaves without brown
spots. Fresh herbs are highly perishable, so
buy as you need them—or, better yet, grow
them in a pot in your windowsill or in your
garden.

To store fresh herbs, cut $\frac{1}{2}$ inch from the
stem ends. Stand stems in a small jar with
some water. Loosely cover leaves with a
plastic bag and store in the refrigerator. (Do
not refrigerate basil; it may darken.) Discard
wilted leaves as they appear.

Couscous Salad Platter

Spoon the hummus into a small bowl or simply mound it on
the platter to serve.

SERVINGS 4 ($\frac{1}{2}$ cup couscous mixture, $\frac{1}{4}$ cup
cucumber, 2 tablespoons sweet pepper, and 1 tablespoon
hummus each)

CARB. PER SERVING 26 g

PREP 15 minutes **COOK** 22 minutes **STAND** 5 minutes

$\frac{3}{4}$	cup Israeli (large pearl) couscous
$1\frac{1}{4}$	cups reduced-sodium chicken broth
$\frac{1}{4}$	cup chopped tomatoes
1	tablespoon snipped fresh mint
1	tablespoon lemon juice
$\frac{1}{8}$	teaspoon black pepper
1	cup sliced cucumber
$\frac{1}{2}$	cup bottled roasted red sweet peppers, cut into strips
8	pitted Kalamata olives (optional)
$\frac{1}{4}$	cup purchased hummus

1. In a dry medium saucepan toast couscous over medium-
low heat, stirring frequently, for 8 to 10 minutes or until
golden brown. Remove from saucepan; set aside.

2. In the medium saucepan bring broth to boiling. Add
couscous. Return to boiling; reduce heat. Simmer, covered,
for 12 to 15 minutes or until liquid is absorbed. Remove from
heat. Stir in tomatoes, mint, lemon juice, and black pepper.
Cover and let stand for 5 minutes.

3. Transfer couscous to a small platter. Arrange cucumber,
roasted red peppers, olives (if using), and hummus on or
around couscous.

PER SERVING: 138 cal., 1 g total fat (0 g sat. fat), 0 mg chol.,
228 mg sodium, 26 g carb. (3 g fiber, 2 g sugars), 5 g pro.
Exchanges: 1 vegetable, 1.5 starch.

Poblano Pasta Salad

For a Greek version of this family-friendly pasta salad,
substitute green sweet pepper for the poblano, basil for the
cilantro, and reduced-fat feta for the queso fresco.

SERVINGS 6 ($\frac{2}{3}$ cup each)

CARB. PER SERVING 20 g

PREP 20 minutes **ROAST** 20 minutes **STAND** 20 minutes

1	medium fresh poblano chile pepper (see tip, page 20)
1	medium red sweet pepper
$\frac{1}{2}$	of a medium sweet onion, cut into $\frac{1}{2}$-inch slices
4	ounces dried whole wheat rotini pasta, dried whole grain penne pasta, or dried whole grain bow tie pasta (about $1\frac{2}{3}$ cups)
$\frac{1}{4}$	cup chopped tomatoes
2	tablespoons snipped fresh cilantro
2	tablespoons toasted pumpkin seeds (pepitas)
2	tablespoons red wine vinegar

1 tablespoon olive oil
1 clove garlic, minced
¼ teaspoon salt
⅛ teaspoon black pepper
1 ounce queso fresco, crumbled

1. Preheat oven to 425°F. Halve poblano pepper and sweet pepper. Remove seeds and membranes. Place poblano pepper, sweet pepper, and onion slices, cut sides down, on foil-lined baking sheet. Roast in oven about 20 minutes or until pepper skins and onion are lightly charred. Wrap peppers in the foil and let stand for 20 to 30 minutes or until cool enough to handle. Peel off skin. Coarsely chop peppers and onion.

2. Meanwhile, cook pasta according to package directions. Drain well. Rinse well with cold water; drain again.

3. In a large bowl combine cooked pasta, chopped peppers, onion, tomatoes, cilantro, and pumpkin seeds. Set aside.

4. For dressing, in a screw-top jar combine vinegar, olive oil, garlic, salt, and black pepper. Cover and shake well. Pour dressing over pasta and vegetables; toss gently to combine. Garnish each serving with a sprinkle of queso fresco.

PER SERVING: 146 cal., 5 g total fat (1 g sat. fat), 3 mg chol., 138 mg sodium, 20 g carb. (2 g fiber, 3 g sugars), 5 g pro. Exchanges: 1 vegetable, 1 starch, 1 fat.

Poblano Pasta Salad

Spinach and
Olive Melts

Miso-Ginger Kale

Apple-
Tomato
Salad

Spinach and Olive Melts

Pop these salad-topped muffins under the broiler to melt the cheese and serve alongside a steaming bowl of soup.

SERVINGS 4 (1 open-face melt each)
CARB. PER SERVING 14 g
PREP 10 minutes **BROIL** 3 minutes

- 1 cup fresh spinach, coarsely chopped
- 4 pitted Kalamata olives, chopped
- 2 whole wheat English muffins, split
- 1 teaspoon Dijon-style mustard
- 1 ounce Gouda cheese, shaved or coarsely shredded (1/4 cup)

1. Preheat broiler. In a small bowl combine spinach and olives; set aside. On a baking sheet arrange English muffin halves, cut sides up. Broil 4 inches from the heat about 2 minutes or until golden.

2. Spread English muffin halves lightly with mustard. Top with spinach mixture and cheese. Broil about 1 minute more or until cheese is melted and bubbly. Serve immediately.

PER SERVING: 101 cal., 3 g total fat (1 g sat. fat), 8 mg chol., 298 mg sodium, 14 g carb. (3 g fiber, 3 g sugars), 5 g pro. Exchanges: 1 starch, 0.5 fat.

Miso-Ginger Kale

Kale, a nutrient powerhouse, has some cholesterol-lowering benefits when eaten raw and even more when steamed.

SERVINGS 6 (1 cup each)
CARB. PER SERVING 9 g
PREP 25 minutes **COOK** 10 minutes

- 2 8-ounce bunches fresh kale
- 2 tablespoons rice vinegar
- 2 tablespoons canola oil
- 1/2 teaspoon finely shredded lime peel
- 1 tablespoon lime juice
- 2 teaspoons miso (soybean paste)
- 1 teaspoon grated fresh ginger
- 1 clove garlic, minced
- 2 tablespoons dry-roasted cashews or peanuts, chopped (optional)

1. Rinse and dry kale. Trim and discard tough stems. Stack leaves, then cut crosswise into 1/2-inch strips.

2. Place a steamer basket in a Dutch oven with a tight-fitting lid. Add water to just below the basket. Bring water to boiling over medium-high heat. Place kale in the steamer basket. Cover and steam about 10 minutes or until tender, tossing leaves once or twice. Remove steamer basket with kale and transfer kale to a bowl.

3. For dressing, in a small bowl combine vinegar, oil, lime peel, lime juice, miso paste, ginger, and garlic; whisk to combine. Drizzle dressing mixture over kale. Toss to combine. If desired, serve kale topped with chopped nuts.

PER SERVING: 86 cal., 5 g total fat (0 g sat. fat), 0 mg chol., 103 mg sodium, 9 g carb. (2 g fiber, 2 g sugars), 3 g pro. Exchanges: 1 vegetable, 1 fat.

Apple-Tomato Salad

To toast nuts in the oven, place them in a baking pan and bake in a 350°F oven for 5 to 10 minutes, shaking the pan once or twice. Toast a cup or two at a time and store them in the freezer.

SERVINGS 4 (about 1 1/2 cups salad mixture and 1 tablespoon dressing each)
CARB. PER SERVING 14 g
START TO FINISH 20 minutes

- 2 cups green leaf lettuce, torn into bite size pieces
- 2 cups arugula
- 1 cup cherry tomatoes, halved
- 1 medium Fuji apple or green-skin apple, halved and thinly sliced
- 1/4 of a medium red onion, thinly sliced
- 2 tablespoons crumbled blue cheese
- 4 teaspoons chopped pecans. toasted
- 2 tablespoons cider vinegar
- 4 teaspoons olive oil
- 1 tablespoon honey
- 1/8 teaspoon salt
- 1/8 teaspoon black pepper

1. Arrange leaf lettuce, arugula, tomatoes, apple, and red onion on four salad plates. Sprinkle with blue cheese and pecans.

2. For dressing, in a screw-top jar combine vinegar, olive oil, honey, salt, and pepper. Cover and shake well. Drizzle dressing over salads.

PER SERVING: 128 cal., 8 g total fat (2 g sat. fat), 3 mg chol., 143 mg sodium, 14 g carb. (2 g fiber, 11 g sugars), 2 g pro. Exchanges: 1 vegetable, 0.5 fruit, 1.5 fat.

Porcini Eggplant

The concentrated, nutty flavor of porcini mushrooms is popular in Italian cuisine. Porcinis are pricey because they are not easy to cultivate.

SERVINGS 6 (¹/₂ cup each)
CARB. PER SERVING 8 g
PREP 15 minutes **ROAST** 15 minutes **STAND** 15 minutes
COOK 5 minutes

 1 pound eggplant, peeled and cut into 1-inch cubes
 2 tablespoons olive oil
 ¹/₄ teaspoon salt
 ¹/₄ teaspoon black pepper
 ¹/₂ ounce dried porcini mushrooms
 ¹/₃ cup balsamic vinegar
 1 teaspoon snipped fresh thyme
 ¹/₂ cup grape tomatoes, quartered
 1 tablespoon snipped fresh basil

1. Preheat oven to 425°F. Arrange eggplant in a 15×10×1-inch baking pan. Drizzle with olive oil and sprinkle with the salt and pepper. Toss to coat. Roast for 15 to 20 minutes or until tender and browned, stirring once or twice.

2. Meanwhile, place mushrooms in a small bowl. And 1 cup boiling water to bowl. Let stand for 15 minutes; drain water. Chop mushrooms.

3. In a small saucepan heat balsamic vinegar over medium heat until boiling; reduce heat. Simmer, uncovered, about 5 minutes or until reduced by half. Stir in mushrooms and thyme.

4. To serve, drizzle roasted eggplant with balsamic mixture. Combine grape tomatoes and basil. Sprinkle over the eggplant mixture.

PER SERVING: 77 cal., 5 g total fat (1 g sat. fat), 0 mg chol., 103 mg sodium, 8 g carb. (3 g fiber, 4 g sugars), 1 g pro. Exchanges: 1 vegetable, 1 fat.

comforting
breakfasts

Southwest Breakfast Quesadilla

It's important to begin each day by eating a wholesome breakfast. Whether you indulge in a protein-rich egg dish or a high-fiber cereal, eating healthfully will fuel your body, kick up your metabolic rate, and help balance your blood glucose. Try boosting your morning momentum with one of these tasty new breakfast options.

Southwest Breakfast Quesadilla

If you prefer eggs over egg product, substitute 1 egg in this meatless meal.

SERVINGS 1
CARB. PER SERVING 25 g
START TO FINISH 10 minutes

Nonstick cooking spray
1/4 cup refrigerated or frozen egg product, thawed
1/8 to 1/4 teaspoon salt-free Southwest chipotle seasoning blend
1 8-inch whole wheat flour tortilla
2 tablespoons shredded part-skim mozzarella cheese
2 tablespoons canned no-salt-added black beans, rinsed and drained
2 tablespoons refrigerated fresh pico de gallo or chopped tomato
Refrigerated fresh pico de gallo or chopped tomato (optional)

1. Coat an unheated medium nonstick skillet with cooking spray. Preheat skillet over medium heat. Add egg to hot skillet; sprinkle with seasoning blend. Cook over medium heat, without stirring, until egg begins to set on the bottom and around edge. Using a spatula or a large spoon, lift and fold the partially cooked egg so that the uncooked portion flows underneath. Continue cooking over medium heat for 30 to 60 seconds or until egg is cooked through but is still glossy and moist.
2. Immediately spoon cooked egg onto one side of the tortilla. Top with cheese, beans, and the 2 tablespoons pico de gallo. Fold tortilla over filling to cover; press gently.
3. Wipe out the same skillet with a paper towel. Coat skillet with cooking spray. Preheat skillet over medium heat. Cook filled tortilla in hot skillet about 2 minutes or until tortilla is browned and filling is heated through, turning once. If desired, top with additional pico de gallo.

PER SERVING: 175 cal., 5 g total fat (1 g sat. fat), 9 mg chol., 507 mg sodium, 25 g carb. (14 g fiber, 2 g sugars), 19 g pro. Exchanges: 1.5 starch, 2 lean meat.

Creole Eggplant Eggs Benedict

If the eggplant slices have a diameter greater than 3 inches, use a 3-inch round cutter to cut the slices to size.

SERVINGS 4 (2 eggplant slices, 1 egg, $^1/_2$ cup Creole sauce, and 1 tablespoon hollandaise topper each)
CARB. PER SERVING 20 g or 19 g
START TO FINISH 50 minutes

$^1/_2$	cup chopped onion (1 medium)
$^1/_2$	cup chopped celery (1 stalk)
1	clove garlic, minced
5	teaspoons olive oil
1	14.5-ounce can no-salt-added diced tomatoes, undrained
2	teaspoons Worcestershire sauce
$^1/_2$	teaspoon sugar*
$^1/_2$	teaspoon dried thyme, crushed
$^1/_8$ to $^1/_4$	teaspoon cayenne pepper
1	tablespoon snipped fresh Italian (flat-leaf) parsley
$^1/_2$	cup panko (Japanese-style bread crumbs)
1	teaspoon dried parsley flakes
$^1/_4$	cup refrigerated or frozen egg product, thawed
$^1/_2$	teaspoon garlic powder
$^1/_2$	teaspoon paprika
$^1/_8$ to $^1/_4$	teaspoon black pepper
$^1/_8$	teaspoon salt

8	$^1/_2$-inch-thick slices peeled eggplant (3 inches in diameter)
4	eggs
$^1/_4$	cup plain fat-free Greek yogurt
2	teaspoons lime juice
1	teaspoon yellow mustard
$^1/_8$	teaspoon ground white pepper

1. Preheat oven to 200°F. For Creole sauce, in a medium saucepan cook onion, celery, and garlic in 1 teaspoon of the oil until tender. Add tomatoes, Worcestershire sauce, sugar, thyme, and cayenne pepper. Bring to boiling; reduce heat. Simmer, uncovered, for 10 minutes. Stir in the fresh parsley.

2. In a shallow dish combine panko and dried parsley. Place egg product in another shallow dish. In a small bowl combine garlic powder, paprika, black pepper, and salt.

3. In a very large nonstick skillet heat the remaining oil over medium heat. Sprinkle eggplant slices with the spice mixture. Dip each eggplant slice in the egg product, then dip in the crumb mixture to lightly coat. Add eggplant slices to hot oil; cook for 12 to 14 minutes or until golden brown and tender (if eggplant browns too quickly, reduce heat slightly), turning eggplant once halfway through cooking. Transfer eggplant slices to a baking sheet; place in oven to keep warm.

4. Meanwhile, poach the 4 eggs. In a large skillet bring 1 inch water to boiling; reduce heat to simmering (bubbles should begin to break the surface of the water). Break an egg into a cup and slip egg into the simmering water. Repeat with remaining eggs, allowing each egg an equal amount of space in the water. Simmer eggs, uncovered, for 3 to 5 minutes or until whites are set and yolks begin to thicken but are not hard. Using a slotted spoon, remove eggs from water.

5. To make hollandaise topper, in a small bowl stir together yogurt, lime juice, mustard, and the white pepper.

6. For each serving, place an eggplant slice on a plate; top with $^1/_4$ cup of the Creole sauce, one poached egg, another eggplant slice, another $^1/_4$ cup of the Creole sauce, and about 1 tablespoon of the hollandaise topper. If desired, sprinkle with additional paprika or black pepper.

MAKE-AHEAD TIP: The Creole sauce and hollandaise topper can be made the day ahead. Refrigerate until needed. Reheat the Creole sauce before serving.

*SUGAR SUBSTITUTES: Choose from Splenda Granular, Equal Spoonful or packets, or Sweet'N Low packets or bulk. Follow package directions to use product amount equivalent to $^1/_2$ teaspoon sugar.

PER SERVING: 226 cal., 11 g total fat (3 g sat. fat), 186 mg chol., 296 mg sodium, 20 g carb. (5 g fiber, 8 g sugars), 12 g pro. Exchanges: 2 vegetable, 0.5 starch, 1 medium-fat meat, 1.5 fat.
PER SERVING WITH SUBSTITUTE: Same as above, except 225 cal., 19 g carb.

Creole Eggplant
Eggs Benedict

Hearty Vegetable,
Bacon, and
Quinoa Quiche

Hearty Vegetable, Bacon, and Quinoa Quiche

The pie plate will be full, so carefully transfer it to the oven to avoid spilling. If you wish, place the plate on a baking sheet.

SERVINGS 6 (¹/6 of quiche each)

CARB. PER SERVING 15 g

PREP 25 minutes BAKE 55 minutes

   Nonstick cooking spray
½ cup dry quinoa
8 ounces sliced fresh mushrooms
1 cup loosely packed coarsely chopped fresh spinach
½ cup sliced, halved leeks
4 slices applewood smoked bacon, crisp-cooked, drained, and coarsely crumbled
4 eggs, lightly beaten
1 cup refrigerated or frozen egg product, thawed
1 12-ounce can evaporated fat-free milk
2 ounces Gruyère or Havarti cheese, shredded (½ cup)
½ teaspoon salt
⅛ teaspoon black pepper

1. Preheat oven to 350°F. Coat a deep 10-inch pie plate with cooking spray. Rinse quinoa. Using a rubber spatula, spread quinoa as evenly as possible over the bottom of the prepared pie plate.

2. In a medium bowl stir together mushrooms, spinach, leeks, and bacon. Spread mushroom mixture evenly over the quinoa.

3. In a large bowl whisk together the eggs, egg product, evaporated milk, shredded cheese, salt, and pepper. Pour into the pie plate (it will be full).

4. Bake for 55 to 60 minutes or until set in the center and browned on top.

PER SERVING: 288 cal., 12 g total fat (4 g sat. fat), 163 mg chol., 571 mg sodium, 15 g carb. (1 g fiber, 4 g sugars), 20 g pro. Exchanges: 1 starch, 2.5 lean meat.

Quick Breakfast Pizza

Once toasted, the sandwich thin halves will cool quickly. Immediately add the pizza toppings.

SERVINGS 1

CARB. PER SERVING 23 g

START TO FINISH 10 minutes

    Nonstick cooking spray
    4 slices turkey pepperoni, quartered (0.25 ounce total)
    2 tablespoons diced green sweet pepper
    2 tablespoons sliced mushrooms
    2 egg whites
    1 tablespoon milk
    1 seven-grain sandwich thin roll, split
    2 teaspoons pizza sauce
    1 0.75-ounce slice mozzarella cheese, cut diagonally into quarters
    4 slices roma tomato (optional)

1. Coat a small nonstick saucepan with cooking spray; heat over medium heat. Add pepperoni, sweet pepper, and mushrooms to saucepan; cook for 2 minutes.

2. In a small bowl whisk together egg whites and milk; pour over pepperoni mixture in saucepan. Cook until egg white mixture begins to set. Using a spatula, fold the partially cooked egg white mixture over; cook about 2 minutes more or until egg whites are cooked through.

3. Meanwhile, toast sandwich thin roll halves. Place on a plate, cut sides down. Spread each half with 1 teaspoon pizza sauce; place two cheese quarters on each half.

4. Spoon half of the egg mixture over each of the prepared sandwich thin halves. If desired, top with tomato slices.

PER SERVING: 218 cal., 6 g total fat (3 g sat. fat), 23 mg chol., 563 mg sodium, 23 g carb. (6 g fiber, 5 g sugars), 21 g pro. Exchanges: 1 vegetable, 1 starch, 2.5 lean meat.

Garden Fresh Omelets

Jump-start the meal prep by stirring together the salsa the night before. It can chill for up to 8 hours.

SERVINGS 4 (1 omelet, $^3/_4$ cup salsa, and 1 tablespoon cheese each)

CARB. PER SERVING 9 g

START TO FINISH 35 minutes

    1$^1/_3$ cups coarsely chopped tomatoes, drained
    1 cup coarsely chopped, seeded cucumber
    $^1/_2$ of a ripe avocado, halved, seeded, peeled, and chopped
    $^1/_2$ cup coarsely chopped red onion (1 medium)
    1 clove garlic, minced
    2 tablespoons snipped fresh parsley
    2 tablespoons red wine vinegar
    1 tablespoon olive oil
    2 eggs
    1$^1/_2$ cups refrigerated or frozen egg product, thawed
    $^1/_4$ cup water
    1 tablespoon snipped fresh oregano or 1 teaspoon dried oregano, crushed
    $^1/_4$ teaspoon salt
    $^1/_4$ teaspoon black pepper
    $^1/_8$ teaspoon crushed red pepper
    $^1/_4$ cup crumbled reduced-fat feta cheese (1 ounce)

1. For salsa, in a medium bowl stir together tomatoes, cucumber, avocado, onion, garlic, parsley, vinegar, and 1 teaspoon of the oil. Set aside.

2. In a medium bowl whisk together eggs, egg product, the water, oregano, salt, black pepper, and crushed red pepper. For each omelet, in a medium nonstick skillet with flared sides heat $^1/_2$ teaspoon of the remaining oil over medium heat. Add $^1/_2$ cup of the egg mixture to skillet. Stir eggs with a spatula until mixture resembles cooked egg pieces surrounded by liquid. Stop stirring, but continue cooking until egg is set. Spoon $^1/_3$ cup of the salsa over one side of the cooked egg mixture. Remove from skillet; fold omelet over the filling. Repeat to make four omelets total.

3. Spoon remaining salsa over omelets. Sprinkle 1 tablespoon of the feta cheese over each omelet.

PER SERVING: 181 cal., 10 g total fat (2 g sat. fat), 108 mg chol., 478 mg sodium, 9 g carb. (2 g fiber, 4 g sugars), 15 g pro. Exchanges: 1 vegetable, 2 lean meat, 2 fat.

Quick Breakfast Pizza

Garden Fresh Omelets

QUICK TIP
After you have chopped the tomatoes, place them in a colander to drain for a bit. Otherwise, the salsa will be watery and the omelet will get soggy.

Spinach-and-Feta Omelets
with Banana-Oat Muffins
recipe on page 121

A Bit of Perfection

To make a perfect omelet, use these techniques to ensure success. After the egg has set but while the top is still wet, place the filling on one side of the cooked egg mixture. Don't overfill it or the omelet will be difficult to fold. Use a rubber spatula to fold the unfilled side over the filling. Once the omelet has finished cooking, carefully slide it out of the skillet and onto a plate.

Spinach-and-Feta Omelets

This Mediterranean-style omelet is ideal for a leisurely weekend breakfast. Serve it with muffins or toast.

SERVINGS 2 (1 omelet each)
CARB. PER SERVING 10 g
START TO FINISH 20 minutes

  1 cup refrigerated or frozen egg product, thawed
⅛ teaspoon salt
   Dash black pepper
   Nonstick cooking spray
  1 cup sliced fresh mushrooms
½ cup chopped onion (1 medium)
  2 teaspoons olive oil or canola oil
  2 cups lightly packed fresh baby spinach
¼ cup crumbled feta cheese (1 ounce)

1. In a small bowl whisk together egg, salt, and pepper; set aside. Lightly coat an unheated medium nonstick skillet with flared sides with cooking spray. Preheat skillet over medium heat. Add mushrooms and onion; cook and stir until onion is tender. Remove vegetables from skillet; set aside.
2. Add 1 teaspoon of the oil to skillet; heat over medium heat. Add half of the egg mixture to skillet and immediately begin stirring gently with a wooden or plastic spatula. Stir continuously until the mixture resembles small pieces of cooked egg surrounded by liquid egg. Stop stirring and cook for 30 to 60 seconds more or until egg mixture is set and shiny.
3. Spoon half of the mushroom mixture across one side of the cooked egg mixture. Top with 1 cup of the spinach and 1 tablespoon of the feta cheese. Loosen edge of cooked egg mixture from skillet. Fold unfilled side over the filling. Cook about 1 minute more or just until spinach starts to wilt. Slide omelet onto serving plate; cover and keep warm. Repeat to make a second omelet.
4. To serve, sprinkle omelets with the remaining 2 tablespoons feta cheese.

PER SERVING: 177 cal., 8 g total fat (3 g sat. fat), 13 mg chol., 562 mg sodium, 10 g carb. (2 g fiber, 5 g sugars), 17 g pro. Exchanges: 2 vegetable, 2 lean meat, 1.5 fat.

Country Breakfast Skillet

Breakfast staples hash browns, veggies, ham, and eggs cook together and then get crowned with cheese.

SERVINGS 4 (⅔ cup each)
CARB. PER SERVING 12 g
START TO FINISH 25 minutes

  2 teaspoons canola oil
  1 cup frozen shredded hash brown potatoes, thawed and patted dry
⅓ cup chopped green sweet pepper

      ⅓ cup chopped onion
      1 ounce low-sodium lean ham, finely chopped
      3 eggs or ¾ cup refrigerated or frozen egg product,
         thawed
      4 egg whites
      1 tablespoon fat-free milk
      ¼ teaspoon salt
      ⅛ to ¼ teaspoon black pepper
      ½ cup reduced-fat cheddar cheese (2 ounces)
      1 tablespoon snipped fresh chives

1. In a large nonstick skillet heat oil over medium-high heat. Add potatoes, sweet pepper, onion, and ham; cook for 5 to 8 minutes or until vegetables are just tender, turning mixture occasionally. Reduce heat to medium.

2. In a medium bowl stir together eggs, egg whites, milk, salt, and black pepper. Pour egg mixture into skillet with potato mixture. Cook, without stirring, until mixture begins to set on the bottom and around edge. Using a large spoon or spatula, lift and fold partially cooked egg mixture so uncooked portion flows underneath.

3. Sprinkle with cheese and chives. Continue cooking over medium heat for 2 to 3 minutes or until egg mixture is cooked through but is still glossy and moist. Remove from heat. (Be careful not to overcook the egg mixture.)

PER SERVING: 216 cal., 12 g total fat (5 g sat. fat), 159 mg chol., 426 mg sodium, 12 g carb. (1 g fiber, 5 g sugars), 14 g pro. Exchanges: 1 vegetable, 0.5 starch, 2 lean meat, 1 fat.

Fruit-Topped Breakfast Waffle Pizzas

For an interactive breakfast, put single servings of fruit on each plate and let your family design their own pizza tops.

SERVINGS 4 (1 pizza each)
CARB. PER SERVING 27 g
START TO FINISH 25 minutes

      4 Kashi 7-Grain frozen waffles
      ¼ cup light tub-style cream cheese, softened
      ¼ cup vanilla fat-free yogurt
      1 tablespoon honey
      ¼ teaspoon almond extract
      ½ cup sliced fresh strawberries
      ⅓ cup fresh blueberries
      ⅓ cup fresh raspberries
      1 tablespoon sliced almonds, toasted

1. Prepare waffles according to package directions.
2. In a small bowl use a hand mixer to beat together the cream cheese, yogurt, honey, and almond extract until well combined.
3. For each pizza, spread cream cheese mixture over a prepared waffle. Top with strawberries, blueberries, and raspberries, arranging in a pattern if desired. Sprinkle with almonds. Serve immediately.

PER SERVING: 165 cal., 6 g total fat (2 g sat. fat), 8 mg chol., 212 mg sodium, 27 g carb. (6 g fiber, 11 g sugars), 4 g pro. Exchanges: 0.5 fruit, 1 starch, 1 fat.

Fruit-Topped Breakfast Waffle Pizzas

Buttermilk Bran Cakes with Apple-Walnut Topping

To make 1¼ cups sour milk, place 4 teaspoons lemon juice in a glass measuring cup. Add enough milk to make 1¼ cups liquid; stir. Let stand for 5 minutes before using.

SERVINGS 8 (2 pancakes and about 3 tablespoons topping each)
CARB. PER SERVING 26 g or 21 g
START TO FINISH 30 minutes

- ⅓ cup high-fiber whole bran cereal
- 1¼ cups buttermilk or sour milk
- 1 egg
- 2 tablespoons packed brown sugar*
- 2 teaspoons vegetable oil
- 1 cup flour
- 1 teaspoon baking powder
- ½ teaspoon baking soda
- ¼ teaspoon salt
- 1 cup chopped apple
- ¼ cup coarsely chopped walnuts
- 1 tablespoon granulated sugar*
- ¼ teaspoon ground cinnamon
- ⅓ cup vanilla low-fat yogurt

1. Place cereal in a medium bowl. Add buttermilk, egg, brown sugar, and oil; stir to mix well. Let stand for 10 minutes. Meanwhile, in a small bowl stir together flour, baking powder, baking soda, and salt; set aside.

2. For apple-walnut topping, in another small bowl combine apple and walnuts. Combine granulated sugar and the ¼ teaspoon cinnamon; toss with apple mixture. Stir yogurt until creamy; gently stir into apple mixture.

3. Add flour mixture to buttermilk mixture, stirring until combined. Coat a griddle with *nonstick cooking spray.* Heat griddle to medium-low (about 250°F). For each pancake, pour 2 tablespoons of the batter onto the hot griddle. Cook for 1 to 2 minutes or until bottom is golden. Flip pancake; cook about 1 minute more or until golden. Transfer to a serving platter; keep warm while cooking the remaining pancakes. Serve pancakes with apple-walnut topping.

***SUGAR SUBSTITUTES:** Choose from Sweet'N Low Brown or Sugar Twin Granulated Brown to substitute for the packed brown sugar. Choose from Splenda Granular, Truvia Spoonable, or Sweet'N Low packets or bulk to substitute for the granulated sugar. Follow package directions to use product amounts equivalent to 2 tablespoons brown sugar and 1 tablespoon granulated sugar.

PER SERVING: 159 cal., 5 g total fat (1 g sat. fat), 25 mg chol., 279 mg sodium, 26 g carb. (3 g fiber, 11 g sugars), 5 g pro. Exchanges: 1.5 starch, 1 fat.

PER SERVING WITH SUBSTITUTE: Same as above, except 141 cal., 21 g carb. (6 g sugars), 278 mg sodium.

Mexican Chocolate French Toast

SERVINGS 4 (2 slices French toast, 2 tablespoons syrup, and 1 orange wedge each)
CARB. PER SERVING 34 g
PREP 15 minutes   **COOK** 4 minutes per batch

- ½ cup refrigerated or frozen egg product, thawed, or 2 eggs, lightly beaten
- ½ cup fat-free milk
- 1 tablespoon unsweetened cocoa powder
- ½ teaspoon ground cinnamon
- ½ teaspoon vanilla
- 8 slices 100% whole grain 45-calorie bread
- 1 ounce semisweet chocolate, chopped
- ½ cup sugar-free or light pancake syrup
- 4 orange wedges

1. In a shallow bowl whisk together egg, milk, unsweetened cocoa powder, cinnamon, and vanilla; set aside.

2. Coat an unheated very large nonstick skillet with *nonstick cooking spray.* Preheat over medium heat. Dip bread into egg mixture, turning to coat. Place bread in hot skillet; cook for 4 to 6 minutes or until golden brown, turning once.

3. Meanwhile, in a small saucepan heat chocolate over low heat until just melted. Stir in syrup. Whisk to combine. Continue to heat over low heat until heated through, whisking as needed to keep combined.

4. Serve toast with chocolate syrup and orange wedges.

PER SERVING: 179 cal., 3 g total fat (1 g sat. fat), 1 mg chol., 354 mg sodium, 34 g carb. (5 g fiber, 10 g sugars), 11 g pro. Exchanges: 1 starch, 1 carb., 1 lean meat.

Blueberry Coffee Cake

The juices from the frozen berries may color the batter a bit.

SERVINGS 12 (1 piece each)
CARB. PER SERVING 32 g or 23 g
PREP 25 minutes   **BAKE** 30 minutes   **COOL** 15 minutes

- 1⅔ cups all-purpose flour
- 2½ teaspoons baking powder
- ½ teaspoon salt
- ⅓ cup butter, softened
- ⅔ cup granulated sugar*
- 2 egg whites or ¼ cup refrigerated or frozen egg product, thawed
- 2 teaspoons finely shredded lemon peel
- ¾ cup fat-free milk
- 1⅔ cups fresh or frozen blueberries
- 3 tablespoons packed brown sugar*
- ½ teaspoon ground cinnamon

1. Preheat oven to 350°F. Grease and flour a 9-inch square baking pan. Combine flour, baking powder, and salt.

Blueberry Coffee Cake

2. In a bowl beat butter and granulated sugar on high speed about 4 minutes or until light and fluffy. Add egg whites; beat 2 minutes more. Beat in lemon peel. Reduce speed to low. Add flour mixture alternately with milk, one-third at a time, stopping mixer to scrape bowl. Do not overbeat.

3. Spread half of the batter into prepared pan; sprinkle with half of the blueberries. Spoon remaining batter on top, spreading evenly. Combine brown sugar and cinnamon. Sprinkle brown sugar mixture on top of batter. Swirl through batter several times with a knife; top with remaining berries.

4. Bake for 30 to 35 minutes or until toothpick inserted in center comes out with moist crumbs clinging. Cool in pan on wire rack 15 minutes. Cut into 12 pieces. Serve warm.

*SUGAR SUBSTITUTES: Choose Splenda Baking Blend for the granulated sugar and Sweet'N Low Brown to substitute for the brown sugar. Follow package directions to use product amounts equivalent to $^2/_3$ cup granulated sugar and 3 tablespoons brown sugar.

PER SERVING: 185 cal., 5 g total fat (3 g sat. fat), 14 mg chol., 261 mg sodium, 32 g carb. (1 g fiber, 17 g sugars), 3 g pro. Exchanges: 1 starch, 1 carb., 1 fat.

PER SERVING WITH SUBSTITUTE: Same as above, except 156 cal., 23 g carb. (8 g sugars), 260 mg sodium. Exchanges: 0.5 carb.

QUICK TIP
Knead the dough for these
Maple Bacon Scones
just as the recipe says.
Overkneading may cause
them to be dense and dry.

Maple Bacon Scones

Yummy maple icing and bits of bacon come together for a sweet and salty flavor combo.

SERVINGS 12 (1 scone each)
CARB. PER SERVING 21 g
PREP 25 minutes **BAKE** 13 minutes

1½ cups all-purpose flour
½ cup whole wheat flour
1½ teaspoons baking powder
¼ teaspoon baking soda
¼ teaspoon salt
¼ cup cold butter, cut up
3 tablespoons plain fat-free Greek yogurt
½ cup refrigerated or frozen egg product, thawed, or 2 eggs, lightly beaten
¼ cup buttermilk
¼ cup sugar-free or light pancake syrup
½ teaspoon maple flavoring
2 slices thick-cut bacon, crisp-cooked, drained, and finely chopped
  Buttermilk
⅓ cup powdered sugar
2 teaspoons fat-free milk
½ teaspoon maple flavoring

1. Preheat oven to 400°F. In a large bowl stir together all-purpose flour, whole wheat flour, baking powder, baking soda, and salt. Using a pastry blender, cut in butter until mixture resembles coarse crumbs. Add yogurt and toss until combined. Make a well in the center of the flour mixture.
2. In a small bowl combine egg, ¼ cup buttermilk, syrup, and ½ teaspoon maple flavoring. Stir in the bacon. Add buttermilk mixture all at once to flour mixture. Stir just until moistened.
3. Turn out onto a floured surface. Knead dough for 10 to 12 strokes or until nearly smooth. Pat or lightly roll dough to an 8-inch circle about ¾ inch thick. Brush top with additional buttermilk. Using a floured knife, cut into 12 wedges.
4. Place dough wedges 1 inch apart on an ungreased baking sheet. Bake for 13 to 15 minutes or until edges are lightly browned.
5. For glaze, in a small bowl combine powdered sugar, 2 teaspoons milk, and ½ teaspoon maple flavoring. Add more milk if needed to make drizzling consistency. Drizzle over warm scones.

PER SERVING: 146 cal., 5 g total fat (3 g sat. fat), 12 mg chol., 244 mg sodium, 21 g carb. (1 g fiber, 4 g sugars), 5 g pro. Exchanges: 1.5 starch, 1 fat.

Banana-Oat Muffins

Store these streusel-topped morning favorites in an airtight container at room temperature for up to 2 days or freeze for up to 1 month. *Pictured on page 116.*

SERVINGS 12 (1 muffin each)
CARB. PER SERVING 25 g or 20 g
PREP 20 minutes **BAKE** 20 minutes **COOL** 5 minutes

2 cups regular rolled oats
¾ cup whole wheat flour
⅓ cup sugar*
1 teaspoon baking powder
¾ teaspoon apple pie spice or ground cinnamon
½ teaspoon baking soda
¼ teaspoon salt
1 cup buttermilk
½ cup refrigerated or frozen egg product, thawed, or 2 eggs, lightly beaten
1 large ripe banana, mashed
2 tablespoons butter, melted
1 teaspoon vanilla
¼ cup regular rolled oats
½ teaspoon apple pie spice or ground cinnamon
1 tablespoon butter

1. Preheat oven to 350°F. Line twelve 2½-inch muffin cups with paper bake cups; coat inside of cups lightly with *nonstick cooking spray.* Set aside. Place the 2 cups oats in a food processor or blender; cover and process or blend until finely ground. Transfer ground oats to a large bowl. Stir in whole wheat flour, sugar, baking powder, ¾ teaspoon apple pie spice, baking soda, and salt. Make a well in the center of the flour mixture; set aside.
2. In a medium bowl whisk together buttermilk and eggs; whisk in banana, 2 tablespoons melted butter, and vanilla. Add buttermilk mixture all at once to flour mixture; stir just until moistened (batter should be lumpy). Spoon batter into prepared muffin cups, filling each about three-fourths full.
3. For topping, in a small bowl stir together ¼ cup oats and ½ teaspoon apple pie spice. Using a pastry blender, cut in 1 tablespoon butter until mixture resembles coarse crumbs. Sprinkle the oat mixture on top of muffin batter.
4. Bake for 20 to 22 minutes or until a toothpick inserted in centers comes out clean. Cool in muffin cups on a wire rack for 5 minutes. Remove from muffin cups. Serve warm.
*SUGAR SUBSTITUTES: Choose from Splenda Granular or Sweet'N Low bulk or packets. Follow package directions to use product amount equivalent to ⅓ cup sugar.

PER SERVING: 152 cal., 4 g total fat (2 g sat. fat), 8 mg chol., 183 mg sodium, 25 g carb. (3 g fiber, 8 g sugars), 5 g pro. Exchanges: 1.5 starch, 1 fat.

PER SERVING WITH SUBSTITUTE: Same as above, except 134 cal., 20 g carb. (3 g sugars). Exchanges: 1 starch.

Carrot Cake Breakfast Cookies

Carrot Cake Breakfast Cookies

Baby food is the surprise ingredient that helps to intensify the carrot flavor and adds moistness to these hearty, cakelike cookies.

SERVINGS 18 (1 cookie each)
CARB. PER SERVING 17 g
PREP 25 minutes **BAKE** 10 minutes

- ¾ cup whole wheat pastry flour or whole wheat flour
- ½ cup all-purpose flour
- 1 teaspoon ground cinnamon
- ½ teaspoon baking soda
- ½ teaspoon ground nutmeg
- ¼ teaspoon salt
- 1 tablespoon butter, softened
- ½ cup packed brown sugar*
- ¼ cup canola oil
- 2 egg whites or ¼ cup refrigerated or frozen egg product, thawed
- ¼ cup carrot baby food
- ¼ cup finely shredded carrot
- 1 teaspoon vanilla
- ¾ cup regular rolled oats
- ⅓ cup raisins
- ¼ cup sweetened flake or shredded coconut
- ¼ cup chopped walnuts, toasted

1. Preheat oven to 350°F. In a medium bowl combine wheat flour, all-purpose flour, cinnamon, baking soda, nutmeg, and salt; set aside.

2. In a large bowl beat butter with an electric mixer until light and fluffy. Add brown sugar and oil; beat until well combined and sugar is dissolved. Add egg whites, carrot baby food, carrot, and vanilla; beat until combined. Beat in flour mixture until well combined. Using a wooden spoon, stir in oats, raisins, coconut, and nuts. Dough will be sticky.

3. Line a very large cookie sheet with parchment paper. Scoop about 3 tablespoons dough into 18 mounds on the parchment paper. Bake for 12 to 14 minutes or until bottoms are golden brown. Let cool on cookie sheet for 2 minutes. Transfer to wire rack to cool completely.

*SUGAR SUBSTITUTE: We do not recommend using a sugar substitute for this recipe.

MAKE-AHEAD DIRECTIONS: Layer cookies between sheets of waxed paper in an airtight container; cover. Store in the refrigerator for up to 3 days or freeze for up to 3 months.

PER SERVING: 121 cal., 5 g total fat (1 g sat. fat), 2 mg chol., 87 mg sodium, 17 g carb. (1 g fiber, 8 g sugars), 2 g pro. Exchanges: 1 starch, 1 fat.

Very Cherry Oatmeal

You get a bowl of warm and comforting oatmeal and a double dose of the superfruit cherries. The red little orbs are loaded with antioxidants, vitamins, fiber, and more.

SERVINGS 4 ($^1/_2$ cup each)
CARB. PER SERVING 34 g or 28 g
PREP 15 minutes **COOK** 25 minutes

- 1$^1/_2$ cups water
- 1 cup light vanilla-flavored soymilk
- $^2/_3$ cup steel-cut oats
- $^1/_4$ teaspoon salt
- 2 tablespoons packed brown sugar*
- 1 teaspoon vanilla
- $^1/_2$ cup fresh or frozen dark sweet cherries, thawed, pitted, and halved
- $^1/_4$ cup coarsely chopped pecans, toasted
- 2 tablespoons snipped dried cherries

1. In a medium saucepan combine water, soymilk, oats, and salt. Bring to boiling; reduce heat. Simmer, uncovered, for 25 to 30 minutes or until oats are desired doneness, stirring occasionally. Stir in brown sugar and vanilla.

2. Spoon oatmeal into bowls. Top each serving with fresh cherries, pecans, and dried cherries. Stir gently to combine before eating.

*SUGAR SUBSTITUTE: Choose Sweet'N Low Brown. Follow package directions to use product amount equivalent to 2 tablespoon brown sugar.

PER SERVING: 216 cal., 7 g total fat (1 g sat. fat), 0 mg chol., 178 mg sodium, 34 g carb. (4 g fiber, 14 g sugars), 6 g pro. Exchanges: 1 fruit, 1 starch, 0.5 carb., 1 fat.

PER SERVING WITH SUBSTITUTE: Same as above, except 190 cal., 28 g carb. (8 g sugars), 176 mg sodium. Exchanges: 0 carb.

Honey-Sweet Granola

Dried cranberries add a bit of chewy goodness to this crunchy cereal. Eat it dry or serve it with milk or yogurt—either way it's ultimately delicious.

SERVINGS 18 ($^{1}/_{3}$ cup each)
CARB. PER SERVING 21 g or 18 g
PREP 20 minutes BAKE 35 minutes

2$^{1}/_{2}$ cups regular rolled oats
$^{2}/_{3}$ cup chopped walnuts
$^{1}/_{4}$ cup sunflower kernels
$^{1}/_{4}$ cup sesame seeds
$^{1}/_{4}$ cup butter
$^{1}/_{4}$ cup packed brown sugar*
$^{1}/_{4}$ cup honey
1$^{1}/_{2}$ teaspoons vanilla
$^{1}/_{2}$ cup toasted wheat germ
$^{1}/_{4}$ cup oat bran
$^{1}/_{2}$ cup dried cranberries
    Fat-free milk or yogurt (optional)

1. Preheat oven to 300°F. Lightly grease a 13×9×2-inch baking pan. Add oats, walnuts, sunflower kernels, and sesame seeds; spread evenly. Bake for 20 minutes, stirring twice.
2. Meanwhile, in a small saucepan combine butter, brown sugar, and honey. Cook over medium heat, stirring constantly, until butter is melted and mixture is combined. Remove from heat. Stir in vanilla.
3. Remove pan from the oven; place on a wire rack. Increase oven temperature to 350°F. Add wheat germ and oat bran to the oat mixture. Pour warm brown sugar mixture over oat mixture. Using a fork or spatula, stir the oat mixture until it is thoroughly coated with brown sugar mixture. Bake for 5 minutes more. Remove pan from oven; place on a wire rack.
4. Stir cranberries into oat mixture. With a spatula, firmly press down the granola in the pan, making an even layer. Bake for 10 to 15 minutes more or until golden brown. Remove pan from oven and place on a wire cooling rack. With a spatula, remove the granola from the pan (mixture will be crumbly). Spread the pieces on a large piece of foil. Cool completely.
5. Store in an airtight container for up to 2 weeks. For breakfast, serve granola with milk or yogurt if desired.

*SUGAR SUBSTITUTE: Choose Sweet'N Low Brown sugar substitute. Follow package directions to use product amount equivalent to $^{1}/_{4}$ cup brown sugar.

PER SERVING: 167 cal., 9 g total fat (2 g sat. fat), 7 mg chol., 31 mg sodium, 21 g carb. (3 g fiber, 10 g sugars), 4 g pro. Exchanges: 1 starch, 0.5 carb., 1.5 fat.

PER SERVING WITH SUBSTITUTE: Same as above, except 155 cal., 18 g carb. (7 g sugars). Exchanges: 0 carb.

Wake-Me-Up Smoothies

You can skip the coffee shop drive-through when you make this eye-opening drink at home.

SERVINGS 4 (8 ounces each)
CARB. PER SERVING 12 g or 7 g
START TO FINISH 5 minutes

2 cups ice cubes
1 cup fat-free milk
$^{3}/_{4}$ cup double-strength coffee
2 tablespoons sugar*
1 tablespoon sugar-free caramel ice cream topping
    Fat-free frozen whipped dessert topping, thawed (optional)
    Chocolate-covered espresso beans, coarsely chopped (optional)

1. In a blender combine ice, milk, coffee, sugar, and ice cream topping. Cover and blend until smooth. Serve immediately. If desired, top with whipped topping and chocolate-covered espresso beans.

*SUGAR SUBSTITUTES: Choose from Splenda Granular or Sweet'N Low bulk or packets. Follow package directions to use product amount equivalent to 2 tablespoons sugar.

PER SERVING: 57 cal., 0 g total fat, 1 mg chol., 36 mg sodium, 12 g carb. (0 fiber, 9 g sugars), 2 g pro. Exchanges: 1 carb.

PER SERVING WITH SUBSTITUTE: Same as above, except 36 cal., 7 g carb. (4 g sugars). Exchanges: 0.5 carb.

Eat-Your-Veggie Smoothies

This icy treat is a great way to sneak in some veggies—the flavors of sweet peach and banana mask those of the nutrition-packed Swiss chard.

SERVINGS 4 (10 ounces each)
CARB. PER SERVING 17 g
START TO FINISH 10 minutes

2 cups ice cubes
2 cups V8 V-Fusion Light peach mango juice
1 medium peach, halved and pitted
1 medium banana
2 leaves Swiss chard, ribs removed
    Mango wedges (optional)

1. In a blender combine ice, juice, peach, banana, and Swiss chard. Cover and blend until smooth. Serve immediately. If desired, garnish with mango wedges.

PER SERVING: 68 cal., 0 g total fat, 41 mg sodium, 17 g carb. (1 g fiber, 12 g sugars), 1 g pro. Exchanges: 1 fruit.

good-for-you
snacks

Rice Cakes with Fire Jelly

Keeping your blood sugar in line from one meal to the next is important, so turn to these good-for-you snacks to get you through. From creamy dips and chunky salsas to frozen fruits and crunchy rice cakes, each recipe here is easy to make, tasty to eat, and, best of all, nutrtionally balanced. Take your pick—each is super satisfying.

Rice Cakes with Fire Jelly

Experiment with other flavors of sugar-free preserves to vary the taste and appearance.

SERVINGS 4 (3 mini cakes each)
CARB. PER SERVING 12 g
START TO FINISH 10 minutes

- ⅓ cup sugar-free apricot preserves
- 2 teaspoons minced fresh jalapeño chile pepper (see tip, page 20)
- 12 miniature salt-and-pepper rice cakes, such as Quaker Quakes
- ⅓ cup fat-free tub-style cream cheese
- 1 teaspoon snipped fresh rosemary

1. In a small bowl combine preserves and chile pepper. Spread rice cakes with cream cheese; top with preserves mixture. Sprinkle with rosemary.

PER SERVING: 56 cal., 1 g total fat (0 g sat. fat), 2 mg chol., 200 mg sodium, 12 g carb. (0 g fiber, 1 g sugars), 3 g pro. Exchanges: 1 starch.

Cottage Cheese with Raspberry Honey

This quick snack is perfect for a side dish or dessert, too. Garnish each serving with a lemon peel twist.

SERVINGS 4 (⅔ cup each)
CARB. PER SERVING 20 g
START TO FINISH 15 minutes

- 2 cups fresh raspberries
- 2 tablespoons honey
- 1 teaspoon finely shredded lemon peel
- 2 cups low-fat cottage cheese
- 2 tablespoons roasted, salted sunflower kernels

1. Place 1 cup of the raspberries in a food processor; cover and process until pureed. Strain raspberry mixture through a fine-mesh sieve. In a small bowl combine the raspberry puree, honey, and shredded lemon peel.

2. Divide cottage cheese among four bowls. Top with raspberry-honey mixture; gently stir once or twice. Top with the remaining 1 cup raspberries and the sunflower kernels.

PER SERVING: 169 cal., 4 g total fat (1 g sat. fat), 5 mg chol., 476 mg sodium, 20 g carb. (4 g fiber, 15 g sugars), 16 g pro. Exchanges: 1 fruit, 2 lean meat, 0.5 fat.

Citrus Fruit Bowl

Vary the colors of the fruit: Try blood oranges paired with yellow grapefruit.

SERVINGS 4 (1 cup fruit slices, $1/2$ tablespoon honey, $1/2$ tablespoon cheese, and $3/4$ teaspoon mint each)
CARB. PER SERVING 27 g
START TO FINISH 10 minutes

      3 oranges, peeled and sliced crosswise
      1 pink grapefruit, peeled and sliced crosswise
      2 tablespoons honey
      2 tablespoons crumbled fat-free feta cheese
      1 tablespoon snipped fresh mint

1. Arrange orange and grapefruit slices in four shallow bowls. Drizzle with honey; sprinkle with feta cheese and snipped fresh mint. If desired, cover and chill for up to 4 hours before serving.

PER SERVING: 110 cal., 0 g total fat, 0 mg chol., 32 mg sodium, 27 g carb. (3 g fiber, 22 g sugars), 2 g pro. Exchanges: 1 fruit, 1 carb.

Buffalo Chicken Wings with Blue Cheese Dressing

If you can't find chicken drummettes, start with 6 chicken wings. Cut off the wing tips; discard or save for making stock. Cut wings at joints to form 12 pieces.

SERVINGS 12 (1 drummette, $1^{1}/3$ tablespoons dressing, 2 carrot sticks, and 2 celery sticks each)
CARB. PER SERVING 4 g
PREP 20 minutes **BROIL** 15 minutes

     12 chicken drummettes (2 ounces each)
      2 tablespoons bottled cayenne pepper sauce, such as Frank's RedHot
      1 teaspoon cider vinegar
     $1/4$ teaspoon garlic powder
     $1/4$ teaspoon ground ginger
     $3/4$ cup fat-free sour cream
     $1/2$ cup crumbled blue cheese (2 ounces)
      1 green onion, chopped
      1 tablespoon cider vinegar
      1 tablespoon lemon juice
      1 teaspoon sugar*
      2 medium carrots, each cut into twelve 3-inch sticks
      2 stalks celery, each cut into twelve 3-inch sticks

1. Remove skin from chicken by grasping the edge of the skin with a paper towel and pulling it away from the drummette. In a large bowl toss the drummettes with 1 tablespoon of the cayenne pepper sauce, $1/2$ teaspoon of the vinegar, the garlic powder, and the ginger.

2. Preheat the broiler. Arrange drummettes on the unheated rack of a broiler pan. Broil 4 to 5 inches from the heat for 15 to 20 minutes or until chicken is tender and no longer pink, turning once. Drizzle chicken with remaining 1 tablespoon cayenne pepper sauce and $1/2$ teaspoon cider vinegar.

3. For dressing, in a small bowl combine sour cream, blue cheese, green onion, 1 tablespoon vinegar, the lemon juice, and sugar. Serve dressing with chicken drummettes and carrot and celery sticks.

*SUGAR SUBSTITUTES: Choose from Splenda Granular, Equal Spoonful or packets, or Sweet'N Low packets or bulk. Follow package directions to use product amount equivalent to 1 teaspoon sugar.

PER SERVING: 62 cal., 2 g total fat (1 g sat. fat), 16 mg chol., 228 mg sodium, 4 g carb. (1 g fiber, 1 g sugars), 6 g pro. Exchanges: 1 vegetable, 0.5 lean meat, 0.5 fat.

PER SERVING WITH SUBSTITUTE: Same as above, except 61 cal.

Asparagus-Ricotta Bruschetta

If your herb garden doesn't include rosemary, you can substitute fresh thyme, basil, oregano, or parsley.

SERVINGS 6 (2 slices each)
CARB. PER SERVING 15 g
START TO FINISH 30 minutes

      8 ounces asparagus spears
      1 teaspoon olive oil
     $1/8$ teaspoon salt
     $1/8$ teaspoon black pepper
     $1/2$ cup part-skim ricotta cheese
     $1/2$ teaspoon finely shredded lemon peel
      1 small clove garlic, minced
     $1/4$ teaspoon snipped fresh rosemary
     12 $1/2$-inch-thick slices whole grain baguette-style French bread (6 ounces total), toasted

1. Preheat the broiler. Snap off and discard woody bases from asparagus. Arrange spears in a 9×9×2-inch baking pan. Brush with olive oil and sprinkle with half of the salt and pepper. Broil 3 to 4 inches from the heat for 3 to 5 minutes or until crisp-tender, rearranging halfway through cooking time. Cool; bias-slice asparagus into 2-inch pieces.

2. In a medium bowl combine ricotta, lemon peel, garlic, rosemary, and remaining salt and pepper. Spread ricotta mixture on toasted bread slices. Arrange cooked asparagus pieces on ricotta mixture.

PER SERVING: 110 cal., 4 g total fat (1 g sat. fat), 6 mg chol., 195 mg sodium, 15 g carb. (1 g fiber, 1 g sugars), 5 g pro. Exchanges: 1 starch, 1 lean meat, 0.5 fat.

Citrus Fruit
Bowl

Buffalo Chicken
Wings with Blue
Cheese Dressing

Asparagus-Ricotta
Bruschetta

Avocado-Poblano Pico de Gallo

This intriguing fresh avocado and tomato salsa boasts a blend of poblano and sweet peppers. For a milder version, use all sweet peppers.

SERVINGS 12 ($^1/_4$ cup salsa and $^1/_2$ ounce chips each)
CARB. PER SERVING 12 g
PREP 25 minutes **BROIL** 7 minutes **STAND** 15 minutes

- 1 fresh poblano chile pepper or 1 yellow, red, or green sweet pepper
- 1 yellow, red, or green sweet pepper
- 1 medium tomato, chopped
- $^1/_3$ cup finely chopped red onion
- 2 tablespoons snipped fresh cilantro
- $^1/_2$ teaspoon finely shredded lime peel
- 1 tablespoon lime juice
- $^1/_4$ teaspoon salt
- 1 small avocado, halved, seeded, peeled, and chopped
- 6 ounces baked tortilla chips

1. Preheat the broiler. Place whole peppers on a foil-lined baking sheet. Broil 4 inches from the heat for 7 to 10 minutes

Avocado-Poblano
Pico de Gallo

or until skins are bubbly and blackened, turning occasionally. Carefully bring the foil up and around the peppers to enclose. Let stand about 15 minutes or until cool enough to handle. Pull the skins off gently and slowly using a paring knife (see tip, page 20). Discard skins. Remove pepper stems, seeds, and membranes; chop the peppers.

2. In a medium bowl combine peppers, tomato, red onion, cilantro, lime peel, lime juice, and salt; gently toss to combine. Stir in the avocado. Cover and chill for up to 4 hours before serving. (For longer storage, prepare as directed, except do not stir in the avocado. Cover and chill mixture for up to 24 hours. Stir in the avocado just before serving.) Serve with baked tortilla chips.

PER SERVING: 94 cal., 5 g total fat (1 g sat. fat), 0 mg chol., 106 mg sodium, 12 g carb. (2 g fiber, 1 g sugars), 2 g pro. Exchanges: 1 vegetable, 0.5 starch, 1 fat.

Sweet Pepper-Green Onion Quesadillas

A little adobo sauce from a can of chipotle peppers flavors the cream cheese. To store the peppers, divide them among cups in an ice cube tray and freeze. Pop the peppers from the cups and transfer them to a resealable freezer bag and freeze for other uses.

SERVINGS 4 (1 quesadilla each)
CARB. PER SERVING 12 g
START TO FINISH 20 minutes

- 2 ounces reduced-fat cream cheese (Neufchâtel), softened
- 1/2 teaspoon adobo sauce from canned chipotle chile peppers
- 4 6-inch whole wheat flour tortillas
- 1/2 cup chopped red sweet pepper (1 small)
- 1/4 cup chopped green onions (2)
- 4 teaspoons finely chopped fresh jalapeño chile pepper (see tip, page 20)
  Nonstick cooking spray
  Avocado slices (optional)

1. In a small bowl stir together cream cheese and adobo sauce until smooth. Spread over half of each tortilla. Sprinkle cream cheese mixture with sweet pepper, green onions, and jalapeño chile pepper. Fold over unfilled sides to make quesadillas.

2. Coat an unheated large nonstick skillet with cooking spray. Preheat over medium heat. Cook quesadillas, two at a time, about 4 minutes or until golden and heated through, turning once halfway through cooking. Halve crosswise. If desired, top with avocado slices.

PER SERVING: 132 cal., 6 g total fat (2 g sat. fat), 10 mg chol., 265 mg sodium, 12 g carb. (7 g fiber, 2 g sugars), 7 g pro. Exchanges: 1 starch, 1 fat.

Hummus with Roasted Red Peppers

Chickpeas are the main attraction in this zesty Middle Eastern spread.

SERVINGS 8 (1/4 cup hummus and 1/2 cup vegetable dippers each)
CARB. PER SERVING 17 g
PREP 20 minutes BROIL 10 minutes

- 2 medium red sweet peppers, quartered
- 4 unpeeled cloves garlic
- 1 15-ounce can no-salt-added garbanzo beans (chickpeas), rinsed & drained
- 2 tablespoons tahini (sesame seed paste)
- 1 tablespoon lemon juice
- 1 to 2 teaspoons bottled mild chile pepper sauce
- 1/4 cup chopped fresh cilantro
- 4 cups assorted vegetable dippers, such as carrot sticks, celery sticks, and/or cherry tomatoes

1. Preheat the broiler. Place the pepper quarters on a foil-lined baking sheet. Wrap the garlic cloves in foil and place on the baking sheet with the peppers. Broil 4 to 5 inches from the heat for 10 to 15 minutes or until pepper skins are charred. Place on a wire rack and carefully wrap the pepper quarters in the foil. Let peppers and garlic stand until cool enough to handle.

2. When garlic is cool enough to handle, peel the garlic cloves and place in a food processor. Cover and process until finely chopped. When the peppers are cool enough to handle, peel off and discard the skins. (You should have about 1 cup of roasted peppers.) Add the peppers, garbanzo beans, tahini, lemon juice, and pepper sauce to the garlic in the food processor. Cover and process until smooth. Transfer to a serving bowl. Stir in cilantro. For best flavor, cover and refrigerate for at least 4 hours or up to 3 days. Serve with vegetable dippers.

PER SERVING: 108 cal., 3 g total fat (0 g sat. fat), 0 mg chol., 53 mg sodium, 17 g carb. (4 g fiber, 4 g sugars), 5 g pro. Exchanges: 0.5 vegetable, 1 starch, 0.5 fat.

Caprese Stuffed Cherry Tomatoes

Use a flatware teaspoon to hollow out the tomatoes, being careful not to split the sides.

SERVINGS 4 (6 stuffed tomatoes each)
CARB. PER SERVING 7 g
START TO FINISH 15 minutes

24	cherry tomatoes
4	ounces part-skim mozzarella cheese
2	tablespoons snipped fresh basil
1	tablespoon white balsamic vinegar
¼	teaspoon black pepper

1. Using a sharp knife, cut off the top third of each cherry tomato on the stem end. Hollow out the cherry tomatoes; invert on paper towels to drain. Set aside.

2. Cut the mozzarella into 24 equal cubes. In a medium bowl combine the cheese cubes, basil, vinegar, and pepper. Stuff each tomato with a coated cheese cube.

PER SERVING: 112 cal., 6 g total fat (3 g sat. fat), 15 mg chol., 190 mg sodium, 7 g carb. (1 g fiber, 5 g sugars), 8 g pro. Exchanges: 1 vegetable, 1 medium-fat meat.

Artichoke Spread

Mango-Shrimp
Cracker Topper

Artichoke Spread

This sophisticated spread also tastes terrific on low-sodium whole grain crackers.

SERVINGS 16 (2 tablespoons spread and $^1/_2$ cup vegetables each)
CARB. PER SERVING 8 g
START TO FINISH 15 minutes

- 1 15-ounce can no-salt-added cannellini beans (white kidney beans), rinsed and drained
- 1 9-ounce package frozen artichoke hearts, thawed and well drained
- 1 clove garlic, quartered
- 1 teaspoon finely shredded lemon peel
- 1 tablespoon lemon juice
- $^1/_8$ teaspoon salt
- $^1/_8$ teaspoon cayenne pepper
- 1 green onion, thinly sliced
- 1 tablespoon sliced green onion tops
- 8 cups assorted vegetable dippers, such as carrot sticks, celery sticks, cucumber slices, red sweet pepper strips, cauliflower florets, and/or broccoli florets

1. In a large food processor combine beans, artichoke hearts, garlic, lemon peel, lemon juice, salt, and cayenne pepper. Cover and process until nearly smooth, stopping to scrape down sides as necessary.
2. Transfer bean mixture to a serving bowl; stir in the thinly sliced green onion. Serve immediately or cover and chill for up to 2 days. If chilled, let stand at room temperature for 30 minutes before serving.
3. To serve, garnish with sliced green onion tops. Serve with vegetable dippers.

PER SERVING: 43 cal., 0 g total fat, 0 mg chol., 57 mg sodium, 8 g carb. (3 g fiber, 2 g sugars), 2 g pro. Exchanges: 1.5 vegetable.

Mango-Shrimp Cracker Topper

If fresh mangoes are out of season, substitute 1 cup refrigerated mango slices.

SERVINGS 6 (6 crackers and $^1/_3$ cup topper each)
CARB. PER SERVING 22 g
START TO FINISH 15 minutes

- 1 ripe mango, halved, seeded, and peeled
- 4 ounces cooked, peeled shrimp*
- $^1/_4$ cup snipped fresh cilantro
- 2 tablespoons seasoned rice vinegar
- $^1/_4$ teaspoon crushed red pepper
- 36 low-salt whole wheat crackers

1. Finely chop the mango and shrimp; place in a medium bowl. Add the cilantro, vinegar, and red pepper. Stir to combine. Serve on crackers.
*****TEST KITCHEN TIP:** Purchase cooked, peeled shrimp from the seafood counter at your supermarket or purchase frozen cooked shrimp and thaw before using.

PER SERVING: 151 cal., 5 g total fat (1 g sat. fat), 40 mg chol., 234 mg sodium, 22 g carb. (3 g fiber, 5 g sugars), 7 g pro. Exchanges: 0.5 fruit, 1 starch, 1 lean meat.

QUICK TIP
If you don't have loose or bags of green tea on hand to brew a cup of tea, stop by your favorite coffee shop and order a cup of strong brewed green tea to use to steep these fresh oranges.

Tea-Scented Oranges
Use a sharp paring knife to carefully remove the peel and cut the orange into sections.

SERVINGS 4 (1 sectioned orange, about 1 1/2 tablespoons syrup, and 1 tablespoon yogurt each)
CARB. PER SERVING 21 g
PREP 15 minutes **COOK** 15 minutes **CHILL** 2 hours

> 4 oranges
> 1 cup strong brewed green tea
> 1 tablespoon honey
> 1/4 teaspoon ground cinnamon
> 1/4 cup plain fat-free Greek yogurt
> Ground cinnamon

1. Cut peel from oranges. Section oranges over a small bowl to catch juice. Place the orange sections in another bowl; set aside.
2. In a medium saucepan combine the juice from the oranges with the brewed tea, honey, and 1/4 teaspoon cinnamon. Bring to boiling over medium heat. Boil for 15 to 20 minutes or until reduced to a syrup (1/3 cup). Pour syrup over orange sections; stir to coat. Cover and chill for 2 to 24 hours. Top each serving with 1 tablespoon yogurt and sprinkle with cinnamon.

PER SERVING: 86 cal., 0 g total fat, 0 mg chol., 7 mg sodium, 21 g carb. (3 g fiber, 17 g sugars), 3 g pro. Exchanges: 1 fruit, 0.5 carb.

Green Beans with Lemon-Chili Dip
Rinsing the beans in cold water will stop the cooking process and leave the beans bright green and crisp-tender.

SERVINGS 4 (3/4 cup beans with 2 tablespoons dip each)
CARB. PER SERVING 7 g
PREP 20 minutes **COOK** 3 minutes

> 8 ounces fresh green beans, trimmed
> 1/2 cup light sour cream
> 2 tablespoons chopped green onion (1)
> 1/2 teaspoon finely shredded lemon peel
> 2 teaspoons lemon juice
> 1 clove garlic, minced
> 1/2 teaspoon chili powder

1. Leave beans whole. In a medium saucepan cook beans, covered, in a small amount of boiling water for 3 to 5 minutes or just until crisp-tender; drain. Rinse beans with cold water; drain well. Transfer to a serving bowl.
2. For dip, in a small bowl whisk together the sour cream, green onion, lemon peel, lemon juice, garlic, and chili powder. Serve beans* with sour cream mixture for dipping.
*TEST KITCHEN TIP: If desired, serve dip with roasted asparagus spears. To roast asparagus, preheat oven to 400°F. Snap off and discard woody bases from 8 ounces fresh asparagus spears; scrape off scales. Place asparagus in a 15×10×1-inch baking pan; drizzle with 1 teaspoon olive oil. Spread asparagus in a single layer. Roast, uncovered, for 10 to 12 minutes or until asparagus is crisp-tender.

PER SERVING: 54 cal., 3 g total fat (2 g sat. fat), 8 mg chol., 26 mg sodium, 7 g carb. (2 g fiber, 2 g sugars), 2 g pro. Exchanges: 1 vegetable, 0.5 fat.

Garlic-Chili Popcorn
Turn on the exhaust fan while you pop the corn. The fumes from the chili oil can be a little strong.

SERVINGS 3 (3 cups each)
CARB. PER SERVING 26 g
START TO FINISH 10 minutes

> 1 teaspoon chili oil
> 1/2 cup unpopped popcorn
> 1/4 cup grated Parmesan cheese
> 1/2 teaspoon garlic powder

1. In a stove-top popcorn popper or large heavy saucepan heat chili oil over medium-high heat. Add popcorn; cover. Stir popcorn or shake pan constantly until popcorn has stopped popping.
2. Transfer popcorn to a large bowl. In a small bowl combine the Parmesan cheese with the garlic powder. Sprinkle cheese mixture over hot popcorn; toss well to coat popcorn. Serve immediately.

PER SERVING: 150 cal., 5 g total fat (1 g sat. fat), 6 mg chol., 102 mg sodium, 26 g carb. (5 g fiber, 0 g sugars), 6 g pro. Exchanges: 1.5 starch, 1 fat.

Tea-Scented Oranges

Fruity Applesauce Pops

Strawberry
Iced Tea

Frozen Chocolate
Banana Bites

Snack Right

If you have diabetes, eating healthful snacks is OK as long as you count them as part of your eating plan. Rather than resorting to munching on something from a vending machine, turn to these easy, grab-and-go, and nutritious ideas.

A piece of fruit in between meals might be enough to tame your hunger and hold you over, but to feel fuller longer, pair the fruit with a protein source such as nut spread or reduced-fat cheese. Each is available in single-serving-size packets.

Keep an assortment of vitamin-and-fiber-packed sliced fresh vegetables, such as cucumbers, sweet peppers, carrots, and celery, on hand. Team these veggies with a handful of almonds for something a little more filling.

Fruity Applesauce Pops

When fresh sweet cherries are in season, halve and pit a few to use in combination with the berries.

SERVINGS 16 (1 pop each)
CARB. PER SERVING 8 g
PREP 25 minutes FREEZE overnight

- 1 32-ounce jar unsweetened applesauce
- 2 cups assorted fresh berries, such as raspberries, blackberries, blueberries, and sliced strawberries

1. In a large bowl stir together the applesauce and berries. Spoon into 16 popsicle containers. Cover and freeze overnight. (Or spoon into 5-ounce paper cups. Cover cups with plastic wrap; secure wrap with tape or a rubber band. Insert a popsicle stick through the plastic wrap into applesauce mixture. Freeze overnight.)

PER SERVING: 32 cal., 0 g total fat, 0 mg chol., 1 mg sodium, 8 g carb. (1 g fiber, 6 g sugars), 0 g pro. Exchanges: 0.5 fruit.

Strawberry Iced Tea

You can store a pitcher of this fresh-brewed fruited tea for up to 24 hours.

SERVINGS 7 (8 ounces each)
CARB. PER SERVING 7 g or 4 g
PREP 15 minutes STAND 2 hours

- 1 pound fresh strawberries, trimmed and sliced, or 16 ounces frozen unsweetened whole strawberries, thawed
- 3 tablespoons loose black tea
- 2 tablespoons sugar*
- 4 teaspoons finely shredded lemon peel
- 7 cups boiling water
  Ice cubes
  Fresh whole strawberries (optional)

1. Place strawberries in a large heatproof pitcher or glass measure. Crush berries. Add loose tea, sugar, and lemon peel. Add boiling water. Let mixture steep for 3 to 5 minutes. Pour mixture through a fine-mesh sieve or cheesecloth; discard strawberry pulp, lemon peel, and tea leaves. Cool tea mixture at room temperature about 2 hours. Store tea in the refrigerator.
2. To serve, fill tall glasses with ice. Pour tea into glasses. If desired, add a fresh whole strawberry to each glass.

*SUGAR SUBSTITUTES: Choose from Splenda Granular, Equal Spoonful or packets, or Sweet'N Low packets or bulk. Follow package directions to use product amount equivalent to 2 tablespoons sugar.

PER SERVING: 27 cal., 0 g total fat, 0 mg chol., 8 mg sodium, 7 g carb. (1 g fiber, 5 g sugars), 0 g pro. Exchanges: 0.5 carb.

PER SERVING WITH SUBSTITUTE: Same as above, except 14 cal., 4 g carb. (2 g sugars), 7 mg sodium. Exchanges: 0 carb.

Frozen Chocolate-Banana Bites

Not only do bananas provide lots of potassium to help lower your blood pressure, they also help improve your body's ability to absorb vitamins and minerals, especially calcium.

SERVINGS 4 ($^{1}/_{2}$ banana each)
CARB. PER SERVING 20 g
PREP 15 minutes FREEZE 1 hour

- 2 medium bananas
- 1$^{1}/_{2}$ ounces dark chocolate pieces (about $^{1}/_{3}$ cup)

1. Peel bananas. Slice bananas into $^{1}/_{2}$-inch-thick pieces. Line baking sheet with waxed paper. Arrange banana pieces in a single layer on the prepared baking sheet.
2. In a heavy small saucepan melt chocolate over low heat. Cool slightly. Place melted chocolate in a small resealable plastic bag. Seal bag and snip off a tiny corner. Drizzle chocolate over banana slices. Cover and freeze for 1 to 2 hours or until frozen.
3. Divide banana pieces among four freezer containers or small resealable freezer bags. Freeze for up to 3 days.

PER SERVING: 112 cal., 4 g total fat (0 g sat. fat), 1 mg chol., 1 mg sodium, 20 g carb. (2 g fiber, 12 g sugars), 1 g pro. Exchanges: 1 fruit, 1 high-fat meat, 1 fat.

Pineapple-Melon Slushy

The frozen fruit takes the place of ice in this frosty, fresh drinkable snack.

SERVINGS 4 (1$^{1}/_{4}$ cups each)
CARB. PER SERVING 23 g
PREP 20 minutes FREEZE 2 hours

- 3 cups cubed honeydew melon
- 1$^{1}/_{2}$ cups cold water
- $^{1}/_{2}$ cup orange juice
- $^{1}/_{2}$ of a 16-ounce package frozen pineapple chunks (2 cups)
  Orange peel twists

1. Place melon chunks in a 13x9x2-inch baking pan. Freeze about 2 hours or until solidly frozen.
2. Place the water, orange juice, and about $^{1}/_{3}$ cup of the fruit in a blender. Cover and process until smooth. Gradually add remaining fruit, processing after each addition until smooth. Divide among four tall glasses. Garnish each serving with an orange peel twist.

PER SERVING: 96 cal., 0 g total fat, 0 mg chol., 30 mg sodium, 23 g carb. (2 g fiber, 19 g sugars), 1 g pro. Exchanges: 1.5 fruit.

delightful
desserts

Banana Split Cake Roll

You deserve something sumptuously sweet once in a while. Keep a tally of your numbers and plan for one of these lightened-up desserts, from fancy cakes and swirl-topped cheesecake to chewy cookies, fruit-filled pastries, and frozen treats. They've all been made more healthful for you, so enjoy every sweet little bite!

Banana Split Cake Roll

A clean thin kitchen towel (not terry cloth) is perfect for rolling up the cake.

SERVINGS 10 (1 slice each)
CARB. PER SERVING 29 g
PREP 25 minutes STAND 30 minutes BAKE 12 minutes
CHILL 3 hours

5	egg whites
3	egg yolks
	Nonstick cooking spray
1/2	cup sifted cake flour
1	teaspoon baking powder
1/4	teaspoon salt
1	teaspoon vanilla-butter-nut flavoring or 2 teaspoons vanilla
1/2	cup sugar*
1 1/2	cups fat-free milk
1	4-serving-size package fat-free, sugar-free, reduced-calorie vanilla instant pudding mix
1	cup frozen sugar-free whipped dessert topping, thawed
2	bananas
1/2	cup sliced fresh strawberries
2	tablespoons sugar-free chocolate-flavor syrup

1. For cake, place egg whites in a large bowl and egg yolks in a medium bowl; let stand at room temperature for 30 minutes. Meanwhile, coat a 15×10×1-inch baking pan with cooking spray. Line bottom of pan with parchment paper. Coat parchment paper with cooking spray; set aside. In a small bowl stir together cake flour, baking powder, and salt; set aside.

2. Preheat oven to 350°F. Add flavoring to egg yolks; beat with an electric mixer on high speed about 5 minutes or until thick and lemon color. Gradually beat in 1/4 cup of the sugar, beating on high speed until sugar is almost dissolved. Sprinkle flour mixture over egg yolk mixture; gently fold in just until combined. Thoroughly wash beaters. Beat egg whites with an electric mixer on medium speed until soft peaks form (tips curl). Gradually add the remaining 1/4 cup sugar, beating until stiff peaks form (tips stand straight). Fold 1/2 cup of the beaten egg whites into the egg yolk mixture to lighten. Fold in the remaining egg whites. Spread batter evenly in prepared pan.

3. Bake about 12 minutes or until cake springs back when lightly touched. Immediately loosen edges of cake from pan; turn cake out onto a clean dish towel. Remove parchment paper. Starting from a short side, roll towel and cake into a spiral. Cool on a wire rack.

Continued on page 140

Continued from page 139

4. For filling, in a medium bowl whisk together milk and pudding mix just until thickened. Fold in whipped topping. Cover and chill for at least 1 hour.

5. Unroll cooled cake; remove towel. Spread filling to within 1 inch of edges. Thinly slice one of the bananas; arrange slices over the filling. Roll up cake. Cover and chill for at least 2 hours or up to 8 hours. To serve, thinly slice the remaining banana. Top cake roll with banana and strawberry slices. Drizzle with chocolate syrup. Cut into 10 slices.

*SUGAR SUBSTITUTE: We do not recommend using a sugar substitute for this recipe.

PER SERVING: 155 cal., 2 g total fat (1 g sat. fat), 56 mg chol., 286 mg sodium, 29 g carb. (1 g fiber, 15 g sugars), 5 g pro. Exchanges: 2 starch.

Baked Funnel Cakes

This streamlined, baked recipe lets you treat your family and friends to funnel cakes, a longtime fair favorite, anytime.

SERVINGS 12 (1 mini funnel cake each)
CARB. PER SERVING 9 g
PREP 25 minutes **COOL** 10 minutes **BAKE** 20 minutes

    Nonstick cooking spray
    1   cup water
    $\frac{1}{2}$ cup butter
    $\frac{1}{8}$ teaspoon salt
    1   cup flour
    4   eggs
    2   tablespoons powdered sugar

1. Preheat oven to 400°F. Coat two large baking sheets with cooking spray. Place a wire rack over waxed paper or a large tray. Set aside.

2. In a medium saucepan combine the water, butter, and salt. Bring to boiling. Add flour all at once, stirring vigorously. Cook and stir until mixture forms a ball. Remove from heat. Cool for 10 minutes. Add eggs, one at a time, beating well with a wooden spoon after each addition.

3. Spoon dough into a large resealable plastic bag. Using scissors, snip a $\frac{1}{4}$- to $\frac{1}{2}$-inch hole in one corner of the bag. Pipe dough into twelve 3- to 4-inch circles on prepared baking sheets. Fill in the circles with dough swirls and crisscrosses to resemble funnel cakes.

4. Bake about 20 minutes or until puffed and golden brown. Transfer to the wire rack. Sift powdered sugar over warm cakes. Serve warm.

PER SERVING: 134 cal., 9 g total fat (5 g sat. fat), 91 mg chol., 103 mg sodium, 9 g carb. (0 g fiber, 1 g sugars), 3 g pro. Exchanges: 0.5 starch, 1.5 fat.

Tropical Cake Squares

Save prep time by purchasing a container of chopped fresh pineapple instead of cleaning and chopping a whole one.

SERVINGS 24 (1 cake square, 1 tablespoon cream cheese mixture, $1\frac{1}{2}$ tablespoons fruit, and 1 teaspoon coconut each)
CARB. PER SERVING 20 g or 18 g
PREP 40 minutes **BAKE** 18 minutes **COOL** 5 minutes

    Nonstick cooking spray
    1   package 2-layer-size sugar-free yellow cake mix
    1   cup water
    6   egg whites or $\frac{3}{4}$ cup refrigerated or frozen egg product, thawed
    $\frac{1}{3}$ cup canola oil
    $1\frac{1}{4}$ cups plain fat-free Greek yogurt
    6   ounces fat-free cream cheese, softened
    $\frac{1}{3}$ cup sugar*
    $1\frac{1}{2}$ teaspoons vanilla
    1   cup chopped fresh pineapple
    1   cup fresh blueberries
    $\frac{1}{2}$ cup shredded coconut, toasted

1. Preheat oven to 325°F. Coat a 15×10×1-inch baking pan with cooking spray. Line bottom of pan with parchment paper. Set aside.

2. In a large bowl combine cake mix, the water, egg whites, and oil. Mix according to cake mix package directions. Pour batter into the prepared pan, using the back of a spoon to spread evenly. Bake about 18 minutes or until a wooden pick inserted in the center comes out clean. Cool in pan on a wire rack for 5 minutes. Invert pan and cake together; remove pan. Cool cake completely on wire rack. Carefully remove parchment paper.

3. Meanwhile, in a food processor or blender combine yogurt, cream cheese, sugar, and vanilla. Cover and process or blend until smooth, stopping occasionally to scrape sides and push mixture into blades. Transfer to a small bowl. Chill until needed.

4. To serve, cut the cake into $2\frac{1}{2}$-inch squares. Spoon 1 tablespoon of the cream cheese mixture onto each square. Top each square with about $1\frac{1}{2}$ tablespoons pineapple and/or blueberries and 1 teaspoon coconut.

*SUGAR SUBSTITUTES: Choose from Splenda Granular, Equal Classic Spoonful or packets, or Sweet'N Low bulk or packets. Follow package directions to use product amount equivalent to $\frac{1}{3}$ cup sugar.

PER SERVING: 130 cal., 5 g total fat (2 g sat. fat), 1 mg chol., 210 mg sodium, 20 g carb. (0 g fiber, 5 g sugars), 4 g pro. Exchanges: 1 starch, 1 fat.

PER SERVING WITH SUBSTITUTE: Same as above, except 120 cal., 18 g carb. (3 g sugars).

To transport this crowd-size dessert to a picnic, pack the creamy topping and fruit in separate containers and place in a cooler with ice packs. Top the cake squares just before serving.

Tropical Cake Squares

Sunshine Cupcakes

Sunshine Cupcakes

You can bake these tender cakes ahead and freeze them in a freezer container for up to 1 month.

SERVINGS 24 (1 cupcake each)
CARB. PER SERVING 14 g or 11 g
PREP 30 minutes **STAND** 30 minutes **BAKE** 10 minutes

> 1 cup egg whites (7 to 9 large)
> ¾ cup sifted cake flour
> 1 cup sugar*
> 2 teaspoons vanilla
> 1 teaspoon cream of tartar
> 3 egg yolks
> 1 recipe Lemon Fluff
> Fresh raspberries (optional)
> Orange and/or lemon peel strips (optional)

1. In a very large bowl allow egg whites to stand at room temperature for 30 minutes. Meanwhile, sift cake flour and ½ cup of the sugar together three times. Line twenty-four 2½-inch muffin cups with paper bake cups;* set aside.

2. Preheat oven to 375°F. Add vanilla and cream of tartar to egg whites; beat with an electric mixer on medium to high speed until soft peaks form (tips curl). Gradually add the remaining ½ cup sugar, beating until stiff peaks form (tips stand straight). Sift about one-fourth of the flour mixture over egg white mixture; fold in gently. Repeat sifting and folding with the remaining flour mixture, using one-fourth of the flour mixture each time. Transfer half of the egg white mixture to another bowl; set both bowls aside.

3. In a medium bowl beat egg yolks with an electric mixer on high speed about 5 minutes or until thick and lemon color. Fold egg yolk mixture into one portion of the egg white mixture. Alternately spoon dollops of yellow and white batters into paper bake cups, filling cups two-thirds full. Gently cut through batters with a knife.

4. Bake for 10 to 12 minutes or until cupcakes spring back when lightly touched near the center. Remove from cups; cool completely on a wire rack. Frost with Lemon Fluff. If desired, garnish with raspberries and orange and/or lemon peel strips. Store cupcakes in the refrigerator.

LEMON FLUFF: In a bowl fold together ½ of an 8-ounce container frozen light whipped dessert topping, thawed; ½ teaspoon finely shredded lemon peel; and 1 tablespoon lemon juice just until combined.

***SUGAR SUBSTITUTES:** Choose from Splenda Sugar Blend for Baking or Sun Crystals Granulated Blend. Follow package directions to use product amount equivalent to 1 cup sugar and line only 20 muffin cups with paper bake cups.

PER SERVING: 72 cal., 1 g total fat (1 g sat. fat), 23 mg chol., 18 mg sodium, 14 g carb. (0 g fiber, 9 g sugars), 2 g pro. Exchanges: 0.5 starch, 0.5 carb.

PER SERVING WITH SUBSTITUTE: Same as above, except 28 mg chol., 22 mg sodium, 11 g carb. (6 g sugars).

Apple-Date Cake

Carrot Cake Parfaits

Use a fork to help pull pieces of the cake away to crumble.

SERVINGS 10 (1 parfait each)
CARB. PER SERVING 34 g or 28 g
PREP 30 minutes   BAKE 20 minutes   COOL 10 minutes

1 cup flour
1 teaspoon ground cinnamon
1/2 teaspoon baking soda
1/2 teaspoon ground nutmeg
1/2 cup unsweetened applesauce
1/4 cup granulated sugar*
1/4 cup packed brown sugar*
1 egg, lightly beaten
2 tablespoons vegetable oil
2 cups shredded carrots (4 medium)
1 8-ounce container frozen fat-free whipped dessert topping, thawed
2 tablespoons pureed baby food carrots
1/4 teaspoon ground ginger
1 cup chopped fresh pineapple
1/4 cup finely chopped walnuts

1. Preheat oven to 350°F. Grease a 9-inch round baking pan; set aside. In a small bowl combine flour, cinnamon, baking soda, and nutmeg; set aside.

2. In a medium bowl stir together applesauce, granulated sugar, brown sugar, egg, and oil. Stir in shredded carrots. Add flour mixture, stirring just until combined. Spread batter in the prepared pan.

3. Bake for 20 to 25 minutes or until a toothpick inserted near the center comes out clean. Cool in pan on a wire rack for 10 minutes. Remove from pan. Cool completely on wire rack. Coarsely crumble cooled cake (the crumbles will be dense and moist).

4. In a medium bowl fold together dessert topping, baby food carrots, and ginger just until combined.

5. To assemble desserts, divide half of the crumbled cake among ten 6-ounce parfait glasses or dessert dishes. Top with half of the dessert topping mixture. Top with pineapple, the remaining crumbled cake, and the remaining dessert topping mixture. Sprinkle with walnuts.

*SUGAR SUBSTITUTES: Choose Splenda Sugar Blend for Baking to substitute for the granulated sugar. Choose Splenda Brown Sugar Blend to substitute for the brown sugar. Follow package directions to use product amounts equivalent to 1/4 cup of each sugar.

PER SERVING: 198 cal., 5 g total fat (1 g sat. fat), 21 mg chol., 101 mg sodium, 34 g carb. (2 g fiber, 14 g sugars), 3 g pro. Exchanges: 1 starch, 1 carb., 1 fat.

PER SERVING WITH SUBSTITUTES: Same as above, except 182 cal., 100 mg sodium, 28 g carb. (9 g sugars). Exchanges: 0.5 carb.

Apple-Date Cake

If there is cake left over, warm individual servings in the microwave on 100 percent power (high) for 15 seconds.

SERVINGS 12 (1 piece each)
CARB. PER SERVING 27 g or 24 g
PREP 30 minutes   BAKE 25 minutes

Nonstick cooking spray
2/3 cup fat-free milk
2/3 cup chopped pitted dates
1/4 teaspoon salt
3/4 cup coarsely shredded, peeled cooking apple
1 teaspoon vanilla
1 egg, lightly beaten
2 tablespoons vegetable oil
1/2 cup chopped pecans
1/4 cup packed brown sugar*
1 tablespoon butter, softened
1 teaspoon flour
1 teaspoon ground cinnamon
1 1/2 cups flour
1 teaspoon baking powder
1/2 teaspoon baking soda

1. Preheat oven to 350°F. Lightly coat an 8×8×2-inch baking pan with cooking spray. Set aside.

2. In a small saucepan combine milk, dates, and salt; heat until steaming. Remove from heat. Stir in apple and vanilla; cool. Add egg and oil; stir until combined. Set aside.

3. In a small bowl stir together pecans, brown sugar, butter, the 1 teaspoon flour, and the cinnamon; set aside.

4. In a medium bowl whisk together the 1 1/2 cups flour, the baking powder, and baking soda. Add milk mixture all at once to flour mixture. Stir just until combined. Spoon batter into the prepared baking pan. Sprinkle evenly with pecan mixture.

5. Bake about 25 minutes or until a knife inserted near the center comes out clean. Cool slightly. Cut into 12 pieces and serve warm.

*SUGAR SUBSTITUTE: Choose Splenda Brown Sugar Baking Blend. Follow package directions to use product amount equivalent to 1/4 cup brown sugar.

PER SERVING: 179 cal., 7 g total fat (1 g sat. fat), 18 mg chol., 153 mg sodium, 27 g carb. (2 g fiber, 12 g sugars), 3 g pro. Exchanges: 0.5 fruit, 1 starch, 0.5 carb., 1 fat.

PER SERVING WITH SUBSTITUTE: Same as above, except 171 cal., 24 g carb. (10 g sugars), 152 mg sodium. Exchanges: 0 carb.

No-Bake Cheesecake with Mango Puree

For best flavor, choose a fully ripe mango or ripen the fruit in a paper bag before using it.

SERVINGS 12 (1 wedge cheesecake and 1 tablespoon mango puree each)

CARB. PER SERVING 19 g or 14 g

PREP 35 minutes CHILL 3 hours

Nonstick cooking spray
15 gingersnaps, crumbled

3 tablespoons butter, melted
2 tablespoons sugar*
$\frac{1}{3}$ cup sugar**
1 envelope unflavored gelatin
1 cup boiling water
2 8-ounce packages reduced-fat cream cheese (Neufchâtel), softened
1 teaspoon vanilla
1 ripe medium mango, peeled, seeded, and cut up
1 tablespoon lime juice

No-Bake Cheesecake
with Mango Puree

1. For crust, lightly coat an 8-inch springform pan or a 9-inch pie plate with cooking spray; set aside. Place gingersnaps in a food processor. Cover and process until fine crumbs form. With the machine running, add melted butter and the 2 tablespoons sugar through the opening in the lid; process until crumbs are moistened. Transfer crumb mixture to the prepared pan. Press crumb mixture evenly into the bottom and 1 inch up the sides of the pan. Set aside.
2. In a small bowl combine the $1/3$ cup sugar and the gelatin. Add the boiling water; stir about 5 minutes or until gelatin is dissolved.
3. For cheesecake filling, in a large bowl combine cream cheese and vanilla; beat with an electric mixer on medium speed until combined. Slowly add the gelatin mixture, beating until combined. Pour mixture into the crust.
4. In a food processor combine mango and lime juice; cover and process until a smooth puree forms. Press mango puree through a fine-mesh sieve; discard solids. Drizzle 3 tablespoons of the mango puree on top of the cheesecake filling. Draw a toothpick through the puree and filling to create a marbled effect. Cover and chill the cheesecake and the remaining mango puree about 3 hours or until cheesecake is firm.
5. To serve, remove sides of the springform pan; cut cheesecake into 12 wedges. Serve the remaining mango puree with cheesecake wedges.
*SUGAR SUBSTITUTE: We do not recommend using a sugar substitute for the crust portion of this recipe.
**SUGAR SUBSTITUTES: Choose from Splenda Granular, Equal Spoonful or packets, or Sweet'N Low bulk or packets. Follow package directions to use product amount equivalent to $1/3$ cup sugar.

PER SERVING: 202 cal., 12 g total fat (7 g sat. fat), 36 mg chol., 206 mg sodium, 19 g carb. (1 g fiber, 13 g sugars), 5 g pro. Exchanges: 1 starch, 2.5 fat.

PER SERVING WITH SUBSTITUTE: Same as above, except 183 cal., 14 g carb. (8 g sugars).

Brownie Raspberry Tart

To make a clean cut, dip the knife in hot water before each cut and wipe the knife with a paper towel between cuts.

SERVINGS 10 (1 wedge each)
CARB. PER SERVING 25 g or 19 g
PREP 25 minutes BAKE 10 minutes

    Nonstick cooking spray
$1/2$ cup granulated sugar*
  3 tablespoons canola oil
  2 egg whites
$2/3$ cup flour
$1/2$ cup unsweetened cocoa powder
$1/4$ teaspoon salt
$1/4$ cup water

Brownie Raspberry Tart

$1/2$ cup tub-style light cream cheese
  3 tablespoons powdered sugar**
  1 tablespoon light chocolate-flavor syrup
$1/4$ cup sliced almonds, toasted (see tip, page 107)
  1 to $1 1/2$ cups fresh raspberries

1. For brownie crust, preheat oven to 350°F. Coat a 12-inch pizza pan with cooking spray; set aside.
2. In a medium bowl combine the granulated sugar and the oil. Beat with an electric mixer on medium speed until well mixed. Add egg whites, one at a time, beating well after each addition. In a small bowl stir together flour, cocoa powder, and salt. Add flour mixture and the water to the beaten mixture. Beat just until combined. Spread in the prepared pan. Bake for 10 minutes. Cool in pan on a wire rack.
3. Just before serving, stir together cream cheese, powdered sugar, and chocolate-flavor syrup until well mixed. Spread evenly over the brownie crust. Sprinkle with almonds and top with raspberries. Cut into 10 wedges.
*SUGAR SUBSTITUTE: Choose Splenda Sugar Blend for Baking for the granulated sugar. Follow package directions to use product amount equivalent to $1/2$ cup granulated sugar.
**SUGAR SUBSTITUTE: We do not recommend using a sugar substitute for the powdered sugar.

PER SERVING: 175 cal., 8 g total fat (2 g sat. fat), 6 mg chol., 132 mg sodium, 25 g carb. (3 g fiber, 14 g sugars), 4 g pro. Exchanges: 1 starch, 0.5 carb., 1.5 fat.

PER SERVING WITH SUBSTITUTE: Same as above, except 160 cal., 19 g carb. (9 g sugars).

QUICK TIP
To turn the **Amazing Apple Tart** out of the pie plate,
place a platter over the top, hold them together while
you flip them over, and lift off the pie plate.

Amazing Apple Tart

Juicy baked apples, a tender biscuitlike crust, and a sweet and spicy sauce add up to this diabetes-friendly dessert that bakes upside down. Amazing!

SERVINGS 8 (1 apple half with pastry and $1/2$ tablespoon sauce each)
CARB. PER SERVING 24 g or 18 g
PREP 30 minutes COOL 30 minutes BAKE 37 minutes

- $1/4$ cup apple juice or apple cider
- 3 tablespoons packed brown sugar*
- 2 teaspoons butter or tub-style vegetable oil spread
- $1/4$ teaspoon ground cinnamon
  Dash salt
- $1/2$ teaspoon vanilla
  Nonstick cooking spray
- 4 small apples, such as Jonathan, Winesap, or Empire, cored and halved lengthwise (about 1 pound total)
- 1 recipe Biscuit Pastry

1. Preheat oven to 400°F. For sauce, in a small saucepan combine apple juice, brown sugar, butter, cinnamon, and salt. Bring to boiling; reduce heat. Simmer, uncovered, for 2 minutes. Remove from heat. Stir in vanilla.
2. Place a 6-ounce custard cup upside down in the center of a 9-inch pie plate. Lightly coat the outside of the custard cup with cooking spray. Using the tines of a fork, score the uncut sides of apple halves. Place apple halves, cut sides up, in pie plate around the custard cup. Drizzle apples with sauce.
3. Prepare Biscuit Pastry. On a well-floured surface slightly flatten dough. Roll dough into a 10-inch circle. Place pastry over apples and custard cup (pastry will sink down over apples). Tuck dough between apples and pie plate (do not crimp or flute). Bake for 12 minutes.
4. Reduce oven temperature to 350°F. Bake for 25 to 30 minutes more or until pastry is golden and apples are tender. Cool on a wire rack for 30 minutes. Invert onto a 10- to 12-inch serving plate. To serve, cut into eight wedges; spoon sauce from custard cup over apple and pastry wedges.

BISCUIT PASTRY: In a medium bowl stir together $3/4$ cup flour, $1^1/4$ teaspoons baking powder, 1 teaspoon granulated sugar,* and $1/8$ teaspoon salt. Using a pastry blender, cut in 3 tablespoons butter until mixture resembles coarse crumbs. Using a fork, stir in 3 tablespoons fat-free milk until combined. Gather mixture together and knead gently just until dough forms a ball.

*SUGAR SUBSTITUTES: Choose Sweet'N Low Brown to substitute for the brown sugar. Choose Splenda Granular or Sweet'N Low bulk or packets to substitute for the granulated sugar. Follow package directions to use product amounts equivalent to 3 tablespoons brown sugar and 1 teaspoon granulated sugar.

PER SERVING: 147 cal., 6 g total fat (3 g sat. fat), 14 mg chol., 143 mg sodium, 24 g carb. (2 g fiber, 13 g sugars), 2 g pro. Exchanges: 0.5 fruit, 0.5 starch, 0.5 carb., 1 fat.

PER SERVING WITH SUBSTITUTES: Same as above, except 126 cal., 18 g carb. (7 g sugars), 141 mg sodium. Exchanges: 0 carb.

Bananas Foster Mini Pies

Use a fine-mesh sieve to give the pies a light dusting of powdered sugar. *Pictured on page 149.*

SERVINGS 12 (1 mini pie each)
CARB. PER SERVING 20 g or 19 g
PREP 30 minutes CHILL 1 hour BAKE 15 minutes

- $1/3$ cup butter, softened
- 1 tablespoon granulated sugar*
- $1/4$ teaspoon salt
- 1 egg
- 2 tablespoons cold water
- $1^1/2$ cups flour
- 1 banana, chopped (about $3/4$ cup)
- $1/4$ cup sugar-free caramel-flavor ice cream topping
- $1/4$ cup chopped pecans, toasted
- 1 tablespoon bourbon
- $1/4$ teaspoon ground cinnamon
- 1 tablespoon butter, melted
- 2 teaspoons powdered sugar

1. Line a baking sheet with parchment paper; set aside. In a large bowl beat the $1/3$ cup butter with an electric mixer on medium to high speed for 30 seconds. Add granulated sugar and salt. Beat for 3 minutes on medium speed. Add egg and the water; beat until combined. Beat in as much of the flour as you can. Stir in any remaining flour. Shape dough into a disk. Wrap in plastic wrap; chill 1 hour or until easy to handle.
2. Preheat oven to 400°F. For filling, in a bowl combine banana, ice cream topping, pecans, bourbon, and cinnamon.
3. On a lightly floured surface roll dough to $1/8$ inch thick. Using a 4-inch round cutter, cut dough into rounds, rerolling scraps as necessary. Place about 1 tablespoon of the filling in the center of each round. Brush edges of pastry circles with a little water. Fold each circle in half over filling; press edges to seal. Place pies on prepared baking sheet. Brush pies with the 1 tablespoon melted butter.
4. Bake about 15 minutes or until lightly browned. Sift powdered sugar over pies. Serve warm.

*SUGAR SUBSTITUTES: Choose from Splenda Granular, Truvia Spoonable, or Sweet'N Low packets or bulk. Follow package directions to use product amount equivalent to 1 tablespoon granulated sugar.

PER SERVING: 165 cal., 8 g total fat (4 g sat. fat), 32 mg chol., 118 mg sodium, 20 g carb. (1 g fiber, 3 g sugars), 3 g pro. Exchanges: 1 starch, 1.5 fat.

PER SERVING WITH SUBSTITUTE: Same as above, except 161 cal., 19 g carb. (2 g sugars). Exchanges: 1 fat.

Chocolate-Filled Lemon Meringues

Mascarpone is a rich, extra-creamy cheese with a mild flavor that works well in both savory and sweet dishes. Here it enhances a filling of unsweetened cocoa powder and vanilla, a beguiling match for crisp, low-fat lemon meringues.

SERVINGS 12 (1 filled meringue each)

CARB. PER SERVING 15 g or 14 g

PREP 35 minutes BAKE 25 minutes STAND 1 hour

> 2 egg whites
> 2/3 cup sugar*
> 1 teaspoon finely shredded lemon peel
> 1/4 teaspoon cream of tartar
> 4 teaspoons sugar**
> 1 tablespoon unsweetened cocoa powder
> 1/3 cup mascarpone cheese or reduced-fat cream cheese (Neufchâtel), softened (about 3 ounces)
> 1/2 teaspoon vanilla
> 2 to 3 tablespoons fat-free milk
> 1 cup fresh raspberries and/or blueberries
> Finely shredded lemon peel and/or unsweetened cocoa powder (optional)

1. In a large bowl let egg whites stand at room temperature for 30 minutes. Meanwhile, cover a large baking sheet with parchment paper or foil. Draw twelve 2-inch circles 3 inches apart on the paper or foil; set aside.

2. Preheat oven to 300°F. For meringues, in a small bowl stir together the 2/3 cup sugar and the lemon peel; set aside. Add cream of tartar to egg whites. Beat with an electric mixer on medium speed until soft peaks form (tips curl). Add the sugar-peel mixture, 1 tablespoon at a time, beating on high speed until stiff peaks form (tips stand straight). Spoon egg white mixture into the circles on the prepared baking sheet, building up sides slightly.

3. Bake for 25 minutes. Turn off oven. Let meringues dry in oven with door closed for 1 hour. Remove from oven; cool completely on baking sheet.

4. For filling, in a bowl stir together the 4 teaspoons sugar and the cocoa powder. In another bowl stir together the mascarpone cheese and vanilla. Stir in the cocoa mixture and enough of the milk to make spreading consistency.

5. Spread filling into cooled meringues. Top with berries. If desired, garnish with additional lemon peel and/or unsweetened cocoa powder.

MAKE-AHEAD DIRECTIONS: Prepare as directed through Step 3. Transfer meringues to an airtight storage container. Store at room temperature for up to 1 week. To serve, prepare filling and serve as above.

*TEST KITCHEN TIP: We do not recommend using sugar substitute for the meringues.

**SUGAR SUBSTITUTES: Choose from Splenda Granular, Equal Spoonful or packets, or Sweet'N Low packets or bulk. Follow package directions to use product amount equivalent to 4 teaspoons sugar.

PER SERVING: 91 cal., 3 g total fat (2 g sat. fat), 9 mg chol., 15 mg sodium, 15 g carb. (1 g fiber, 13 g sugars), 2 g pro. Exchanges: 1 carb., 0.5 fat.

PER SERVING WITH SUBSTITUTE: Same as above, except 86 cal., 14 g carb. (12 g sugars).

Apple Crumble with Oats

Leaving the skins on the apples provides fiber and vitamins, so this dessert is not only good-tasting but also good for you.

SERVINGS 6 (2/3 cup crumble each)

CARB. PER SERVING 30 g or 26 g

PREP 20 minutes BAKE 40 minutes

> 1/2 cup regular rolled oats
> 2 tablespoons whole wheat pastry flour
> 2 tablespoons packed brown sugar*
> 1/2 teaspoon ground cinnamon
> 1 tablespoon cold butter, cut into small pieces
> 3 medium Golden Delicious apples, cored and cut into thin wedges
> 2 tablespoons water
> 1 tablespoon fresh lemon juice
> 1 tablespoon packed brown sugar*
> Frozen yogurt or low-fat vanilla yogurt (optional)

1. Preheat oven to 350°F. In a medium bowl combine oats, flour, 2 tablespoons brown sugar, and cinnamon. Mix with fork until combined. Add the butter and work it in with your fingers, the fork, or a pastry blender until the mixture begins to form clumps.

2. In a large bowl toss the apples with the water, lemon juice, and remaining 1 tablespoon brown sugar. Transfer apple mixture to a 9-inch pie plate. Sprinkle the oat mixture evenly over the apples. Bake for 40 to 45 minutes or until the topping is golden and the apples are tender. If desired, serve warm with yogurt.

TEST KITCHEN TIP: To make individual servings, prepare as above, except divide the apple mixture among six 6- to 8-ounce custard cups or ramekins. Sprinkle with oat mixture and bake about 35 minutes or until apples are tender. Serve as above.

*SUGAR SUBSTITUTE: Choose Splenda Brown Sugar Baking Blend. Follow package directions to use product amounts equivalent to 2 tablespoons and 1 tablespoon brown sugar.

PER SERVING: 148 cal., 3 g total fat (1 g sat. fat), 5 mg chol., 20 mg sodium, 30 g carb. (4 g fiber, 16 g sugars), 3 g pro. Exchanges: 1 fruit, 0.5 starch, 0.5 carb., 0.5 fat.

PER SERVING WITH SUBSTITUTE: Same as above, except 137 cal., 26 g carb. (13 g sugars), 18 mg sodium.

Bananas Foster Mini Pies
recipe on page 147

Apple Crumble with Oats

Chocolate-Filled
Lemon Meringues

Gingered
Pears

Almond-Chocolate-
Cherry Cookies

Gingered Pears

To keep the stem intact, insert an apple corer into the bottom of the pear to remove the core. If you do not have an apple corer, use a small paring knife.

SERVINGS 4 (1 pear and about $1^1/_2$ tablespoons sauce each)
CARB. PER SERVING 26 g or 20 g
PREP 15 minutes **COOK** 7 minutes

- 4 small pears, cored (about $1^1/_2$ pounds total)
- 2 tablespoons sugar*
- 2 tablespoons water
- 1 teaspoon finely shredded lemon peel
- 2 tablespoons lemon juice
- 1 tablespoon butter
- $1/_4$ teaspoon ground ginger
- 1 tablespoon chopped crystallized ginger

1. Fill a large Dutch oven with water to a depth of 1 inch. Bring water to boiling. Place a steamer basket in the Dutch oven. Place pears in the steamer basket. Cover and steam for 7 to 9 minutes or until fruit is tender. Remove fruit from steamer basket.
2. Meanwhile, for lemon sauce, in a small saucepan heat and stir sugar, water, lemon peel, lemon juice, butter, and ground ginger over medium heat until butter is melted and sugar is dissolved.
3. To serve, place pears in four dessert dishes. Divide lemon sauce among the dishes and sprinkle with crystallized ginger.
***SUGAR SUBSTITUTES:** Choose from Splenda Granular, Truvia Spoonable, or Sweet'N Low packets or bulk. Follow package directions to use product amount equivalent to 2 tablespoons sugar.

PER SERVING: 122 cal., 3 g total fat (2 g sat. fat), 8 mg chol., 27 mg sodium, 26 g carb. (4 g fiber, 17 g sugars), 1 g pro. Exchanges: 1 fruit, 0.5 carb., 0.5 fat.

PER SERVING WITH SUBSTITUTE: Same as above, except 101 cal., 20 g carb. (12 g sugars). Exchanges: 0 carb.

Almond-Chocolate-Cherry Cookies

Spoon the glaze into a resealable plastic bag, snip off the corner, and lightly squeeze to drizzle over the cookies.

SERVINGS 32 (1 cookie each)
CARB. PER SERVING 14 g or 11 g
PREP 30 minutes **CHILL** 1 hour **BAKE** 10 minutes per batch

- 6 tablespoons butter, softened
- $3/_4$ cup granulated sugar*
- 1 egg
- 1 egg yolk
- 1 teaspoon vanilla
- 1 ounce sweet baking, bittersweet, or semisweet chocolate, melted and cooled slightly
- $1^1/_3$ cups flour
- $1/_2$ cup dried cherries
- $1/_3$ cup sliced almonds
- 1 recipe Chocolate-Almond Glaze

1. In a medium bowl beat butter with an electric mixer on medium-high speed about 2 minutes or until smooth. Add granulated sugar, beating until creamy. Beat in egg, egg yolk, and vanilla until combined. Stir in melted chocolate. Stir in flour. Fold in dried cherries and almonds. Cover and chill dough for 1 hour.
2. Preheat oven to 350°F. Line cookie sheets with parchment paper; set aside. Shape dough into 1-inch balls. Place balls about 1 inch apart on prepared cookie sheets. Bake for 10 to 12 minutes or until centers are set. Transfer cookies to wire racks; cool completely.
3. Drizzle Chocolate-Almond Glaze over cooled cookies. Let stand until glaze is set. To store, layer cookies between sheets of waxed paper in an airtight container. Cover. Store in the refrigerator for up to 3 days or freeze up to 3 months.
CHOCOLATE-ALMOND GLAZE: In a small saucepan combine $1/_2$ ounce sweet baking, bittersweet, or semisweet chocolate

and 1½ teaspoons butter. Heat and stir over low heat until melted and smooth. Remove from heat. Stir in ½ cup powdered sugar, 1 tablespoon fat-free milk, and a dash of almond extract until smooth.

*SUGAR SUBSTITUTE: Use Splenda Sugar Blend. Follow package directions to use product amount equivalent to ¾ cup granulated sugar.

PER SERVING: 88 cal., 4 g total fat (2 g sat. fat), 18 mg chol., 25 mg sodium, 14 g carb. (0 g fiber, 9 g sugars), 1 g pro. Exchanges: 0.5 starch, 0.5 carb., 0.5 fat.

PER SERVING WITH SUBSTITUTE: Same as above, except 81 cal., 11 g carb. (6 g sugars).

Carrot Raisin Cookies

Try dried cranberries in place of the raisins another time.

SERVINGS 36 (1 cookie each)
CARB. PER SERVING 14 g or 11 g
PREP 30 minutes BAKE 8 minutes per batch

½   cup butter, softened
1   cup packed brown sugar*
2   teaspoons baking soda
1   teaspoon ground cinnamon
1   teaspoon ground ginger
¼   teaspoon salt
1   egg
¼   cup unsweetened applesauce
1   teaspoon vanilla
2   cups whole wheat flour
1   cup finely shredded carrots (2 medium)
¾   cup raisins
¾   cup finely chopped walnuts

1. Preheat oven to 375°F. In a large bowl beat butter with an electric mixer on medium speed for 30 seconds. Add brown sugar, baking soda, cinnamon, ginger, and salt; beat until combined. Beat in egg, applesauce, and vanilla. Beat in as much of the flour as you can. Stir in any remaining flour, the carrots, raisins, and walnuts just until combined.
2. Drop by slightly rounded teaspoons 2 inches apart onto ungreased cookie sheets. Bake for 8 to 9 minutes or until edges are firm. Transfer cookies to a wire rack; cool completely. To store, layer between sheets of waxed paper in an airtight container; cover. Store in the refrigerator for up to 3 days or freeze for up to 3 months.

*SUGAR SUBSTITUTE: Choose Splenda Brown Sugar Baking Blend. Follow package directions to use product amount equivalent to 1 cup brown sugar.

PER SERVING: 98 cal., 4 g total fat (2 g sat. fat), 12 mg chol., 115 mg sodium, 14 g carb. (1 g fiber, 8 g sugars), 2 g pro. Exchanges: 0.5 starch, 0.5 carb., 0.5 fat.

PER SERVING WITH SUBSTITUTE: Same as above, except 88 cal., 11 g carb. (5 g sugars), 113 mg sodium. Exchanges: 0 carb., 1 fat.

Chocolate-Coconut Pudding

Chop the chocolate into pieces before adding it to the pudding mixture. The smaller the pieces, the quicker they melt.

SERVINGS 8 (¼ cup each)
CARB. PER SERVING 21 g or 14 g
START TO FINISH 30 minutes

1   cup unsweetened light coconut milk
¼   cup unsweetened cocoa powder
2   tablespoons cornstarch
¼   teaspoon salt
1¼   cups unsweetened almond milk
¼   cup packed brown sugar*
2   tablespoons granulated sugar*
4   ounces semisweet chocolate, chopped
½   teaspoon coconut extract
2   tablespoons unsweetened shredded coconut, toasted

1. In a medium bowl whisk together coconut milk, cocoa powder, cornstarch, and salt. Set aside.
2. In a medium saucepan combine almond milk, brown sugar, and granulated sugar. Cook and stir over medium heat just until boiling. Add coconut milk mixture. Cook and stir just until mixture returns to boiling. Immediately reduce heat to low; cook and stir for 2 minutes more. Remove from heat. Add chocolate; let stand for 30 seconds. Add coconut extract; stir until smooth.
3. Spoon ¼ cup of the pudding into each of eight small dessert dishes, mugs, or pots de crème cups. Sprinkle with toasted coconut. Serve chilled.

*SUGAR SUBSTITUTES: Choose Sweet'N Low Brown to substitute for the packed brown sugar. Choose Splenda Granular, Truvia Spoonable, or Sweet'N Low packets or bulk to substitute for the granulated sugar. Follow package directions to use product amounts equivalent to ¼ cup brown sugar and 2 tablespoons granulated sugar.

PER SERVING: 145 cal., 7 g total fat (4 g sat. fat), 0 mg chol., 114 mg sodium, 21 g carb. (2 g fiber, 14 g sugars), 2 g pro. Exchanges: 0.5 starch, 1 carb., 1 fat.

PER SERVING WITH SUBSTITUTES: Same as above, except 118 cal., 14 g carb. (7 g sugars), 113 mg sodium. Exchanges 0.5 carb.

Carrot Raisin Cookies

Cantaloupe-Tarragon Granita

Honeydew-Mojito Sherbet

Cantaloupe-Tarragon Granita

Its fluffy yet icy texture and pleasant melon-herb flavor make this distinctive dessert a sure-to-please meal ending.

SERVINGS 8 (^{1}/2 cup each)

CARB. PER SERVING 11 g

PREP 20 minutes FREEZE 3 hours

- ¼ cup sugar*
- ¼ cup water
- 2 tablespoons snipped fresh tarragon leaves
- 1 small, ripe cantaloupe (about 1 pound), peeled, seeded, and cut up (about 4 cups)
- 1 teaspoon finely shredded lemon peel
- 2 tablespoons lemon juice
- Lemon peel twists (optional)

1. For tarragon syrup, in a small saucepan combine sugar and the water. Bring to boiling, stirring to dissolve the sugar. Remove saucepan from heat; stir in 1 tablespoon of the tarragon. Let mixture stand for 5 minutes; strain through a fine-mesh sieve. Discard solids.
2. Place cantaloupe in a food processor or blender; cover and process or blend until smooth. Add the tarragon syrup, the remaining 1 tablespoon tarragon, the finely shredded lemon peel, and lemon juice. Cover; process or blend to combine.
3. Pour cantaloupe mixture into a 2-quart baking dish or shallow freezer container. Cover and freeze about 3 hours or until nearly firm, scraping every hour with the tines of a fork so the mixture freezes into coarse crystals.
4. To serve, scrape granita with a fork and scoop into eight dessert dishes. If desired, garnish with lemon peel twists.

*SUGAR SUBSTITUTE: We do not recommend using a sugar substitute for this recipe.

PER SERVING: 45 cal., 0 g total fat, 0 mg chol., 10 mg sodium, 11 g carb. (1 g fiber, 10 g sugars), 1 g pro. Exchanges: 0.5 fruit, 0.5 carb.

Honeydew-Mojito Sherbet

A mojito's signature flavors of lime and mint complement the honeydew and yogurt in this frozen dessert.

SERVINGS 10 (^{1}/2 cup each)

CARB. PER SERVING 23 g or 9 g

PREP 25 minutes FREEZE 3 hours STAND 10 minutes

- ¼ cup cold water
- 1 teaspoon finely shredded lime peel (set aside)
- 3 tablespoons lime juice
- 1 unflavored gelatin
- ¾ cup sugar*
- ½ cup fresh mint leaves
- ½ of a medium honeydew melon, peeled, seeded, and cubed (4 cups)
- ¼ cup low-fat Greek yogurt
- Fresh mint leaves (optional)

1. In a small saucepan combine the cold water and lime juice; sprinkle gelatin over liquid and let stand for 5 minutes to soften.
2. Meanwhile, in a food processor or blender combine sugar, the ½ cup mint leaves, and the lime peel. Cover and process or blend until mint is finely chopped. Add cubed honeydew (half at a time if necessary) and yogurt; cover and process or blend until smooth.
3. Cook and stir gelatin mixture over medium-low heat until gelatin is dissolved. Add gelatin mixture to honeydew mixture; cover and process or blend for 1 minute.
4. Transfer mixture to a 1½- or 2-quart ice cream freezer; freeze according to manufacturer's directions. Spoon into an airtight freezer container; cover and freeze for 3 to 4 hours or until firm.
5. To serve, let stand at room temperature for 10 minutes. Scoop into 10 dessert dishes and, if desired, garnish with additional fresh mint leaves.

*SUGAR SUBSTITUTES: Choose from Splenda Granular, Equal Spoonful or packets, or Sweet'N Low bulk or packets. Follow package directions to use product amount equivalent to ¾ cup sugar.

PER SERVING: 101 cal., 0 g total fat, 0 mg chol., 22 mg sodium, 23 g carb. (1 g fiber, 21 g sugars), 4 g pro. Exchanges: 0.5 fruit, 1 carb., 0.5 lean meat.

PER SERVING WITH SUBSTITUTE: Same as above, except 50 cal., 9 g carb (8 g sugars). Exchanges: 0 carb.

Layered Frozen Chocolate Coffee Pops

One is never too old to enjoy a frosty pop. These layered beauties are designed for the adult palate.

SERVINGS 8 (1 pop each)
CARB. PER SERVING 16 g
PREP 20 minutes FREEZE 12 hours

- 1 4-serving-size package fat-free, sugar-free, reduced-calorie white chocolate instant pudding mix
- 1¼ teaspoons instant espresso coffee powder
- 2 cups fat-free milk
- 8 5-ounce paper or plastic drink cups
- ⅓ cup fat-free sweetened condensed milk
- ¼ cup unsweetened cocoa powder
- ½ teaspoon instant espresso coffee powder
- ½ teaspoon vanilla
- 1½ cups water
- 8 flat wooden crafts sticks

1. In a medium bowl stir together pudding mix and the 1¼ teaspoons espresso powder. Add the 2 cups fat-free milk; whisk about 2 minutes or until smooth and thickened.

2. Evenly spoon the pudding mixture into the paper cups. Cover with foil and chill while preparing the second layer.

3. In a medium bowl whisk together the sweetened condensed milk, cocoa powder, the ½ teaspoon espresso powder, and the vanilla. Whisk in the water until combined. Remove foil from cups and carefully spoon the cocoa powder mixture evenly over the pudding layer.

4. Cover cups with foil again. Cut a slit in the foil over each cup and insert a wooden stick into each slit, pushing the stick down into the layers. Freeze at least 12 hours or until firm.

5. To serve, remove foil and tear away the paper cups or remove pops from plastic cups.

PER SERVING: 78 cal., 0 g total fat, 1 mg chol., 206 mg sodium, 16 g carb. (1 g fiber, 12 g sugars), 4 g pro. Exchanges: 1 starch.

recipe index

recipe guide

See how we calculate nutrition information to help you count calories, carbs, and serving sizes.

Inside Our Recipes

Precise serving sizes (listed below the recipe title) help you to manage portions.

Ingredients listed as optional are not included in the per-serving nutrition analysis.

When kitchen basics such as ice, salt, black pepper, and nonstick cooking spray are not listed in the ingredients list, they are italicized in the directions.

Ingredients

• Tub-style vegetable oil spread refers to 60% to 70% vegetable oil product.

• Lean ground beef refers to 95% or leaner ground beef.

Nutrition Information

Nutrition facts per serving and food exchanges are noted with each recipe.

Test Kitchen tips and sugar substitutes are listed after the recipe directions.

When ingredient choices appear, we use the first one to calculate the nutrition analysis.

Key to Abbreviations

cal. = calories
sat. fat = saturated fat
chol. = cholesterol
carb. = carbohydrate
pro. = protein

metric information

The charts on this page provide a guide for converting measurements from the U.S. customary system, which is used throughout this book, to the metric system.

Product Differences

Most of the ingredients called for in the recipes in this book are available in most countries. However, some are known by different names. Here are some common American ingredients and their possible counterparts:

* All-purpose flour is enriched, bleached or unbleached white household flour. When self-rising flour is used in place of all-purpose flour in a recipe that calls for leavening, omit the leavening agent (baking soda or baking powder) and salt.
* Baking soda is bicarbonate of soda.
* Cornstarch is cornflour.
* Golden raisins are sultanas.
* Light-colored corn syrup is golden syrup.
* Powdered sugar is icing sugar.
* Sugar (white) is granulated, fine granulated, or castor sugar.
* Vanilla or vanilla extract is vanilla essence.

Volume and Weight

The United States traditionally uses cup measures for liquid and solid ingredients. The chart below shows the approximate imperial and metric equivalents. If you are accustomed to weighing solid ingredients, the following approximate equivalents will be helpful.

* 1 cup butter, castor sugar, or rice = 8 ounces = $1/2$ pound = 250 grams
* 1 cup flour = 4 ounces = $1/4$ pound = 125 grams
* 1 cup icing sugar = 5 ounces = 150 grams

Canadian and U.S. volume for a cup measure is 8 fluid ounces (237 ml), but the standard metric equivalent is 250 ml.

1 British imperial cup is 10 fluid ounces.

In Australia, 1 tablespoon equals 20 ml, and there are 4 teaspoons in the Australian tablespoon.

Spoon measures are used for smaller amounts of ingredients. Although the size of the tablespoon varies slightly in different countries, for practical purposes and for recipes in this book, a straight substitution is all that's necessary. Measurements made using cups or spoons always should be level unless stated otherwise.

Common Weight Range Replacements

Imperial / U.S.	Metric
$1/2$ ounce	15 g
1 ounce	25 g or 30 g
4 ounces ($1/4$ pound)	115 g or 125 g
8 ounces ($1/2$ pound)	225 g or 250 g
16 ounces (1 pound)	450 g or 500 g
$1 1/4$ pounds	625 g
$1 1/2$ pounds	750 g
2 pounds or $2 1/4$ pounds	1,000 g or 1 Kg

Oven Temperature Equivalents

Fahrenheit Setting	Celsius Setting*	Gas Setting
300°F	150°C	Gas Mark 2 (very low)
325°F	160°C	Gas Mark 3 (low)
350°F	180°C	Gas Mark 4 (moderate)
375°F	190°C	Gas Mark 5 (moderate)
400°F	200°C	Gas Mark 6 (hot)
425°F	220°C	Gas Mark 7 (hot)
450°F	230°C	Gas Mark 8 (very hot)
475°F	240°C	Gas Mark 9 (very hot)
500°F	260°C	Gas Mark 10 (extremely hot)
Broil	Broil	Grill

Electric and gas ovens may be calibrated using celsius. However, for an electric oven, increase celsius setting 10 to 20 degrees when cooking above 160°C. For convection or forced air ovens (gas or electric), lower the temperature setting 25°F/10°C when cooking at all heat levels.

Baking Pan Sizes

Imperial / U.S.	Metric
9×1$1/2$-inch round cake pan	22- or 23×4-cm (1.5 L)
9×1$1/2$-inch pie plate	22- or 23×4-cm (1 L)
8×8×2-inch square cake pan	20×5-cm (2 L)
9×9×2-inch square cake pan	22- or 23×4.5-cm (2.5 L)
11×7×1$1/2$-inch baking pan	28×17×4-cm (2 L)
2-quart rectangular baking pan	30×19×4.5-cm (3 L)
13×9×2-inch baking pan	34×22×4.5-cm (3.5 L)
15×10×1-inch jelly roll pan	40×25×2-cm
9×5×3-inch loaf pan	23×13×8-cm (2 L)
2-quart casserole	2 L

U.S. / Standard Metric Equivalents

$1/8$ teaspoon = 0.5 ml	
$1/4$ teaspoon = 1 ml	
$1/2$ teaspoon = 2 ml	
1 teaspoon = 5 ml	
1 tablespoon = 15 ml	
2 tablespoons = 25 ml	
$1/4$ cup = 2 fluid ounces = 50 ml	
$1/3$ cup = 3 fluid ounces = 75 ml	
$1/2$ cup = 4 fluid ounces = 125 ml	
$2/3$ cup = 5 fluid ounces = 150 ml	
$3/4$ cup = 6 fluid ounces = 175 ml	
1 cup = 8 fluid ounces = 250 ml	
2 cups = 1 pint = 500 ml	
1 quart = 1 litre